XAVIER BETAUCOURT & YANNICK MARCHAT

NEW LIFE

XAVIER BETAUCOURT
Story

YANNICK MARCHAT
Art

·

MONTANA KANE
Translator

·

FABRICE SAPOLSKY
& ALEX DONOGHUE
US Edition Editors

AMANDA LUCIDO
Assistant Editor

VINCENT HENRY
Original Edition Editor

JERRY FRISSEN
Senior Art Director

FABRICE GIGER
Publisher

Rights and Licensing - licensing@humanoids.com
Press and Social Media - pr@humanoids.com

NEW LIFE. This title is a publication of Humanoids, Inc. 8033 Sunset Blvd. #628, Los Angeles, CA 90046.
Copyright © 2019 Humanoids, Inc., Los Angeles (USA). All rights reserved. Humanoids and its logos are ® and © 2019 Humanoids, Inc.
Library of Congress Control Number: 2018947590

Life Drawn is an imprint of Humanoids, Inc.

First published in France under the title "Trop vieux pour toi" Copyright © 2016 La Boîte à Bulles, Xavier Bétaucourt, Yannick Marchat.
All rights reserved. All characters, the distinctive likenesses thereof and all related indicia are trademarks of La Boîte à Bulles Sarl
and / or of Xavier Bétaucourt, Yannick Marchat.

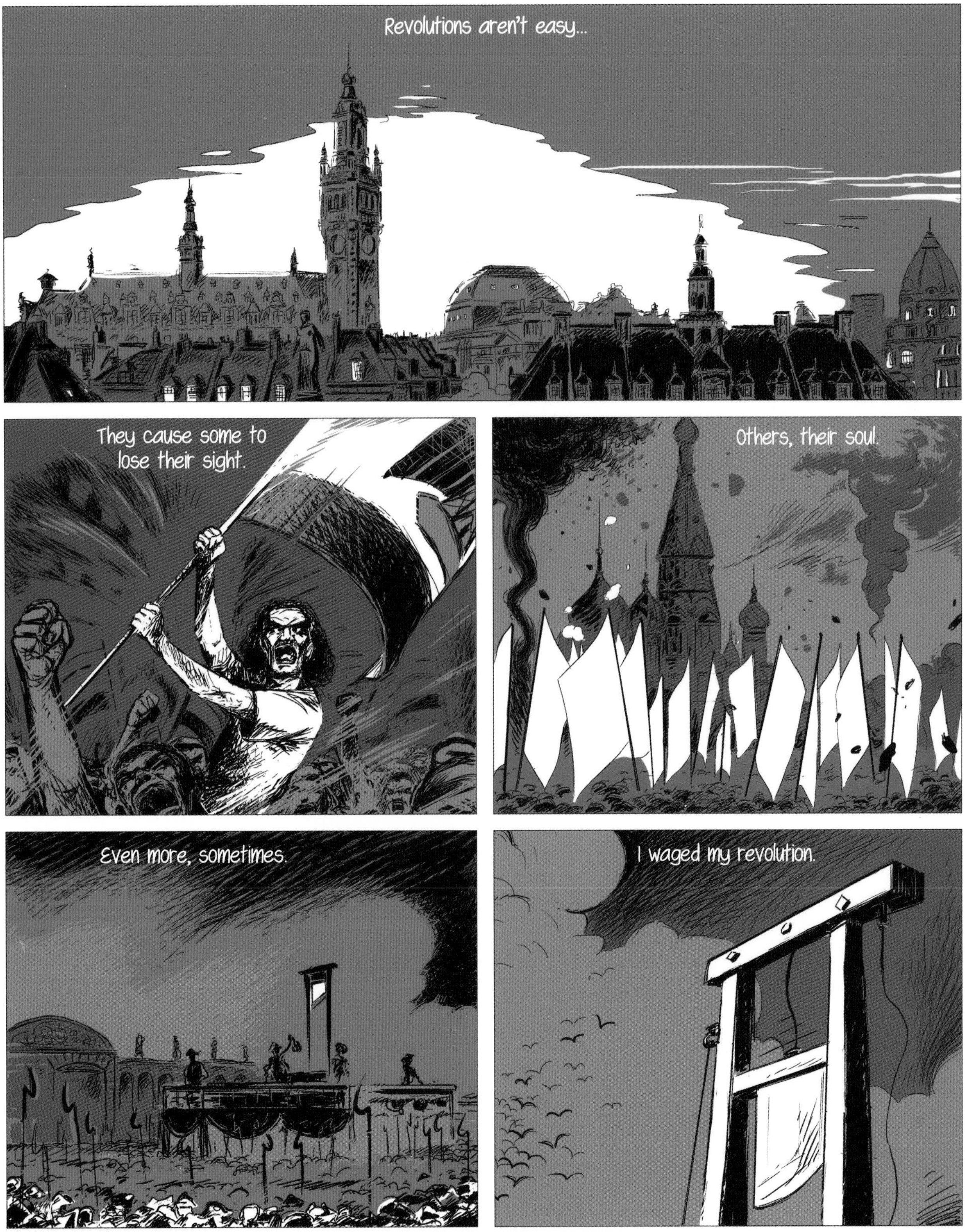
Revolutions aren't easy...
They cause some to lose their sight.
Others, their soul.
Even more, sometimes.
I waged my revolution.

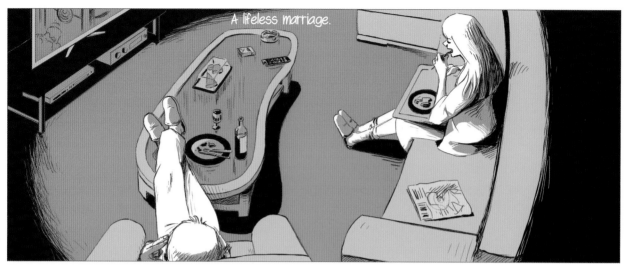

A lifeless marriage.

A child who's all grown up.

A job that no longer inspires me.

HOW'S IT GOING?

LIKE A MONDAY.

A boring life, in other words.

With barely enough comfort to make it bearable.

OH, NO! I'M SICK OF THE MOUNTAINS! I WANT TO GO TO THE BEACH THIS WINTER!

That's when you start feeling that none of it makes sense anymore.

Midlife crisis? I don't know.

Maybe it's realizing you took the wrong path.

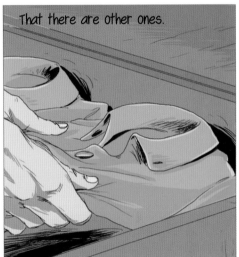

That there are other ones.

That's when you have to make a decision.

A necessarily painful one.

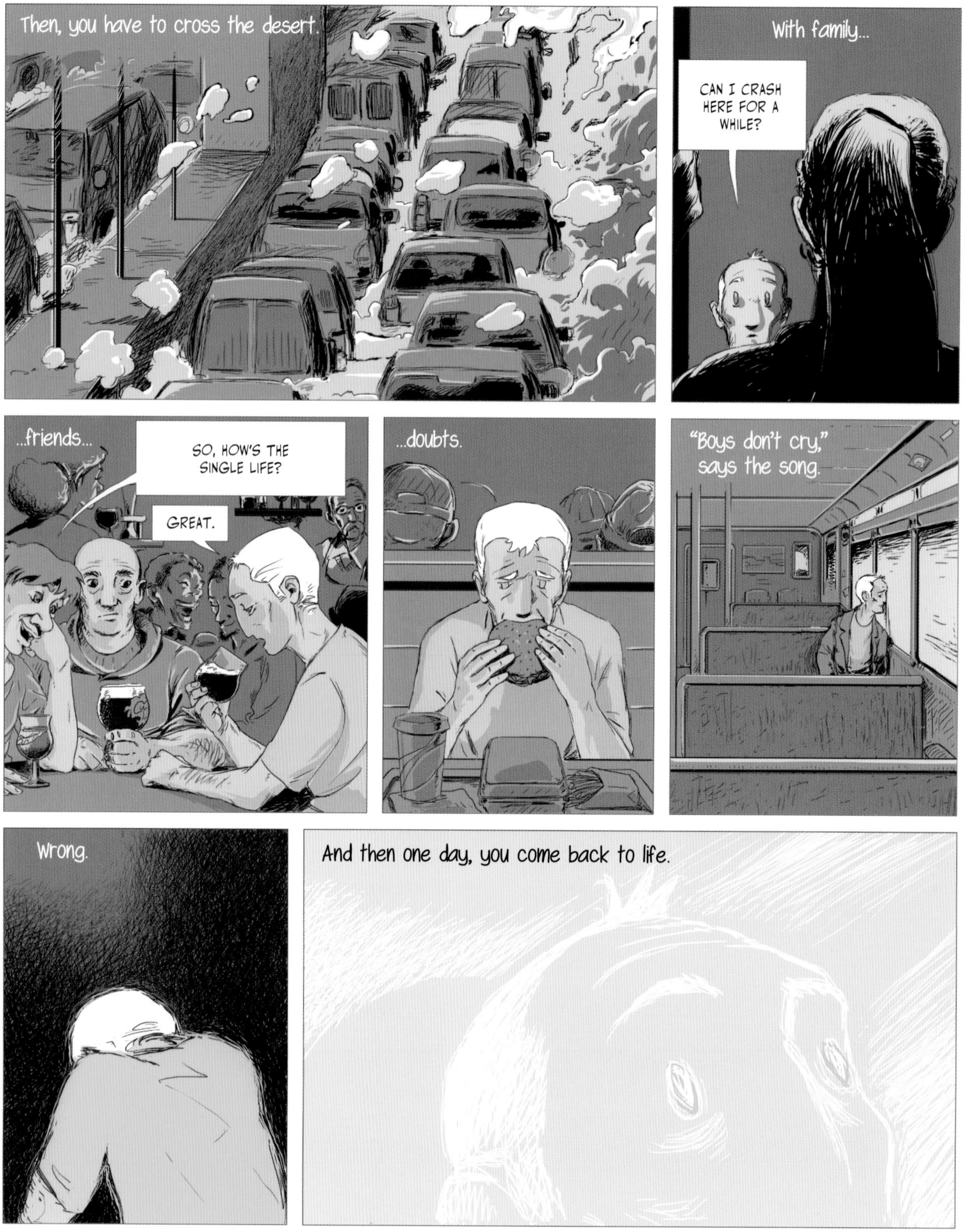
Then, you have to cross the desert.
With family...
CAN I CRASH HERE FOR A WHILE?
...friends...
SO, HOW'S THE SINGLE LIFE?
GREAT.
...doubts.
"Boys don't cry," says the song.
Wrong.
And then one day, you come back to life.

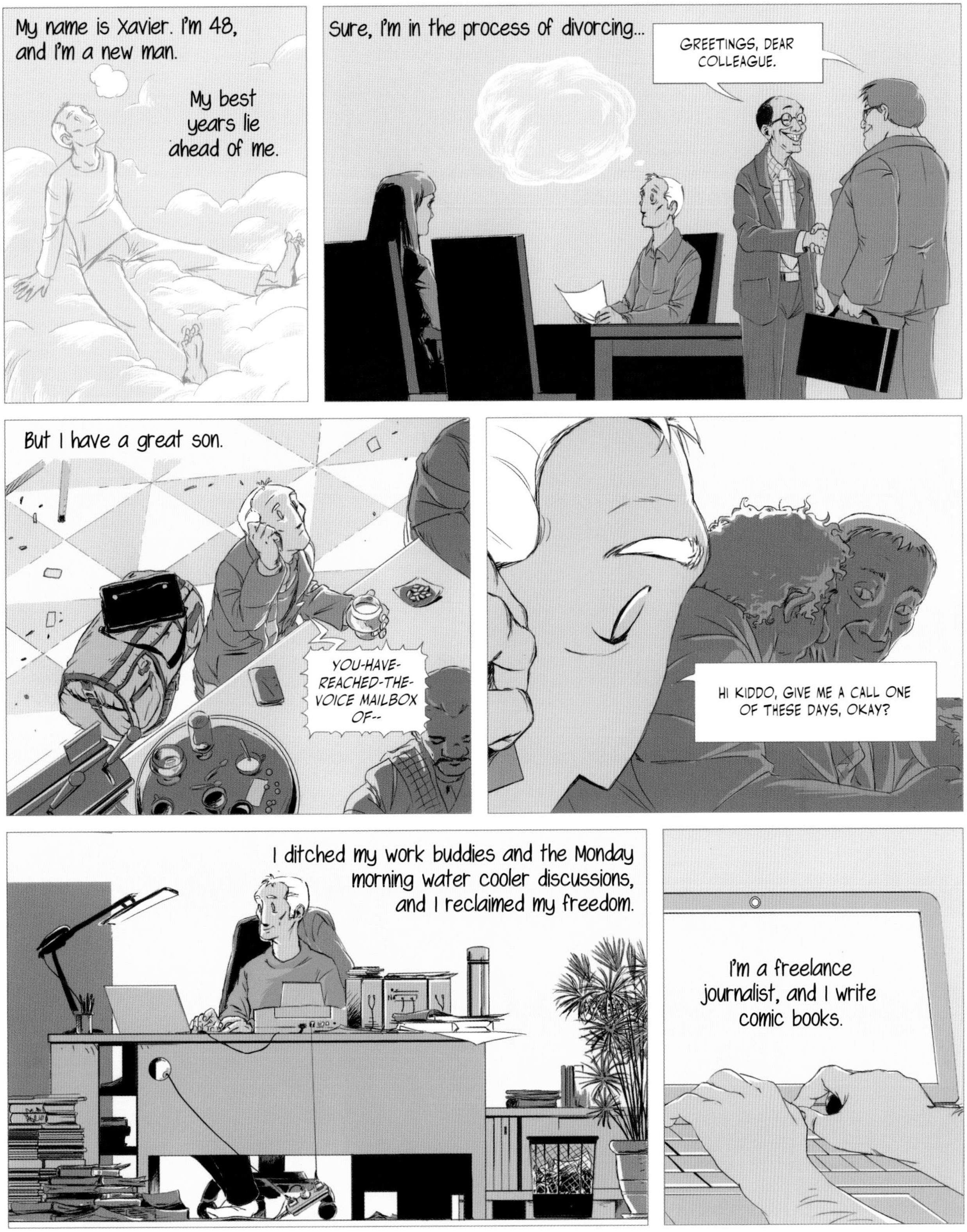
My name is Xavier. I'm 48, and I'm a new man.
My best years lie ahead of me.
Sure, I'm in the process of divorcing...
GREETINGS, DEAR COLLEAGUE.
But I have a great son.
YOU-HAVE-REACHED-THE-VOICE MAILBOX OF--
HI KIDDO, GIVE ME A CALL ONE OF THESE DAYS, OKAY?
I ditched my work buddies and the Monday morning water cooler discussions, and I reclaimed my freedom.
I'm a freelance journalist, and I write comic books.

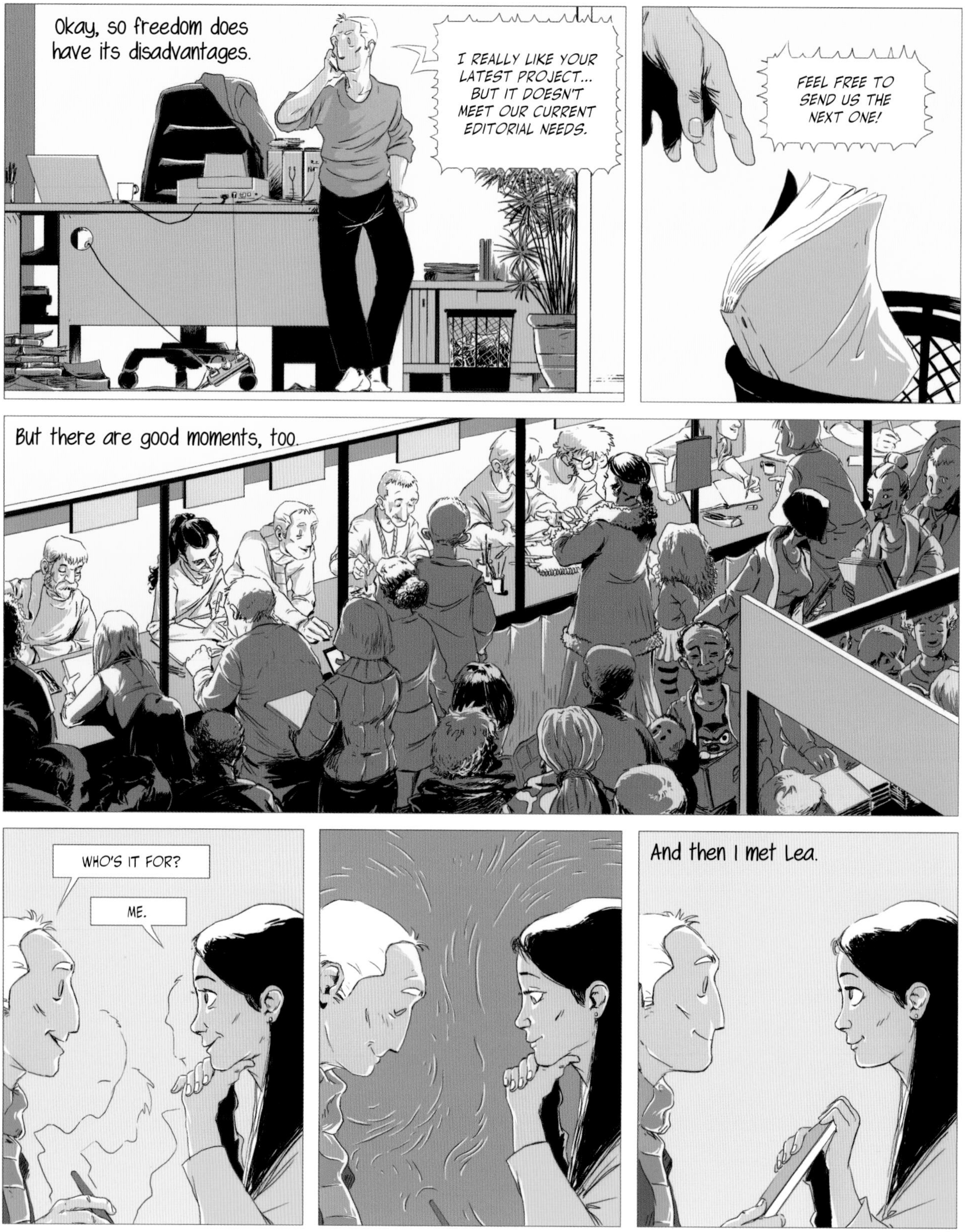
Okay, so freedom does have its disadvantages.
I REALLY LIKE YOUR LATEST PROJECT... BUT IT DOESN'T MEET OUR CURRENT EDITORIAL NEEDS.
FEEL FREE TO SEND US THE NEXT ONE!
But there are good moments, too.
WHO'S IT FOR?
ME.
And then I met Lea.

Lea is vibrant, full of life.

Selfless, too.

ARE YOU BORED? WE CAN GO HOME IF YOU WANT.

NO, I LIKE YOUR FRIENDS. AND THIS IS A GREAT SPREAD.

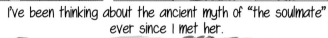

I've been thinking about the ancient myth of "the soulmate" ever since I met her.

BUT LET'S NOT GET HOME *TOO* LATE...

Plato's my buddy now. He totally gets me.

Only practical issues could have ruined things between us.

Or so I thought.

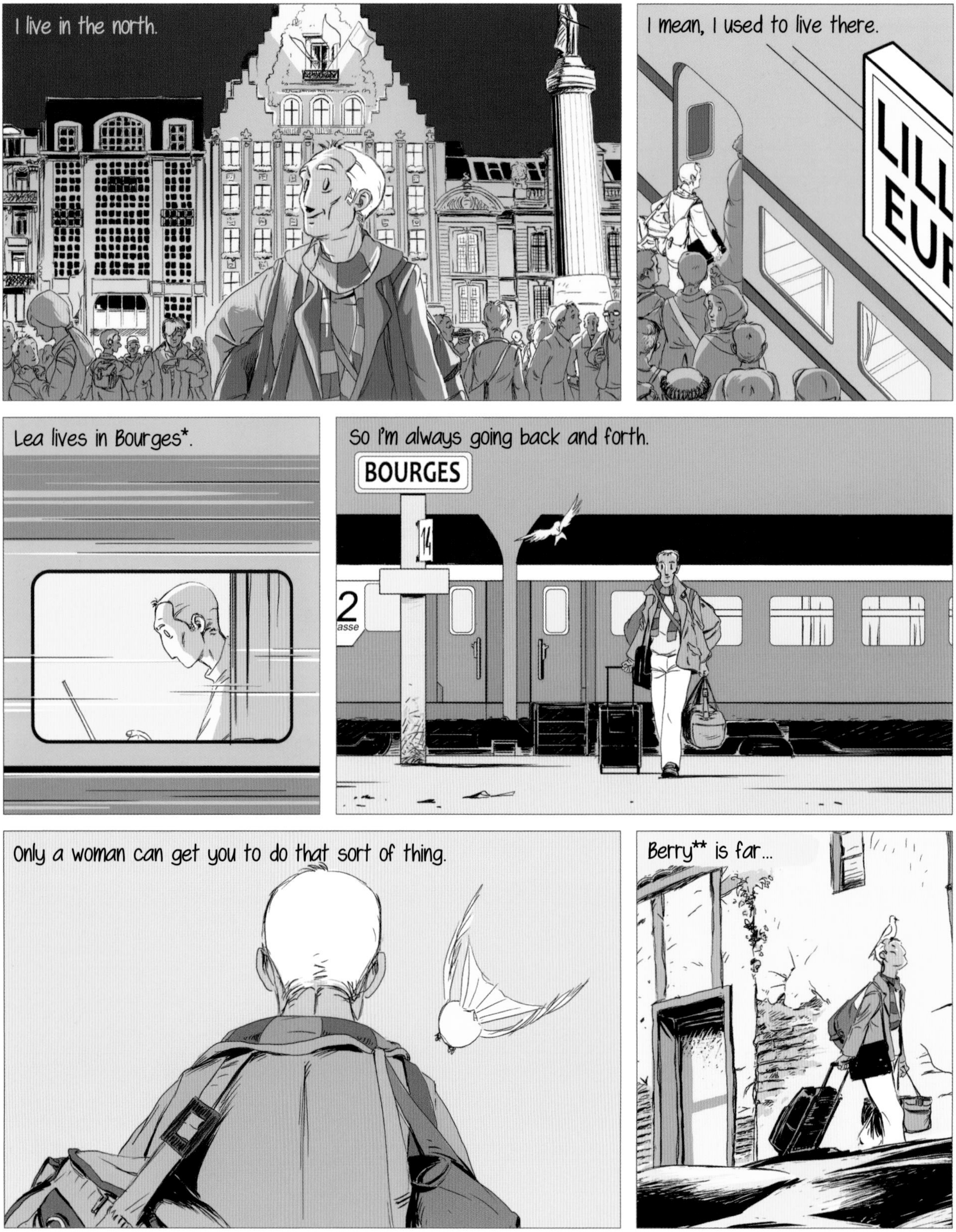
I live in the north.
I mean, I used to live there.
LILL
EUR
Lea lives in Bourges*.
So I'm always going back and forth.
BOURGES
14
2
asse
Only a woman can get you to do that sort of thing.
Berry** is far...

*BOURGES IS LOCATED ABOUT 140 MILES FROM PARIS. **BERRY IS A REGION OF FRANCE, WHERE BOURGES IS LOCATED.

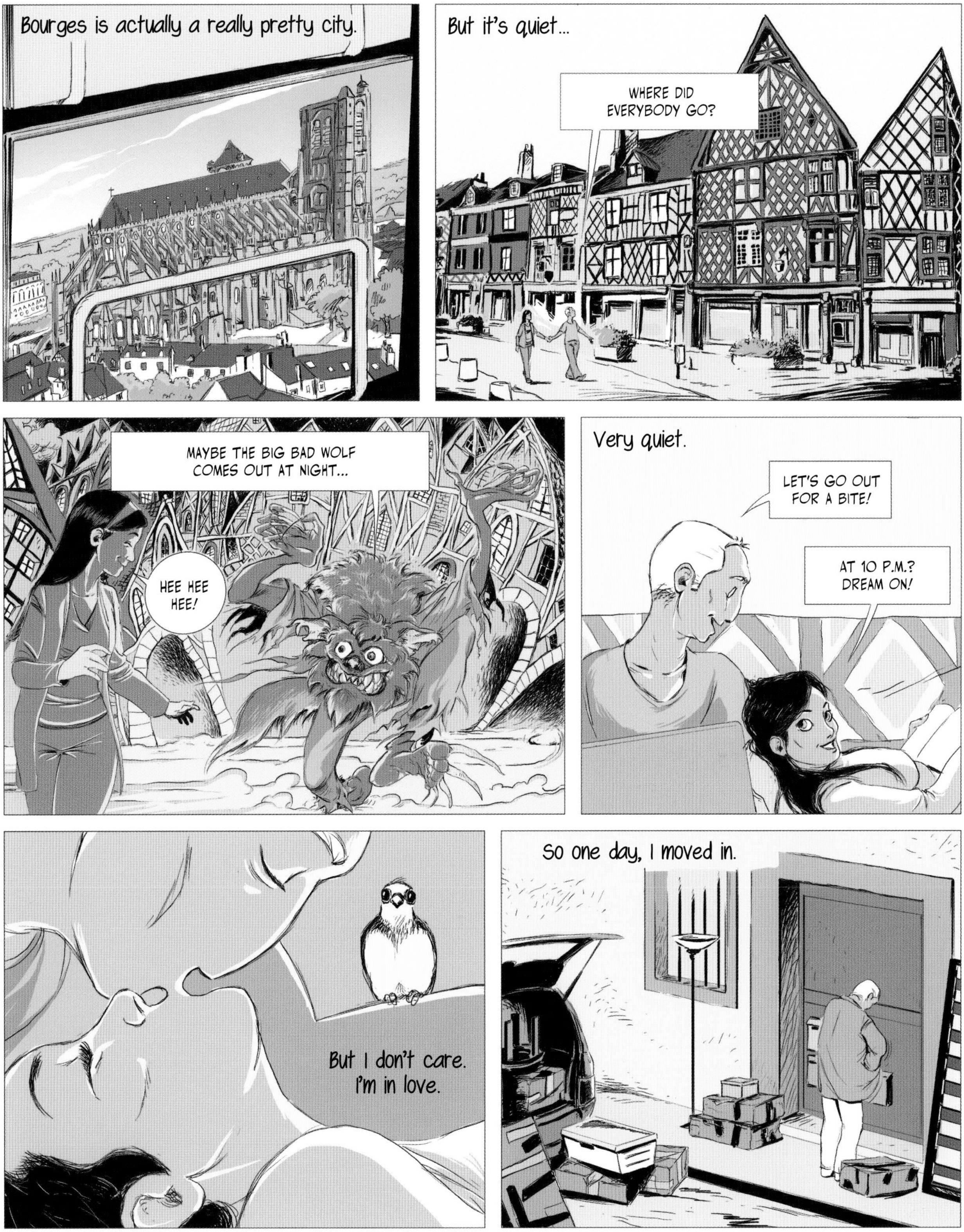
Bourges is actually a really pretty city.
But it's quiet...
WHERE DID EVERYBODY GO?
MAYBE THE BIG BAD WOLF COMES OUT AT NIGHT...
HEE HEE HEE!
Very quiet.
LET'S GO OUT FOR A BITE!
AT 10 P.M.? DREAM ON!
But I don't care. I'm in love.
So one day, I moved in.

Lea is 40 years old.
No kids.

Can't have any.

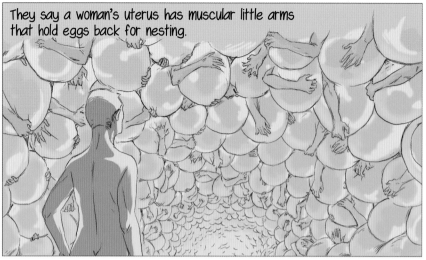

They say a woman's uterus has muscular little arms that hold eggs back for nesting.

Lea has none of those.

To enter motherhood, she'd have to select the Medically Assisted Procreation feature.

She just happened to never opt for it.

Which is fine with me.

It's selfish, I know.

A CROISSANT
AND A CHOCOLATE
BRIOCHE, PLEASE.

But our life will be filled with surprises and experiences.

And I want to fully enjoy my newfound freedom.

WHAT SHOULD WE DO
THIS WEEKEND? STAY
IN BED OR GO TO
THE COAST?

We'll hit the road together this summer.
No obligations and very little baggage.

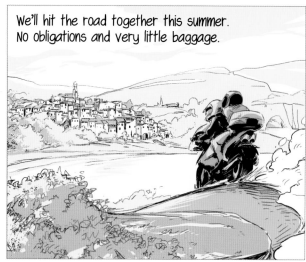

Just the thrill of living in the moment.

SIR?

SIR? IS THIS SEAT TAKEN?

Of course, my work as
a journalist and my family
have me going back up
north on a regular basis.

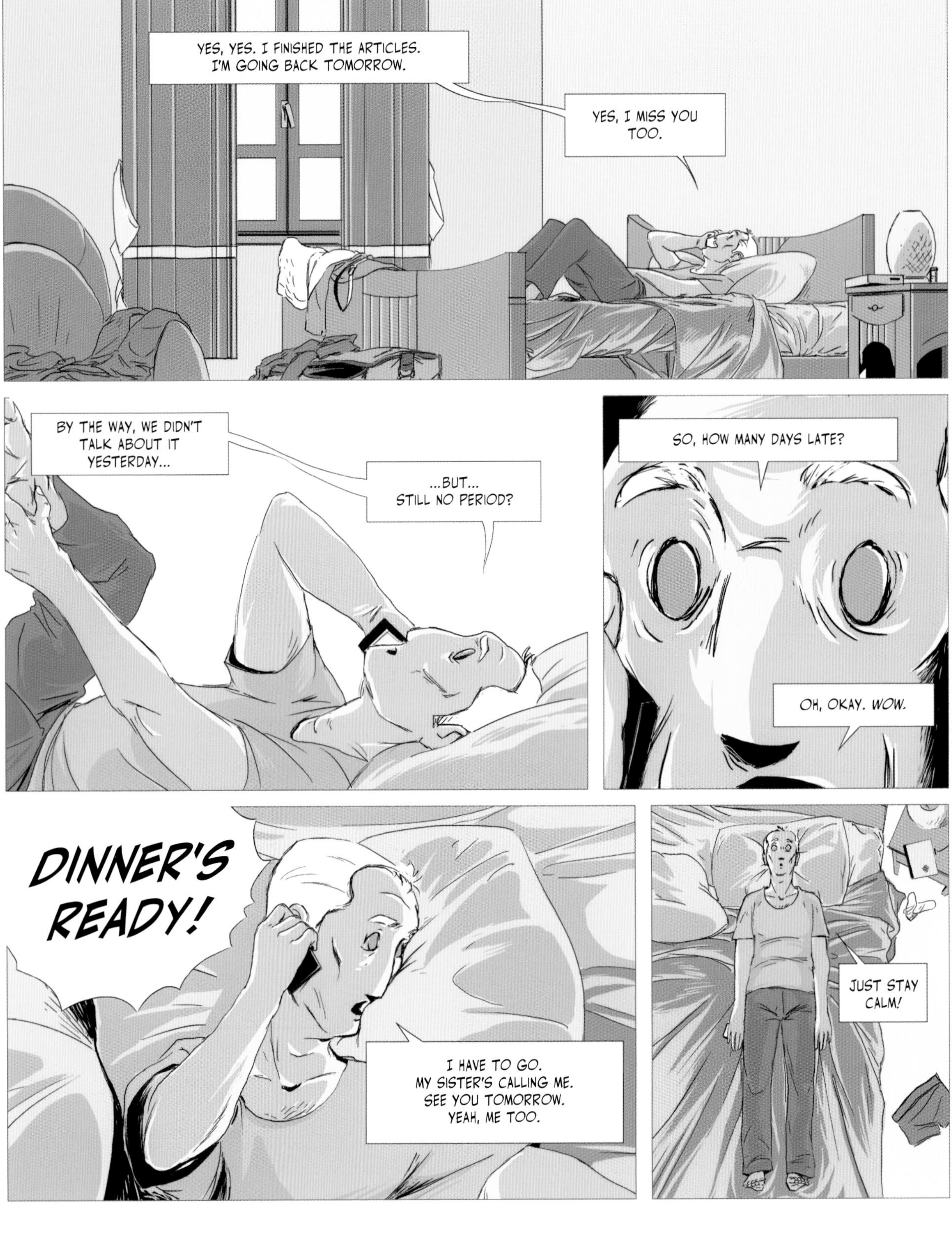
YES, YES. I FINISHED THE ARTICLES. I'M GOING BACK TOMORROW.
YES, I MISS YOU TOO.
BY THE WAY, WE DIDN'T TALK ABOUT IT YESTERDAY...
...BUT... STILL NO PERIOD?
SO, HOW MANY DAYS LATE?
OH, OKAY. WOW.
DINNER'S READY!
I HAVE TO GO. MY SISTER'S CALLING ME. SEE YOU TOMORROW. YEAH, ME TOO.
JUST STAY CALM!

JUNE

1

EARTH

Wednesday the 6th

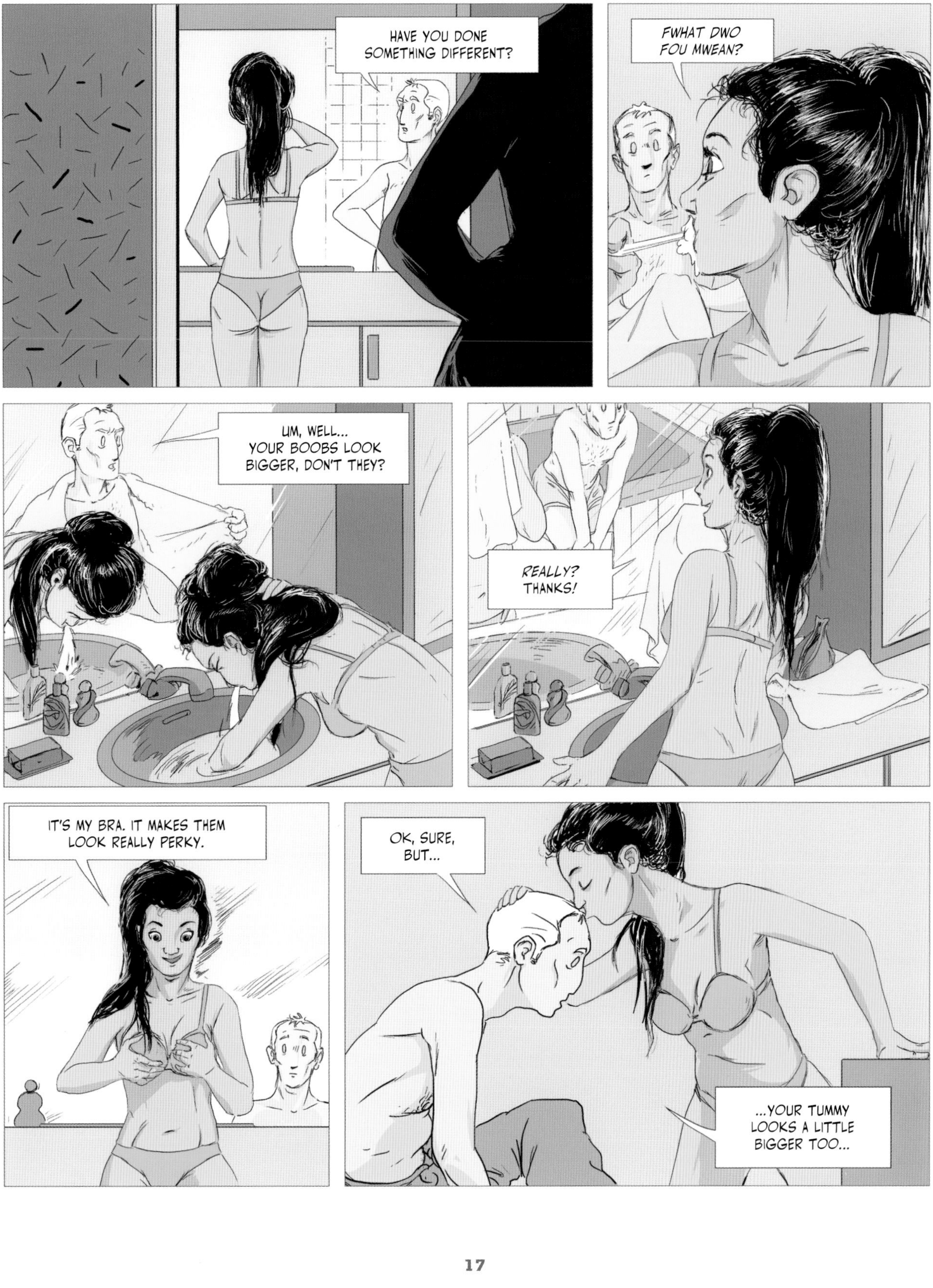
HAVE YOU DONE SOMETHING DIFFERENT?
FWHAT DWO FOU MWEAN?
UM, WELL... YOUR BOOBS LOOK BIGGER, DON'T THEY?
REALLY? THANKS!
IT'S MY BRA. IT MAKES THEM LOOK REALLY PERKY.
OK, SURE, BUT...
...YOUR TUMMY LOOKS A LITTLE BIGGER TOO...

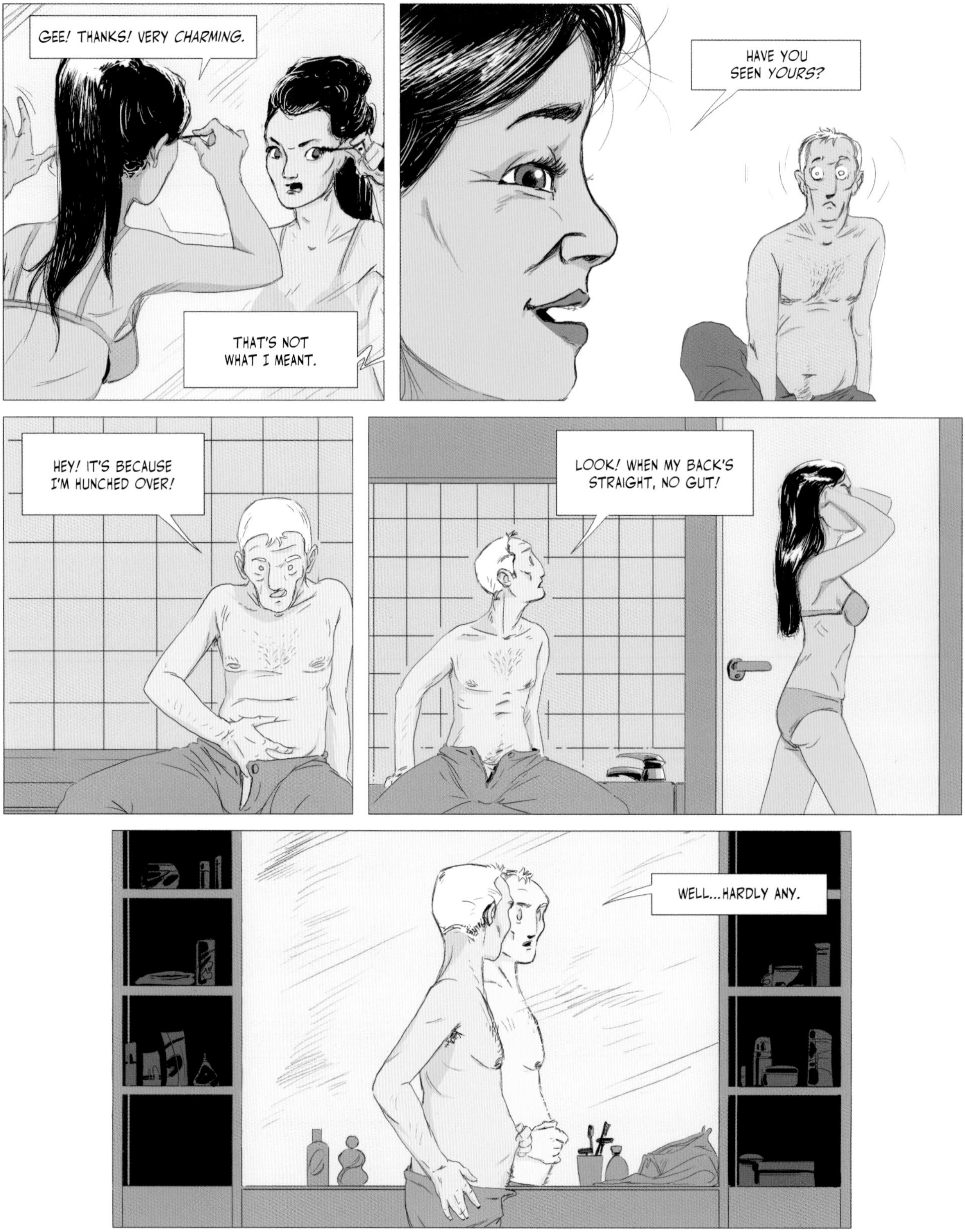
GEE! THANKS! VERY CHARMING.
THAT'S NOT WHAT I MEANT.
HAVE YOU SEEN YOURS?
HEY! IT'S BECAUSE I'M HUNCHED OVER!
LOOK! WHEN MY BACK'S STRAIGHT, NO GUT!
WELL...HARDLY ANY.

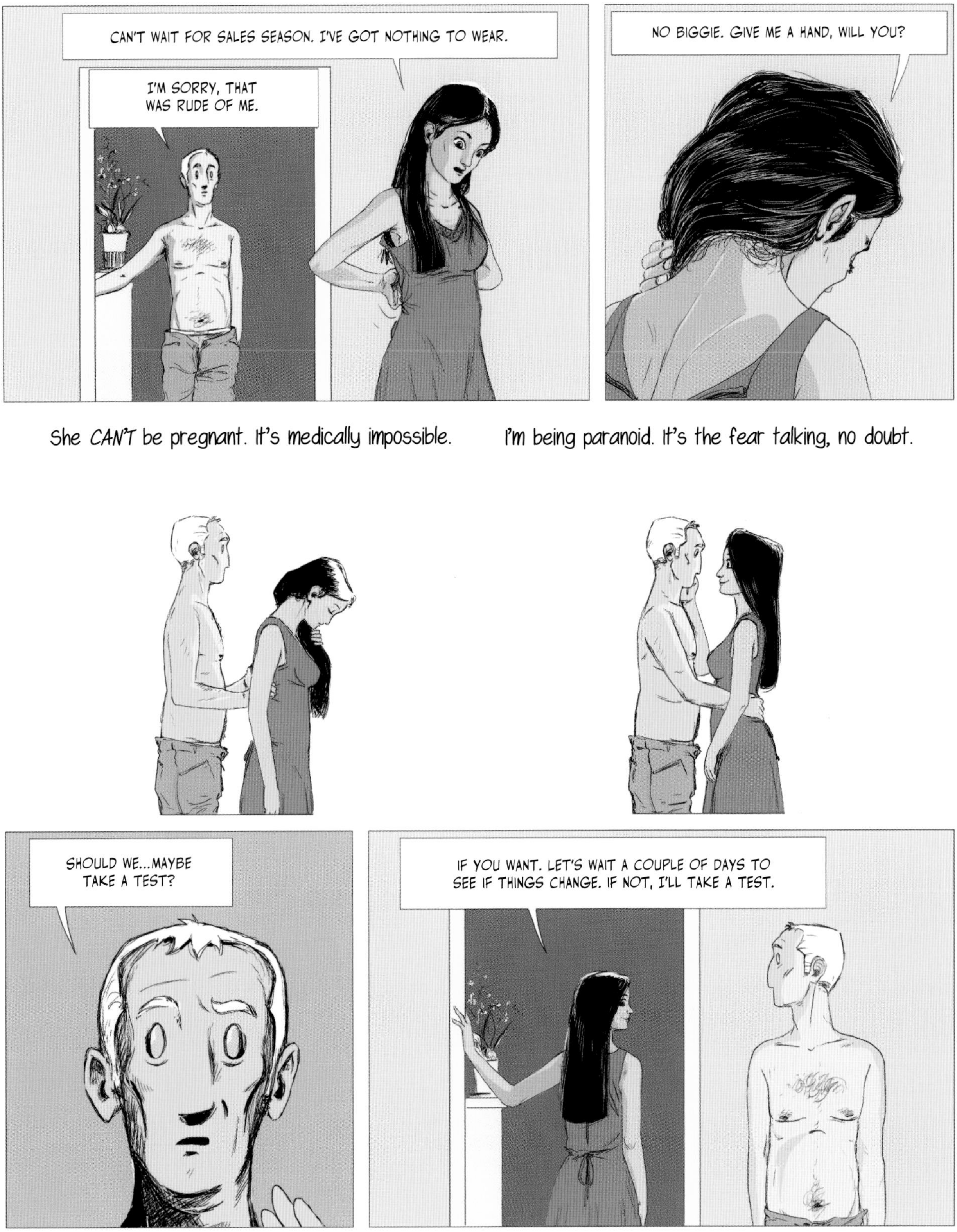
CAN'T WAIT FOR SALES SEASON. I'VE GOT NOTHING TO WEAR.
I'M SORRY, THAT WAS RUDE OF ME.
NO BIGGIE. GIVE ME A HAND, WILL YOU?
She CAN'T be pregnant. It's medically impossible.
I'm being paranoid. It's the fear talking, no doubt.
SHOULD WE...MAYBE TAKE A TEST?
IF YOU WANT. LET'S WAIT A COUPLE OF DAYS TO SEE IF THINGS CHANGE. IF NOT, I'LL TAKE A TEST.

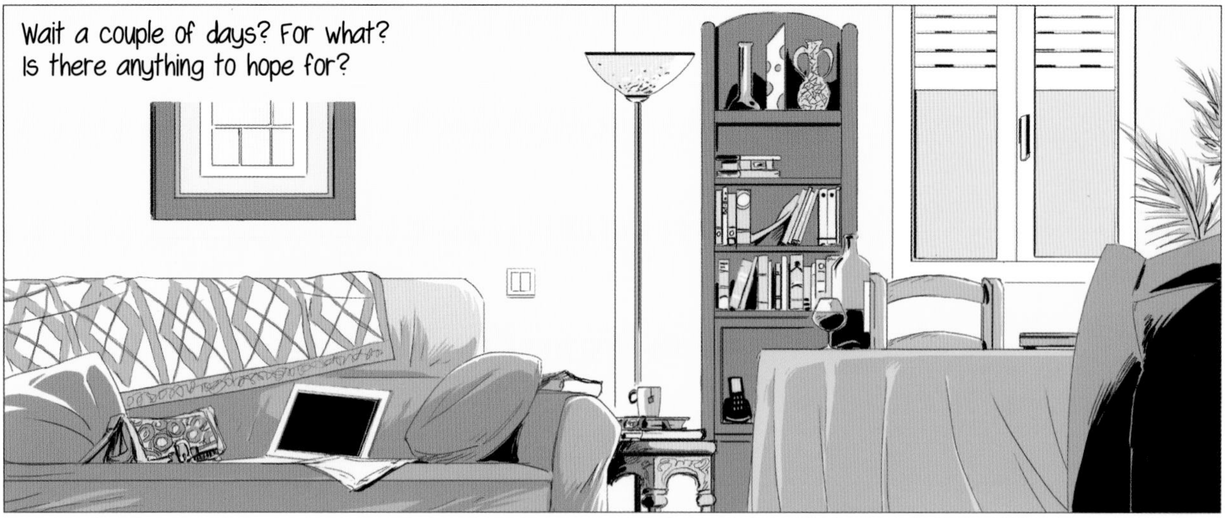
Wait a couple of days? For what?
Is there anything to hope for?

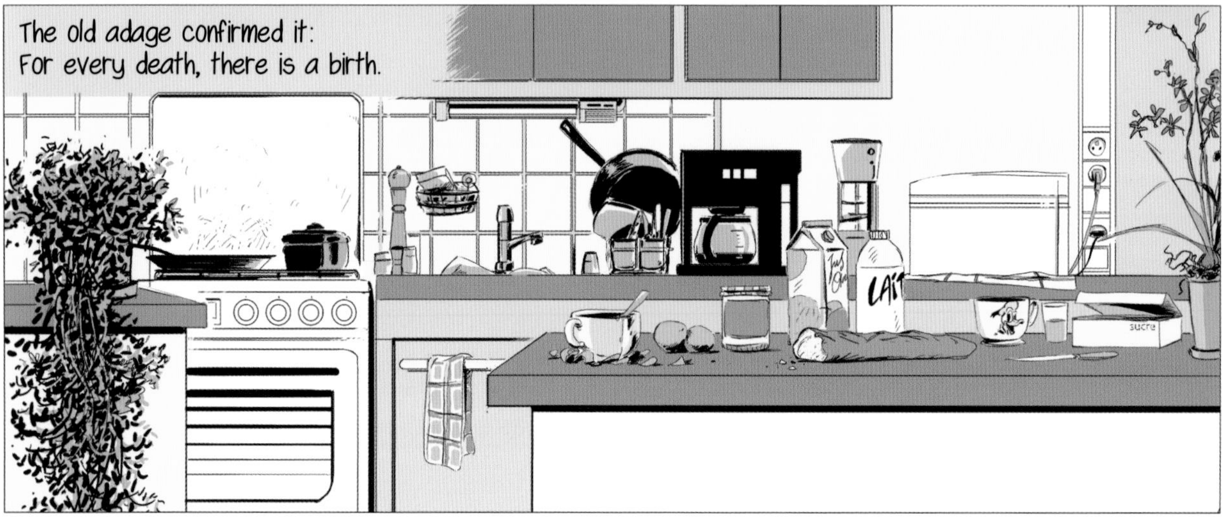
The old adage confirmed it:
For every death, there is a birth.
sucre

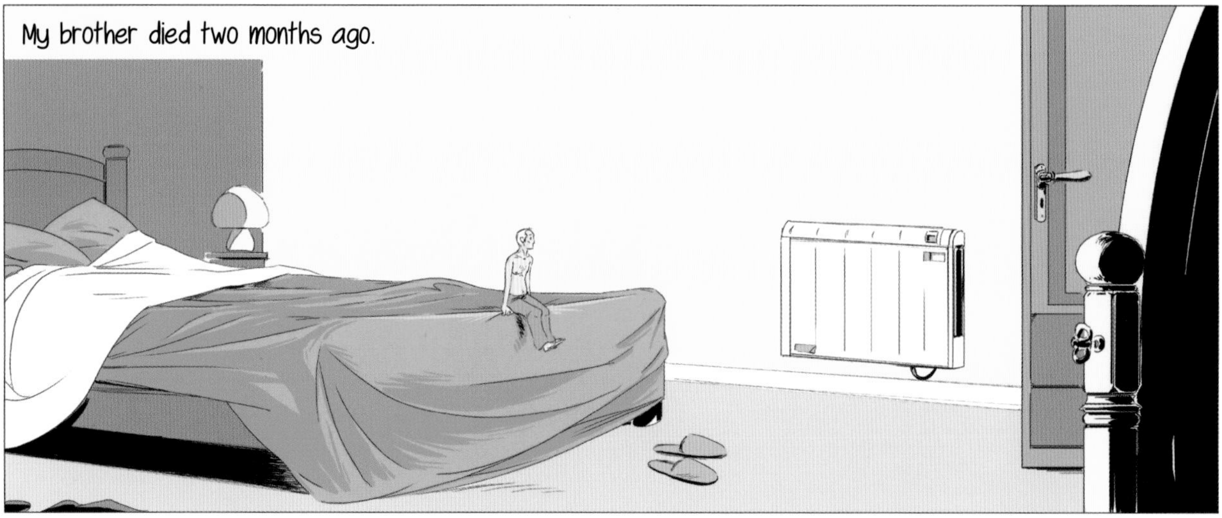
My brother died two months ago.

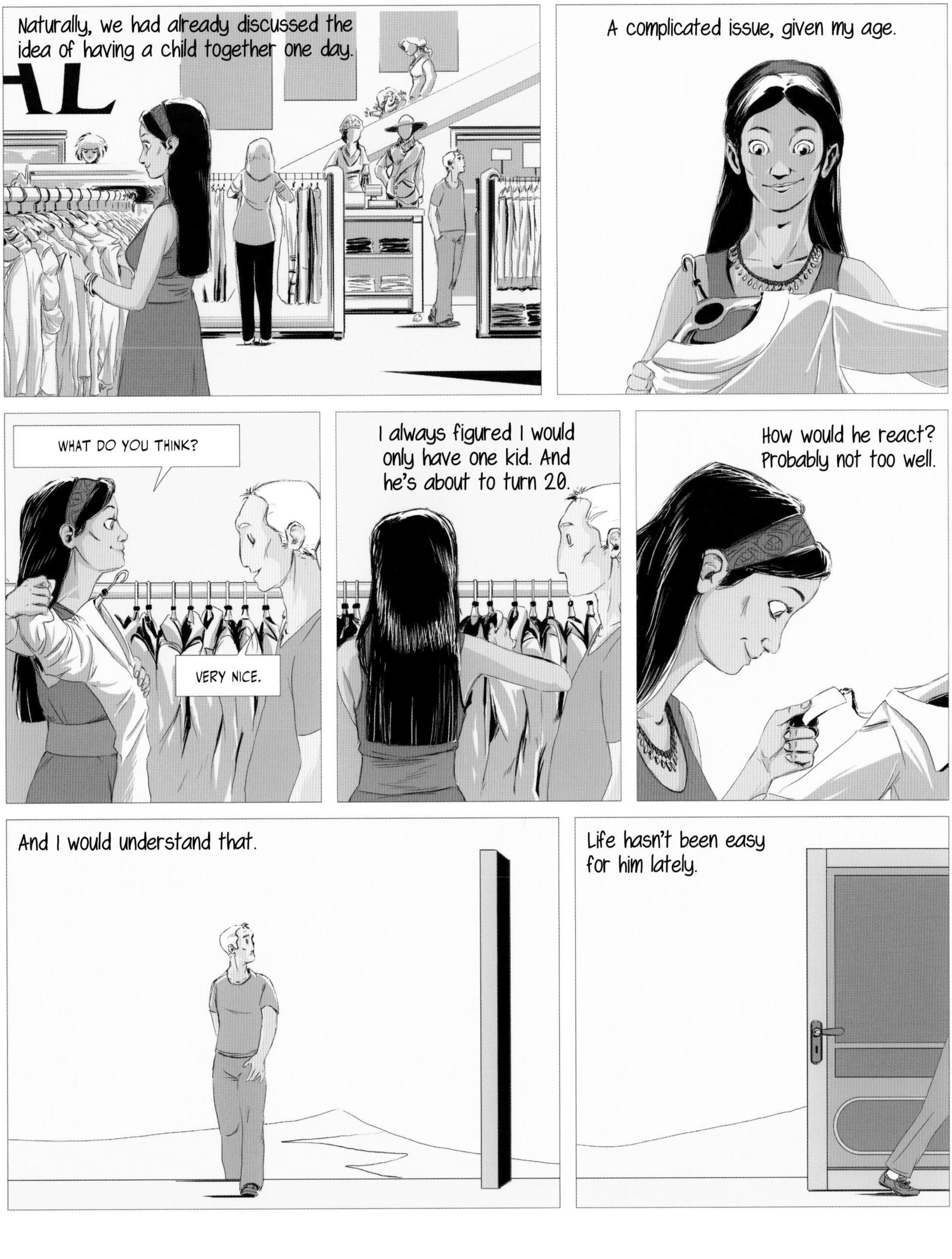
Naturally, we had already discussed the idea of having a child together one day.
A complicated issue, given my age.
WHAT DO YOU THINK?
VERY NICE.
I always figured I would only have one kid. And he's about to turn 20.
How would he react? Probably not too well.
And I would understand that.
Life hasn't been easy for him lately.

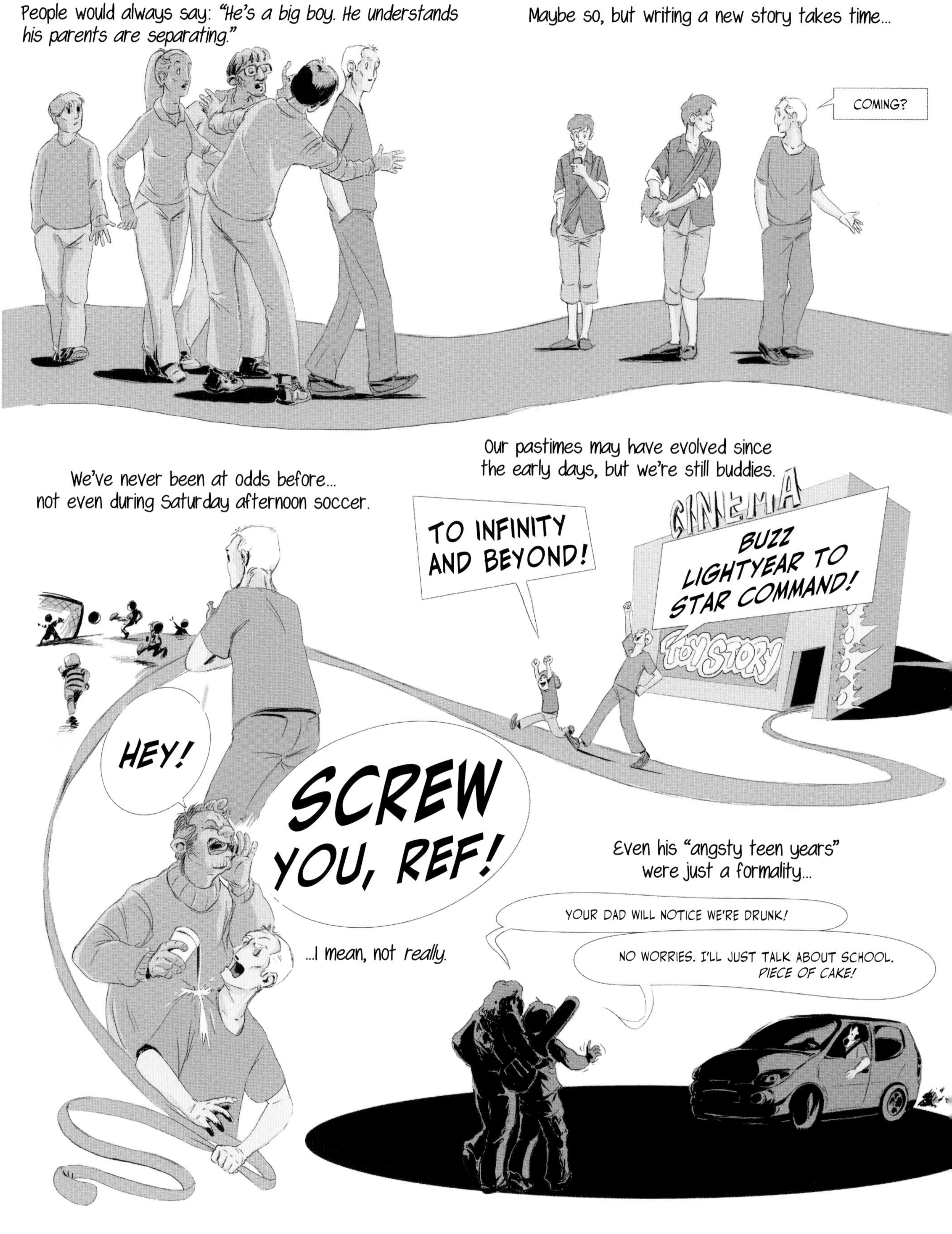
People would always say: "He's a big boy. He understands his parents are separating."
Maybe so, but writing a new story takes time...
COMING?
We've never been at odds before... not even during Saturday afternoon soccer.
HEY!
SCREW YOU, REF!
...I mean, not *really*.
Our pastimes may have evolved since the early days, but we're still buddies.
TO INFINITY AND BEYOND!
CINEMA
BUZZ LIGHTYEAR TO STAR COMMAND!
TOY STORY
Even his "angsty teen years" were just a formality...
YOUR DAD WILL NOTICE WE'RE DRUNK!
NO WORRIES. I'LL JUST TALK ABOUT SCHOOL. PIECE OF CAKE!

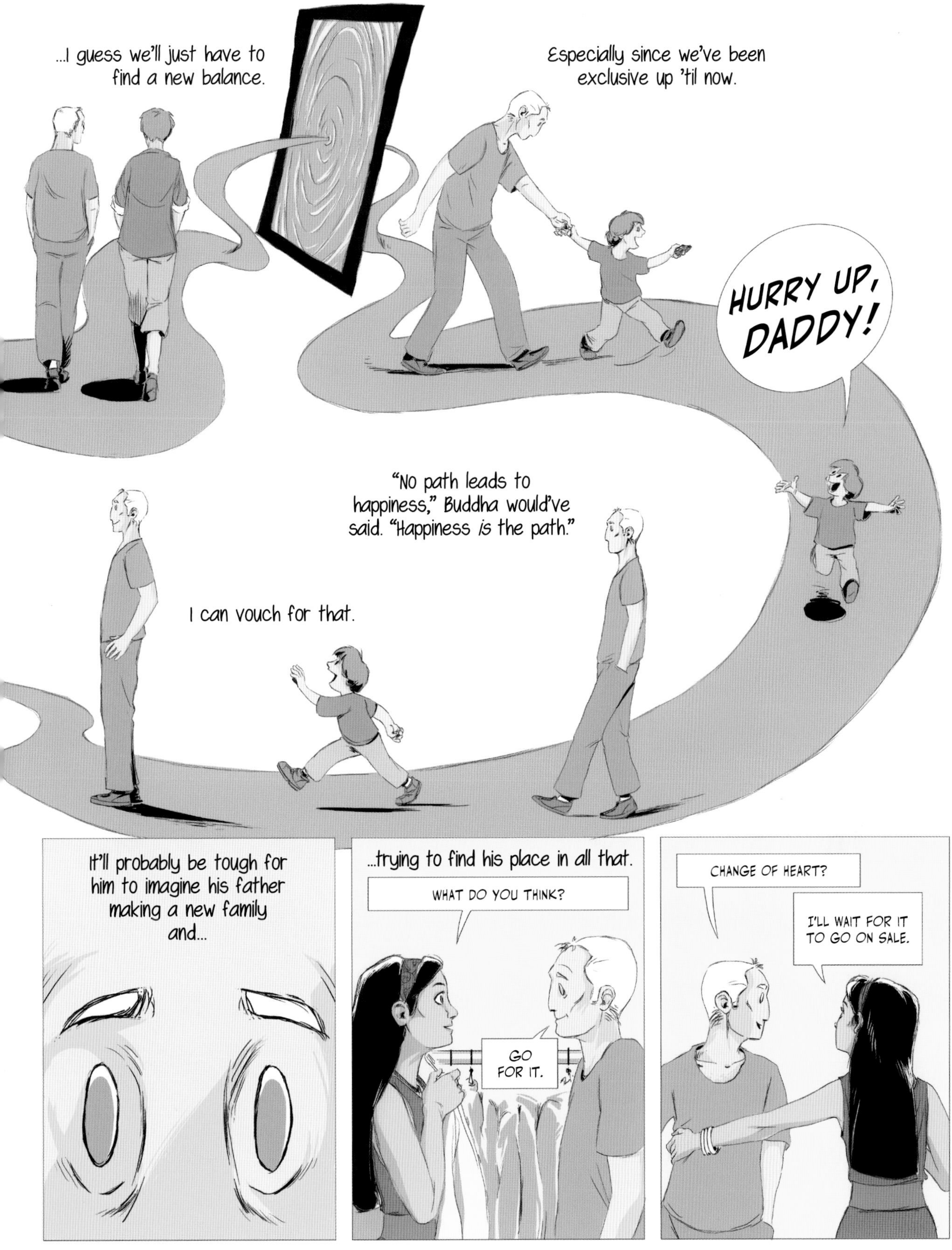

...I guess we'll just have to find a new balance.
Especially since we've been exclusive up 'til now.
HURRY UP, DADDY!
"No path leads to happiness," Buddha would've said. "Happiness *is* the path."
I can vouch for that.
It'll probably be tough for him to imagine his father making a new family and...
...trying to find his place in all that.
WHAT DO YOU THINK?
GO FOR IT.
CHANGE OF HEART?
I'LL WAIT FOR IT TO GO ON SALE.

Saturday the 16th

That thing's been taunting me for two days.

KOF KOF

Lea went to the drugstore.

To put my mind at ease, she said. But also just to know.

I'm waiting.

KOF BEEP BEEP BEEP BEEP BEEP

I CAN'T GO TO WORK LIKE THIS!

YOU MEAN, PREGNANT?

NO, SILLY, I THINK I CAUGHT THE FLU.

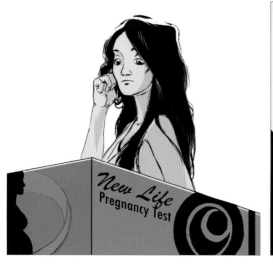

New Life
Pregnancy Test

SHALL I?

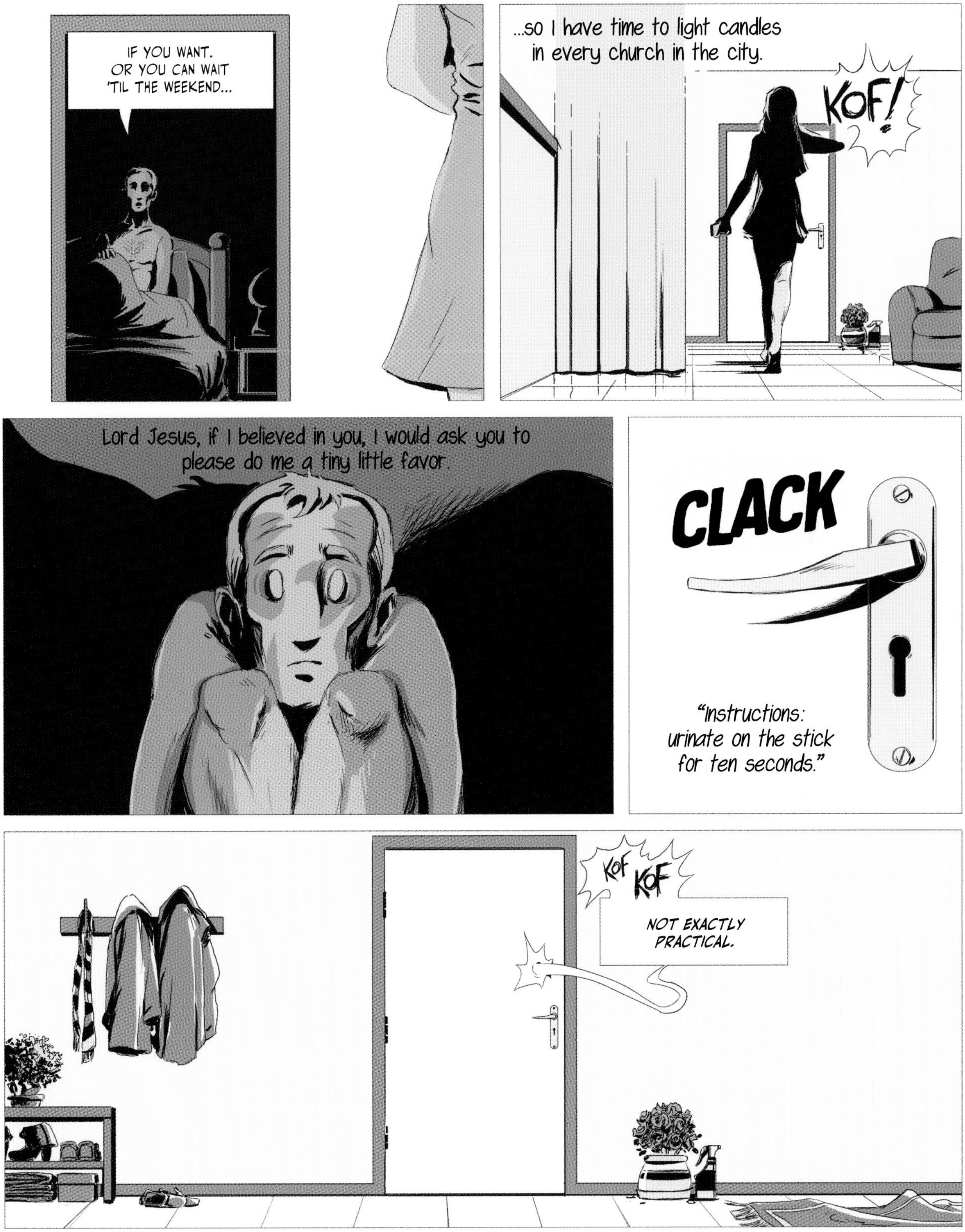
IF YOU WANT.
OR YOU CAN WAIT
'TIL THE WEEKEND...
...so I have time to light candles in every church in the city.
KOF!
Lord Jesus, if I believed in you, I would ask you to please do me a tiny little favor.
CLACK
"Instructions: urinate on the stick for ten seconds."
KOF KOF
NOT EXACTLY PRACTICAL.

"If only the top line appears, it's negative."

"If two lines appear, it's positive."

"If only the bottom line appears, you need to start over."

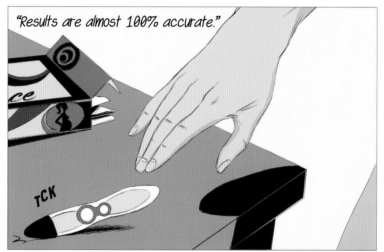

"Results are almost 100% accurate."

TCK

I DON'T GET IT. THERE'S NOTHING TO SEE.

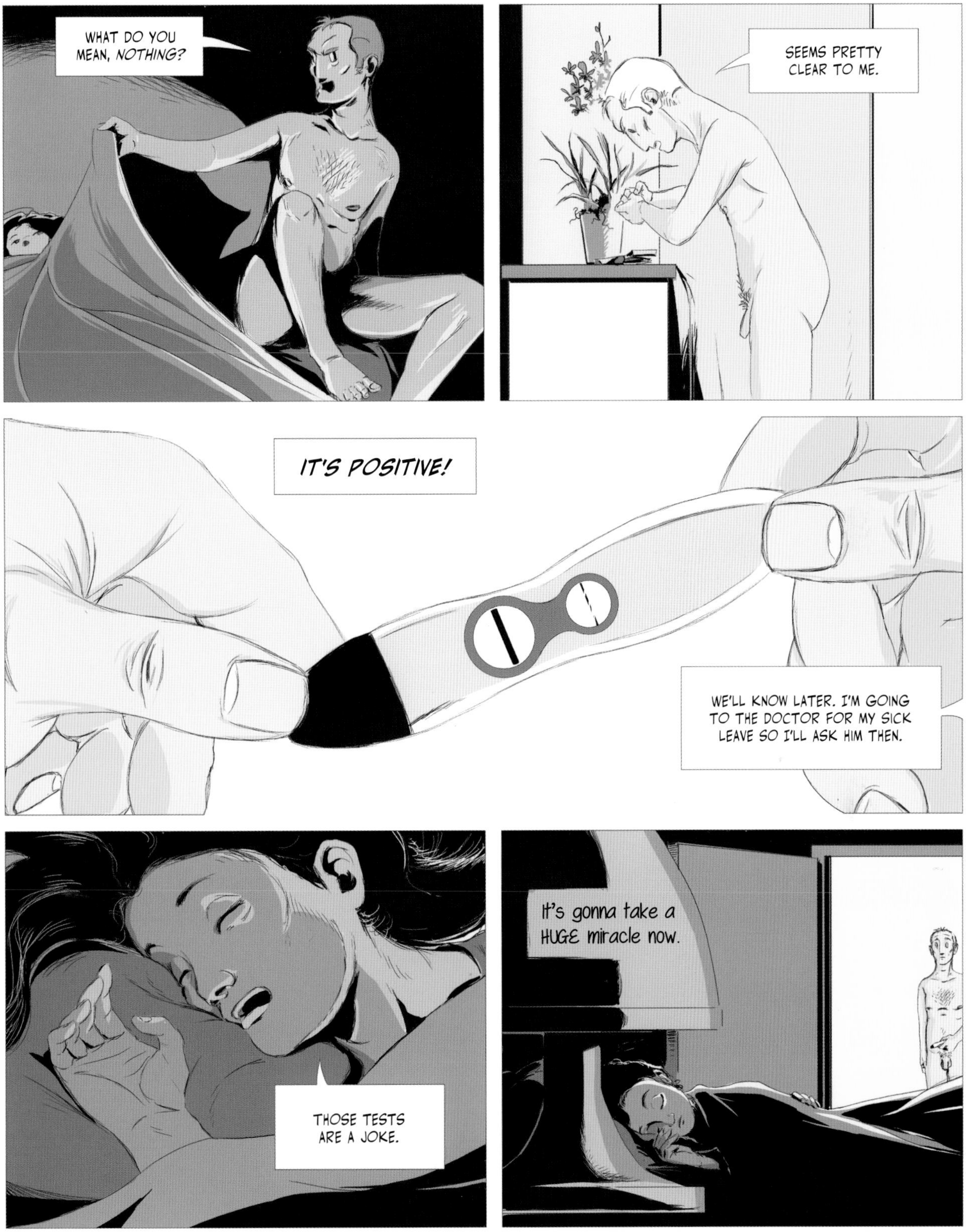
WHAT DO YOU MEAN, *NOTHING?*
SEEMS PRETTY CLEAR TO ME.
IT'S POSITIVE!
WE'LL KNOW LATER. I'M GOING TO THE DOCTOR FOR MY SICK LEAVE SO I'LL ASK HIM THEN.
THOSE TESTS ARE A JOKE.
It's gonna take a HUGE miracle now.

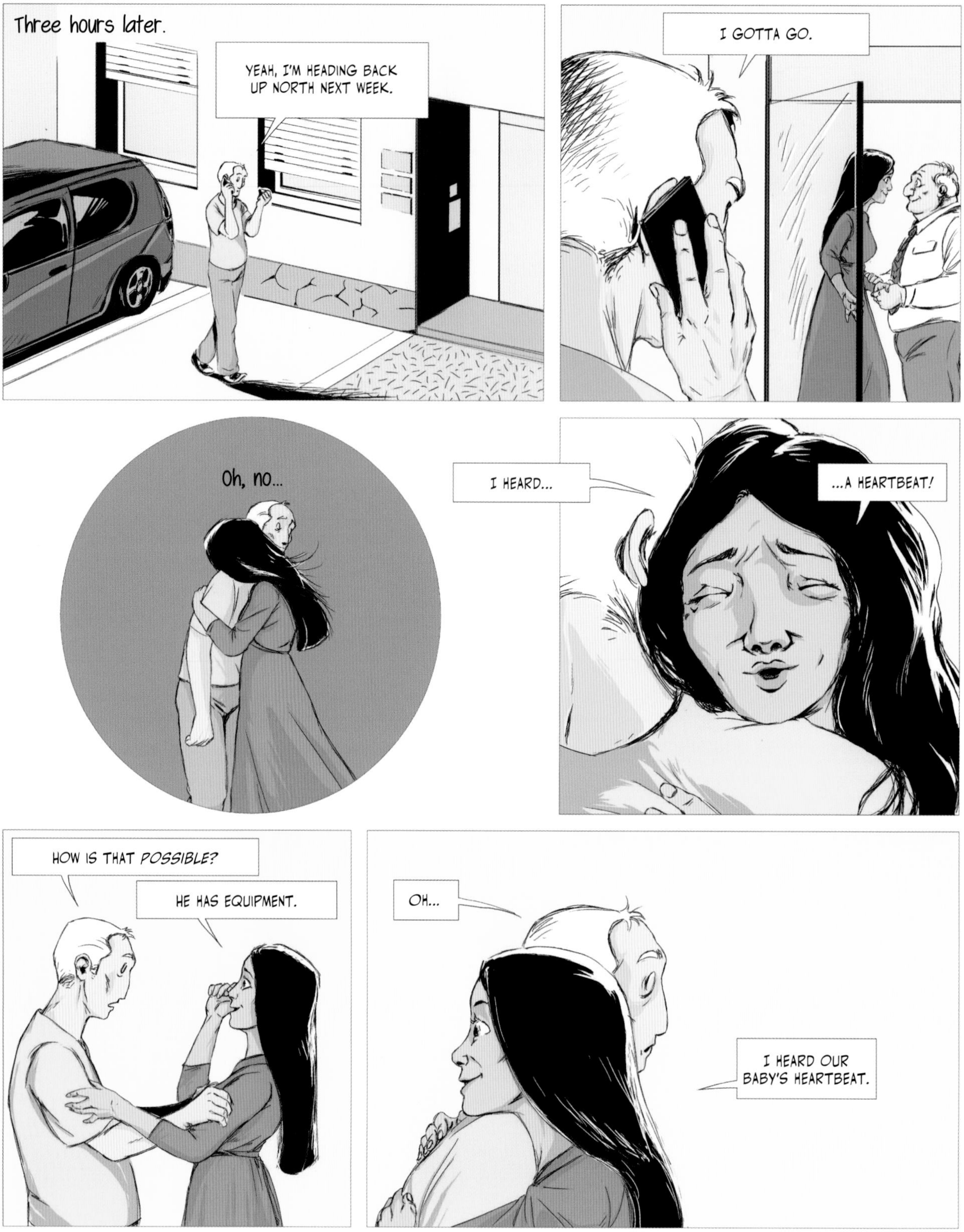
Three hours later.
YEAH, I'M HEADING BACK UP NORTH NEXT WEEK.
I GOTTA GO.
Oh, no...
I HEARD...
...A HEARTBEAT!
HOW IS THAT *POSSIBLE?*
HE HAS EQUIPMENT.
OH...
I HEARD OUR BABY'S HEARTBEAT.

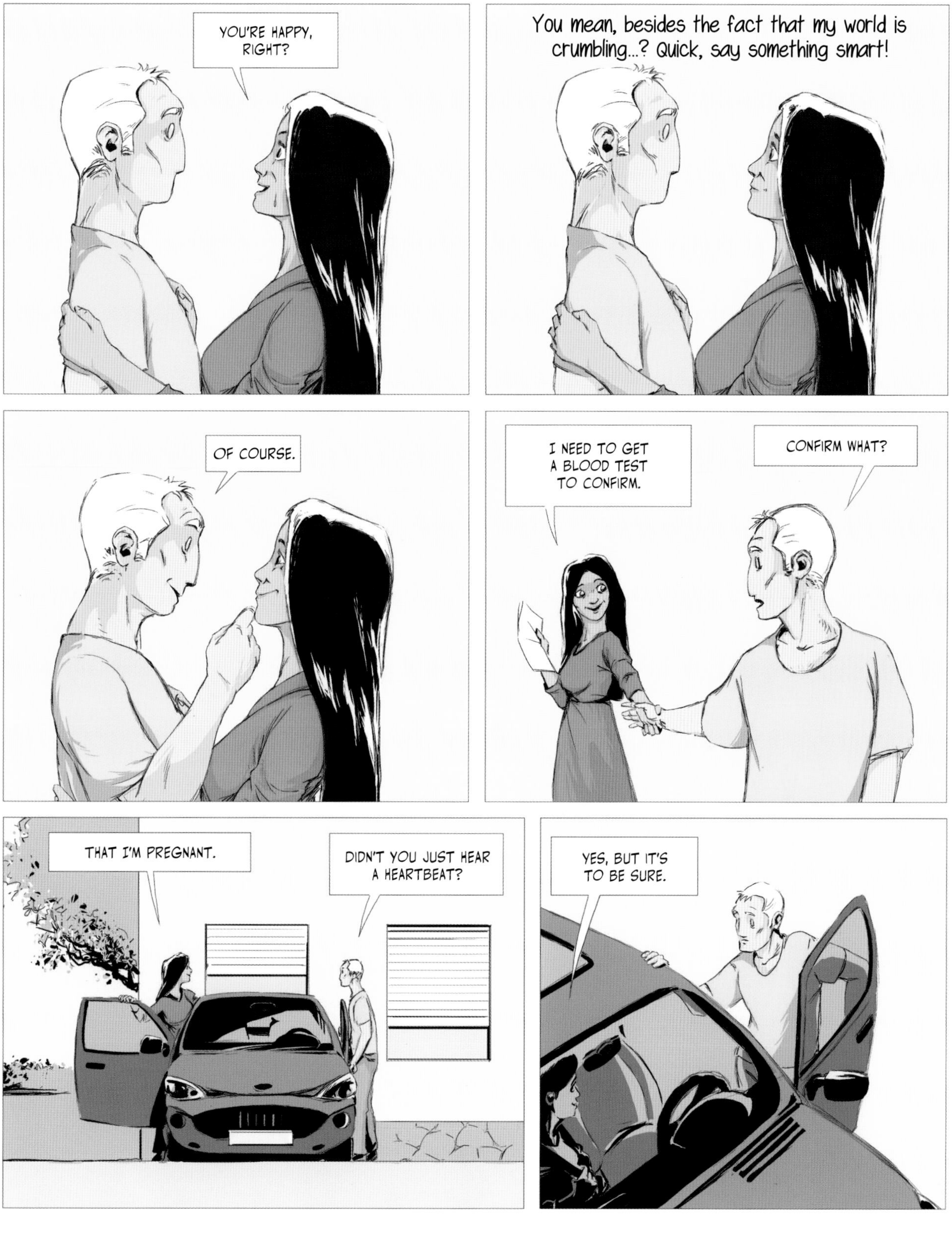
YOU'RE HAPPY, RIGHT?
You mean, besides the fact that my world is crumbling...? Quick, say something smart!
OF COURSE.
I NEED TO GET A BLOOD TEST TO CONFIRM.
CONFIRM WHAT?
THAT I'M PREGNANT.
DIDN'T YOU JUST HEAR A HEARTBEAT?
YES, BUT IT'S TO BE SURE.

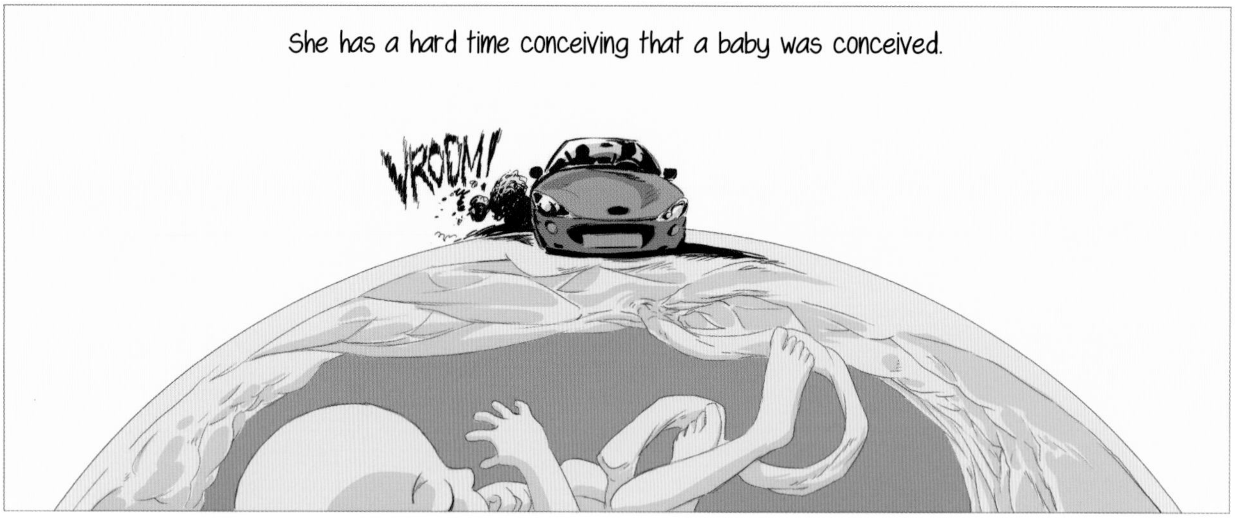
She has a hard time conceiving that a baby was conceived.
VROOM!

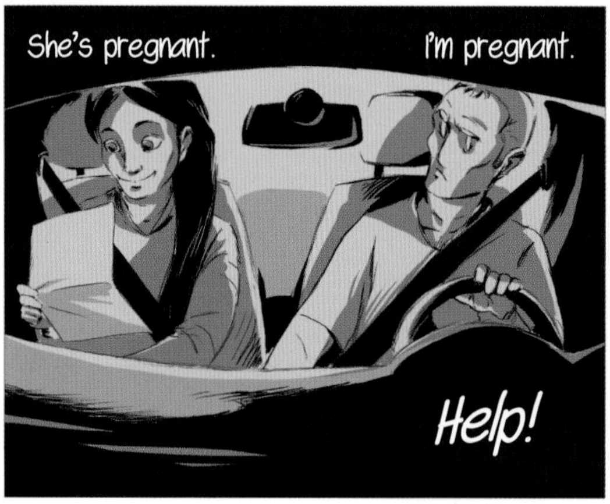
She's pregnant.
I'm pregnant.
Help!

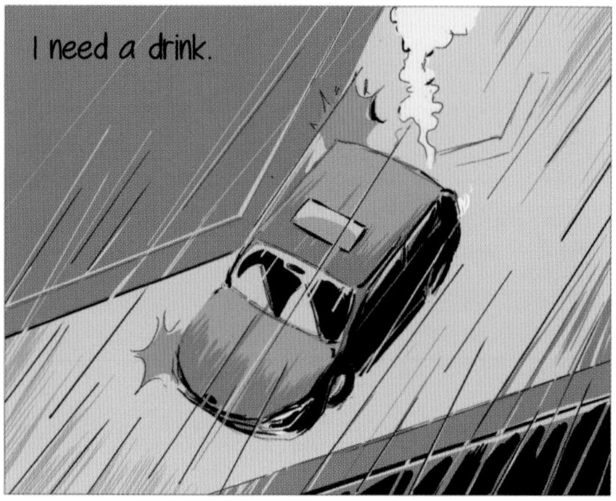
I need a drink.

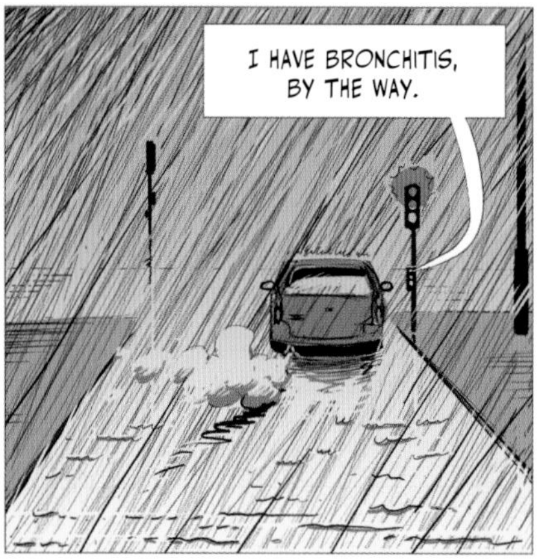
I HAVE BRONCHITIS, BY THE WAY.

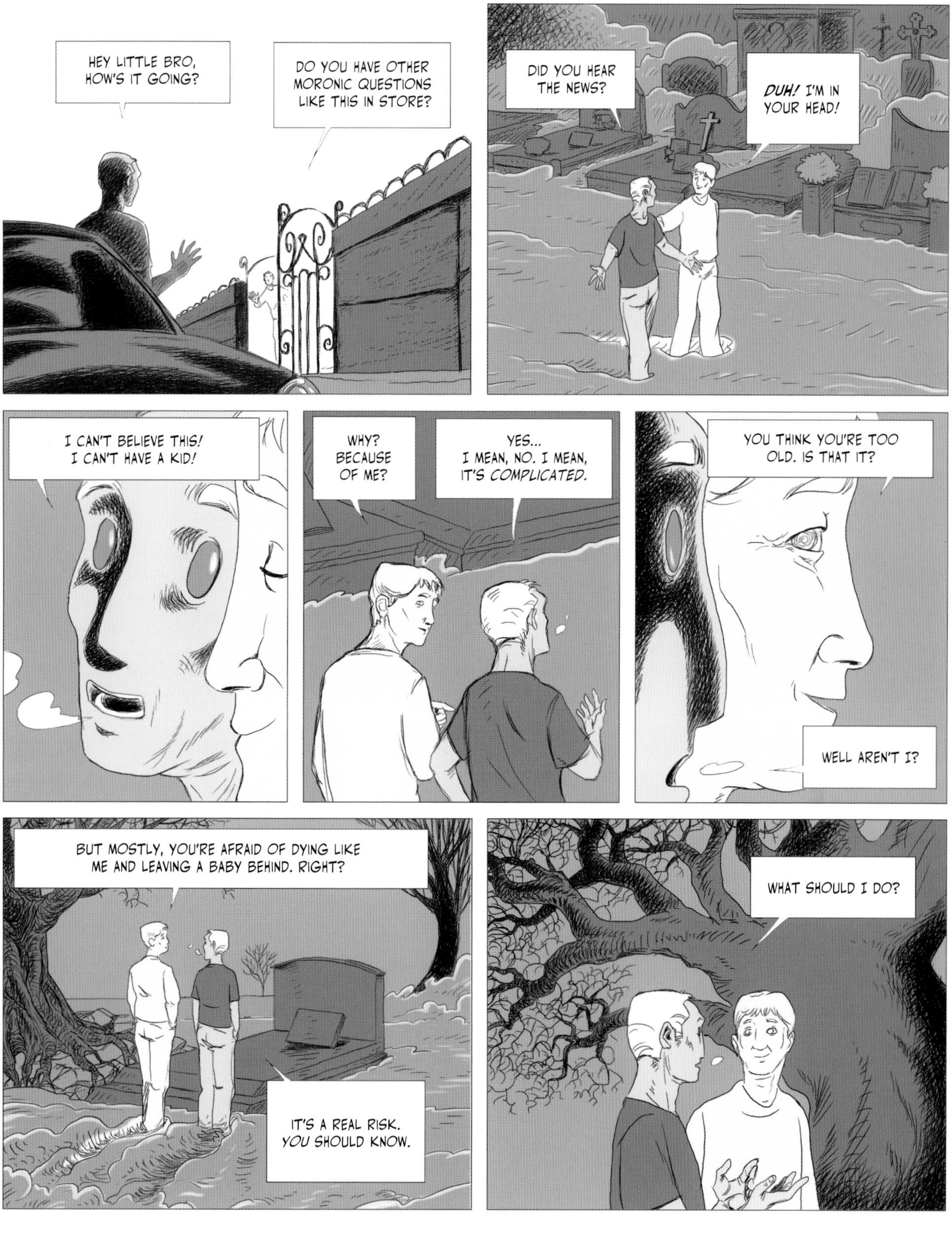
HEY LITTLE BRO, HOW'S IT GOING?
DO YOU HAVE OTHER MORONIC QUESTIONS LIKE THIS IN STORE?
DID YOU HEAR THE NEWS?
DUH! I'M IN YOUR HEAD!
I CAN'T BELIEVE THIS! I CAN'T HAVE A KID!
WHY? BECAUSE OF ME?
YES... I MEAN, NO. I MEAN, IT'S *COMPLICATED.*
YOU THINK YOU'RE TOO OLD. IS THAT IT?
WELL AREN'T I?
BUT MOSTLY, YOU'RE AFRAID OF DYING LIKE ME AND LEAVING A BABY BEHIND. RIGHT?
IT'S A REAL RISK. *YOU* SHOULD KNOW.
WHAT SHOULD I DO?

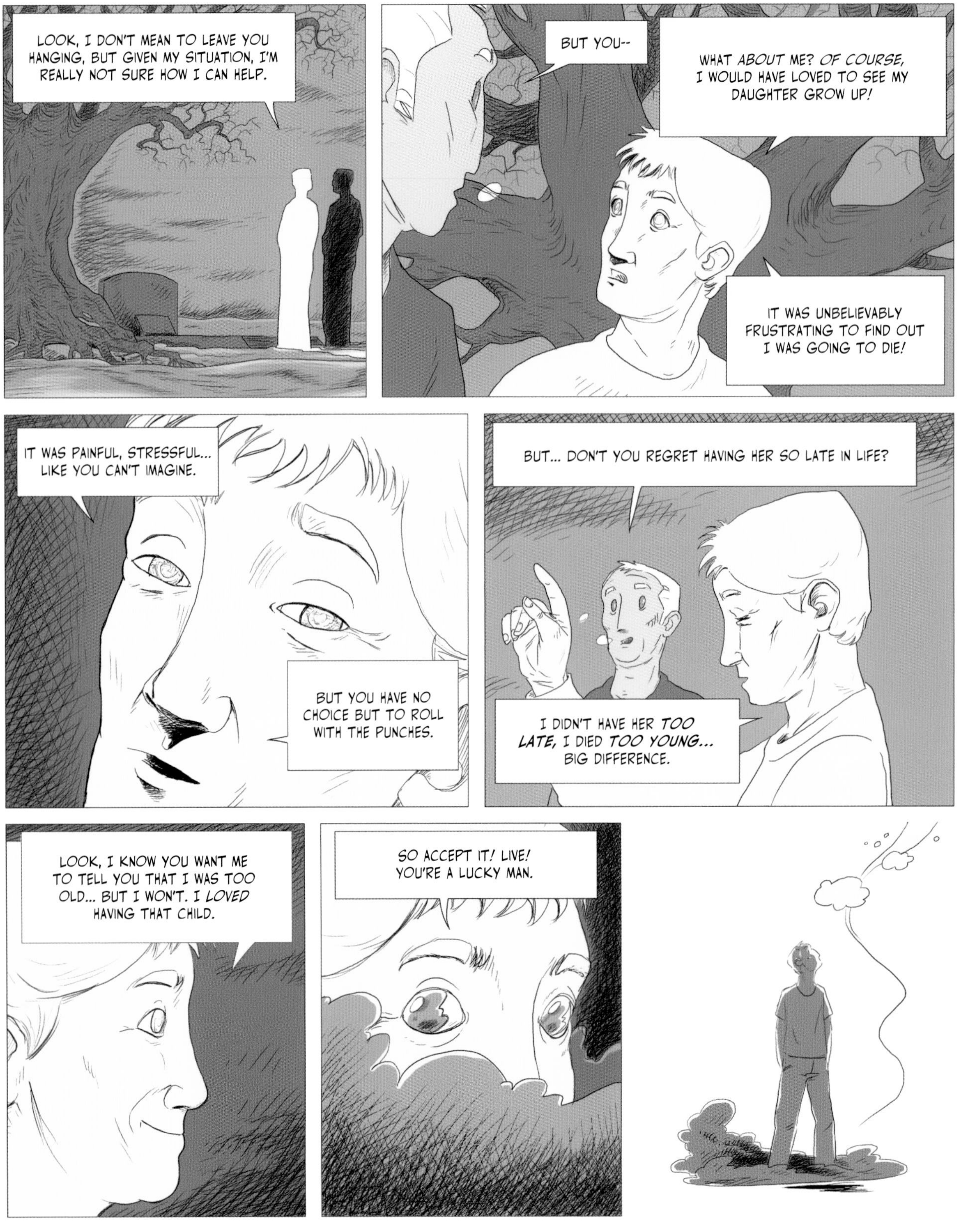
LOOK, I DON'T MEAN TO LEAVE YOU HANGING, BUT GIVEN MY SITUATION, I'M REALLY NOT SURE HOW I CAN HELP.
BUT YOU--
WHAT *ABOUT ME? OF COURSE,* I WOULD HAVE LOVED TO SEE MY DAUGHTER GROW UP!
IT WAS UNBELIEVABLY FRUSTRATING TO FIND OUT I WAS GOING TO DIE!
IT WAS PAINFUL, STRESSFUL... LIKE YOU CAN'T IMAGINE.
BUT YOU HAVE NO CHOICE BUT TO ROLL WITH THE PUNCHES.
BUT... DON'T YOU REGRET HAVING HER SO LATE IN LIFE?
I DIDN'T HAVE HER *TOO LATE,* I DIED *TOO YOUNG...* BIG DIFFERENCE.
LOOK, I KNOW YOU WANT ME TO TELL YOU THAT I WAS TOO OLD... BUT I WON'T. I *LOVED* HAVING THAT CHILD.
SO ACCEPT IT! LIVE! YOU'RE A LUCKY MAN.

Monday the 18th

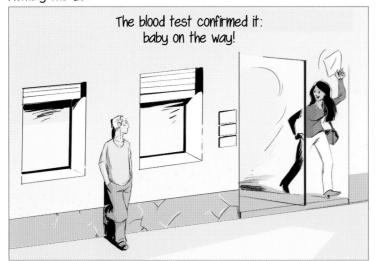

The blood test confirmed it:
baby on the way!

LET'S GO TO MY SISTER'S!

Here we go...
Announcement
Time.

First, Lea's family, of course.

HEY, XAV! WHAT BRINGS
YOU TWO HERE?

DID YOU WIN
THE LOTTERY?

CLOSE.

YOU'RE GONNA BE AN UNCLE!

WAY TO GO, MAN!
THIS CALLS FOR
A TOAST!

!

33

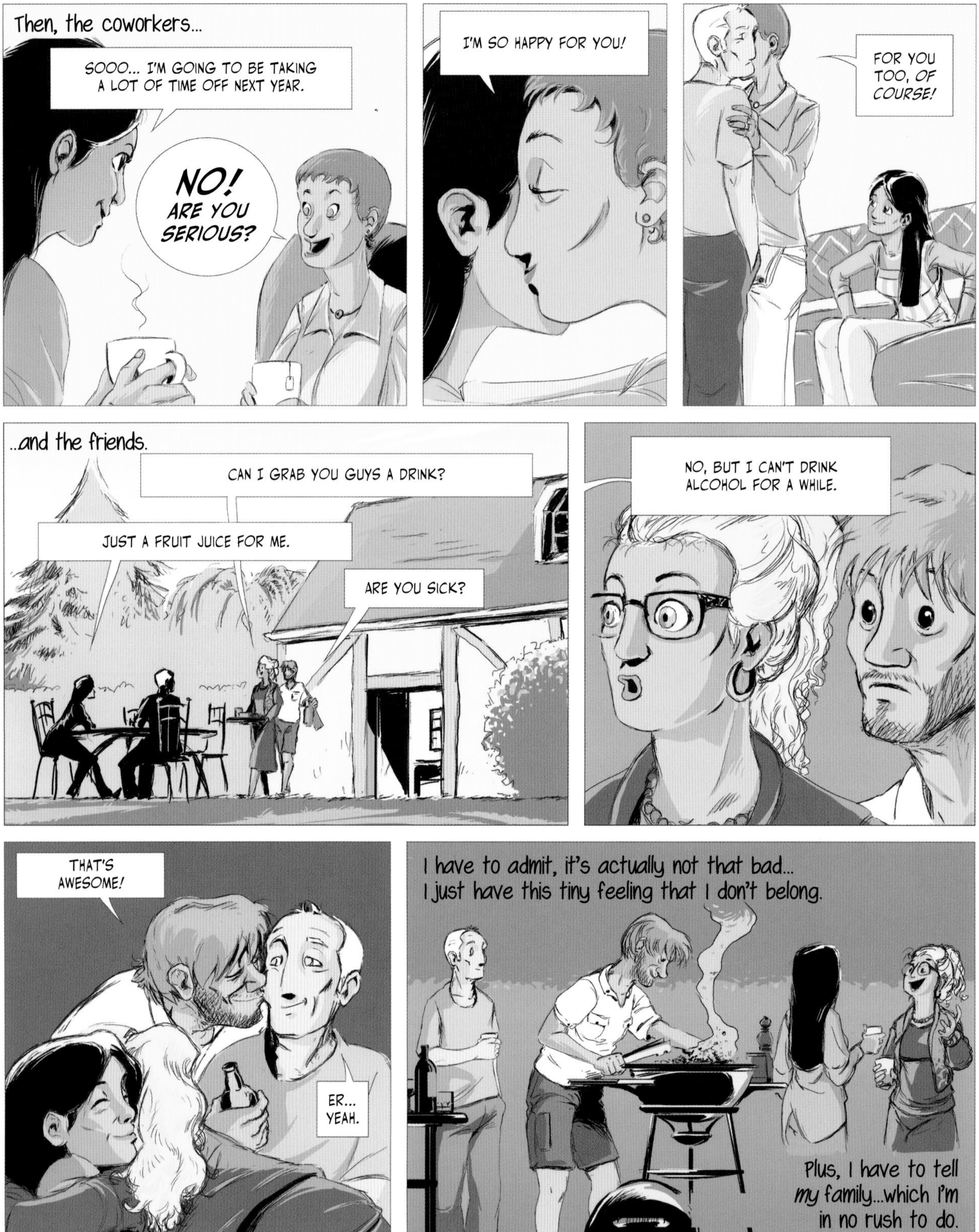
Then, the coworkers...
SOOO... I'M GOING TO BE TAKING A LOT OF TIME OFF NEXT YEAR.
NO! ARE YOU SERIOUS?
I'M SO HAPPY FOR YOU!
FOR YOU TOO, OF COURSE!
..and the friends.
CAN I GRAB YOU GUYS A DRINK?
JUST A FRUIT JUICE FOR ME.
ARE YOU SICK?
NO, BUT I CAN'T DRINK ALCOHOL FOR A WHILE.
THAT'S AWESOME!
ER... YEAH.
I have to admit, it's actually not that bad... I just have this tiny feeling that I don't belong.
Plus, I have to tell *my* family...which I'm in no rush to do.

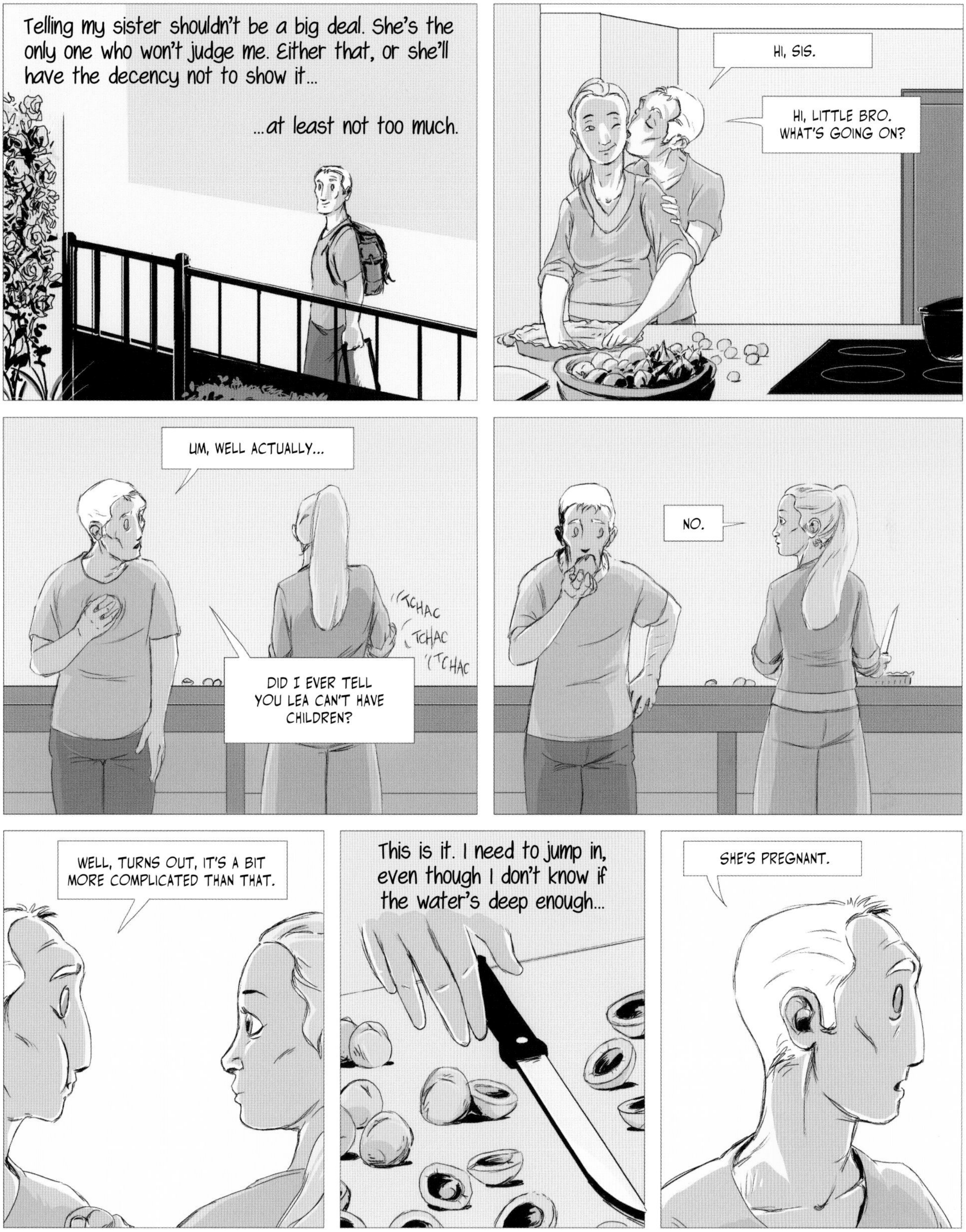
Telling my sister shouldn't be a big deal. She's the only one who won't judge me. Either that, or she'll have the decency not to show it...
...at least not too much.
HI, SIS.
HI, LITTLE BRO. WHAT'S GOING ON?
UM, WELL ACTUALLY...
TCHAC TCHAC TCHAC
DID I EVER TELL YOU LEA CAN'T HAVE CHILDREN?
NO.
WELL, TURNS OUT, IT'S A BIT MORE COMPLICATED THAN THAT.
This is it. I need to jump in, even though I don't know if the water's deep enough...
SHE'S PREGNANT.

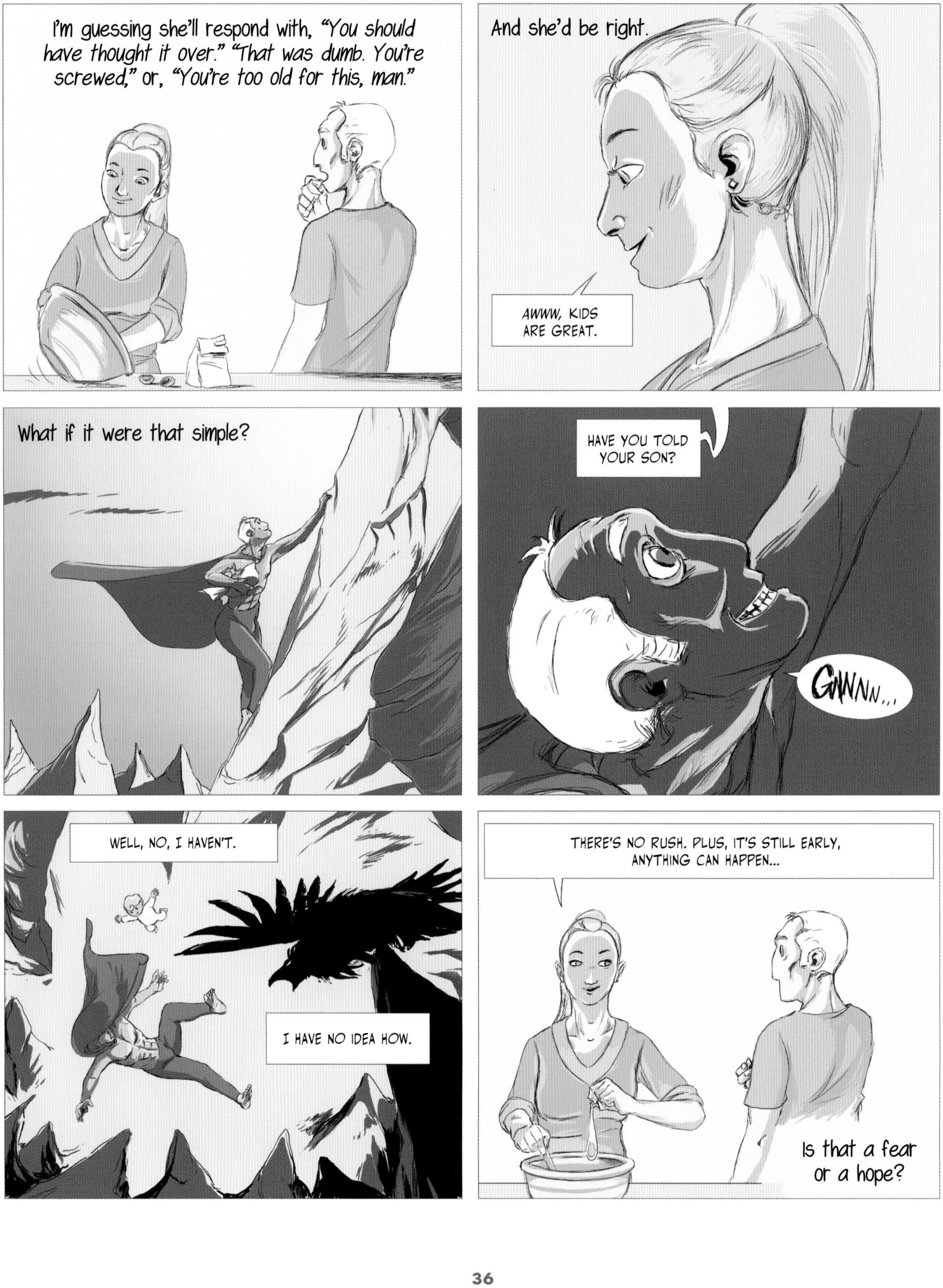
I'm guessing she'll respond with, "You should have thought it over." "That was dumb. You're screwed," or, "You're too old for this, man."
And she'd be right.
AWWW, KIDS ARE GREAT.
What if it were that simple?
HAVE YOU TOLD YOUR SON?
GWNNN...
WELL, NO, I HAVEN'T.
I HAVE NO IDEA HOW.
THERE'S NO RUSH. PLUS, IT'S STILL EARLY, ANYTHING CAN HAPPEN...
Is that a fear or a hope?

JULY

2

1

EARTH

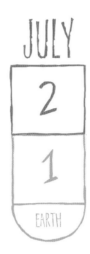

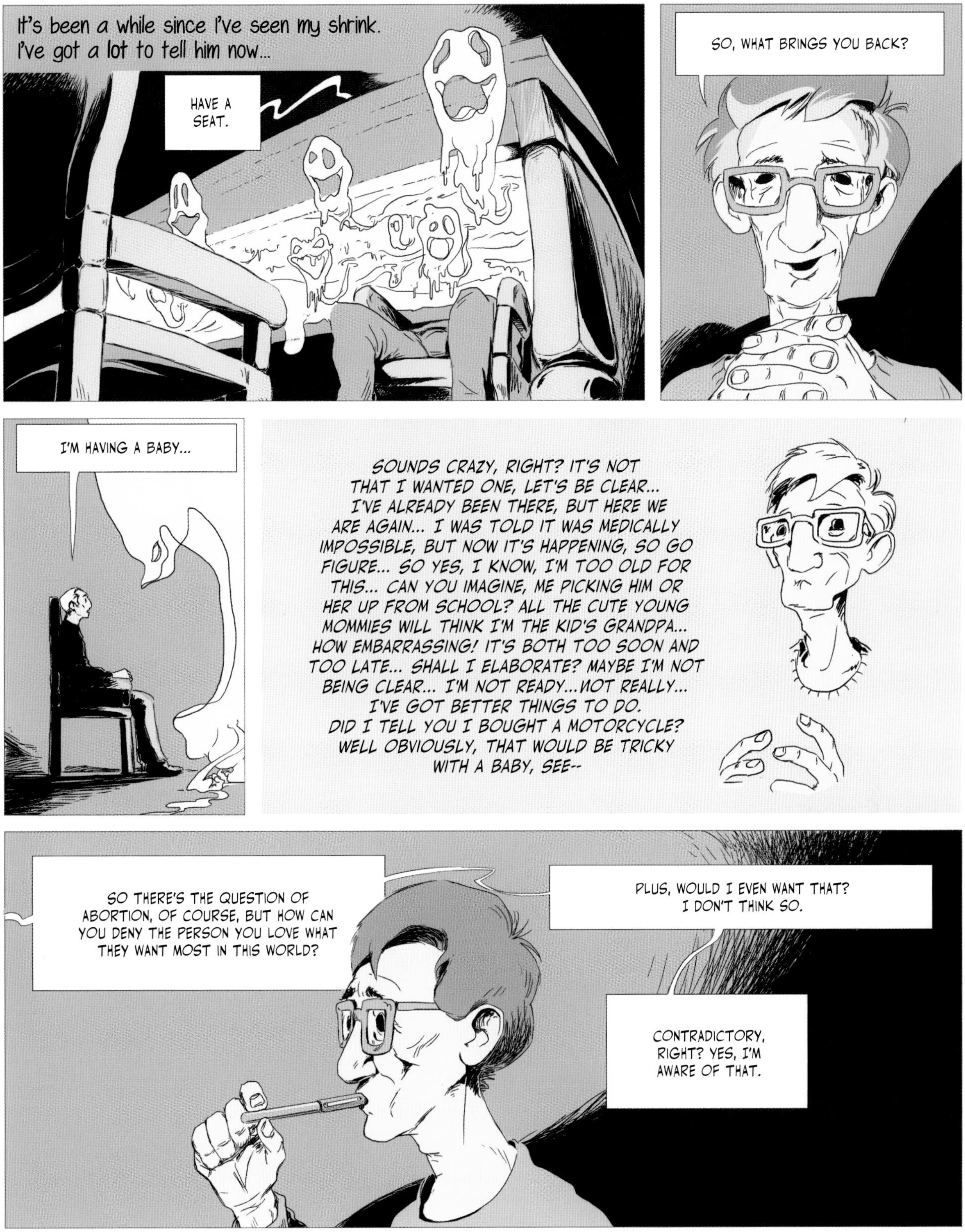
It's been a while since I've seen my shrink.
I've got a lot to tell him now...
HAVE A SEAT.
SO, WHAT BRINGS YOU BACK?
I'M HAVING A BABY...
SOUNDS CRAZY, RIGHT? IT'S NOT THAT I WANTED ONE, LET'S BE CLEAR... I'VE ALREADY BEEN THERE, BUT HERE WE ARE AGAIN... I WAS TOLD IT WAS MEDICALLY IMPOSSIBLE, BUT NOW IT'S HAPPENING, SO GO FIGURE... SO YES, I KNOW, I'M TOO OLD FOR THIS... CAN YOU IMAGINE, ME PICKING HIM OR HER UP FROM SCHOOL? ALL THE CUTE YOUNG MOMMIES WILL THINK I'M THE KID'S GRANDPA... HOW EMBARRASSING! IT'S BOTH TOO SOON AND TOO LATE... SHALL I ELABORATE? MAYBE I'M NOT BEING CLEAR... I'M NOT READY...NOT REALLY... I'VE GOT BETTER THINGS TO DO. DID I TELL YOU I BOUGHT A MOTORCYCLE? WELL OBVIOUSLY, THAT WOULD BE TRICKY WITH A BABY, SEE--
SO THERE'S THE QUESTION OF ABORTION, OF COURSE, BUT HOW CAN YOU DENY THE PERSON YOU LOVE WHAT THEY WANT MOST IN THIS WORLD?
PLUS, WOULD I EVEN WANT THAT? I DON'T THINK SO.
CONTRADICTORY, RIGHT? YES, I'M AWARE OF THAT.

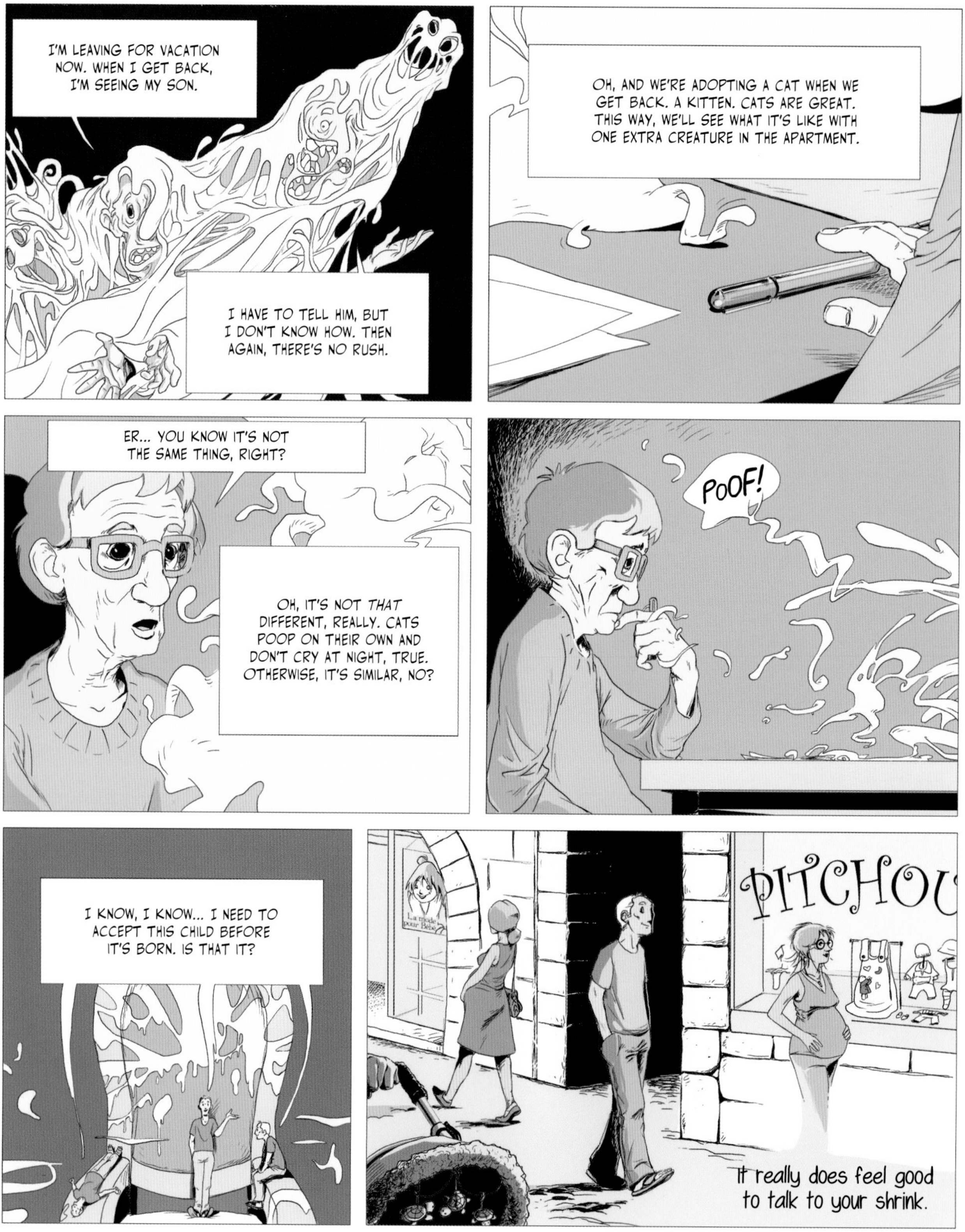
I'M LEAVING FOR VACATION NOW. WHEN I GET BACK, I'M SEEING MY SON.
I HAVE TO TELL HIM, BUT I DON'T KNOW HOW. THEN AGAIN, THERE'S NO RUSH.
OH, AND WE'RE ADOPTING A CAT WHEN WE GET BACK. A KITTEN. CATS ARE GREAT. THIS WAY, WE'LL SEE WHAT IT'S LIKE WITH ONE EXTRA CREATURE IN THE APARTMENT.
ER... YOU KNOW IT'S NOT THE SAME THING, RIGHT?
OH, IT'S NOT *THAT* DIFFERENT, REALLY. CATS POOP ON THEIR OWN AND DON'T CRY AT NIGHT, TRUE. OTHERWISE, IT'S SIMILAR, NO?
POOF!
I KNOW, I KNOW... I NEED TO ACCEPT THIS CHILD BEFORE IT'S BORN. IS THAT IT?
PITCHOU
It really does feel good to talk to your shrink.

We're going on vacation tomorrow! The south, the sun, the sea...nothing too original, but man will it be nice!

I can't wait.

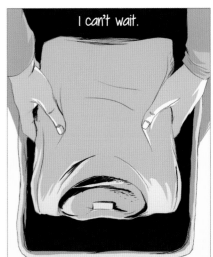

Especially since this is the last time with just the two of us.

HAVE YOU READ *FULL OF LIFE* BY JOHN FANTE? IT'S ABOUT A WRITER WHOSE WIFE IS EXPECTING A BABY.

NOPE, NEVER READ IT!

I'LL BRING IT. SEEMS APPROPRIATE.

ALL *THAT?*

YEAH, WHY?

But before we leave: an ultrasound.

It's THE thing to do in the summer.

GOOD THING WE'RE NOT TAKING THE BIKE.

WE WILL ONE DAY, YOU'LL SEE.

Tomorrow is when we'll see...

HELLO!

HI!

I don't remember coming to a place like this when my son was born. Maybe it wasn't trendy back then...I don't recall.

LOOK, IT'S ALL WOMEN.

IT'S AN OBGYN'S OFFICE. WHAT DID YOU EXPECT?

PLEASE, FOLLOW ME.

I'd always pictured gynecologists as uptight, wrinkled old prunes in Peter Pan collars. But this one's clearly not. Good.

SO, PRESUMED DATE OF CONCEPTION...

WEEKS WITHOUT A PERIOD...CHECK.

BLOOD TEST... VERY GOOD...

OKAY, LET'S GO SEE THIS BABY.

I JUST HAVE ONE QUESTION.

YES?

I THOUGHT LEA COULDN'T HAVE KIDS. NOT EASILY, AT LEAST... ISN'T THAT WHAT YOU TOLD HER?

SIR...

...MEDICINE IS NOT AN *EXACT SCIENCE.*

That's it? One little sentence to satisfy all my questions?

I was expecting some incomprehensible medical explanation or an appropriate "mea culpa," but no. It's simple, it's just nature, no biggie...

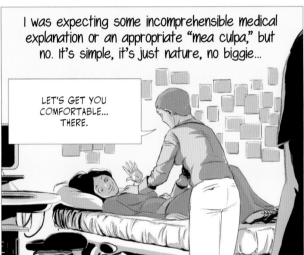

LET'S GET YOU COMFORTABLE... THERE.

Look at them! They're just forging ahead!

IF I CAN'T GET AN IMAGE FROM UP TOP, I'LL HAVE TO GO IN.

BUT DON'T WORRY, IT'S NO BIGGER THAN A SPECULUM.

I guess they have good reason. Just keep moving forward.

IF YOU'RE UNCOMFORTABLE, YOU CAN ASK YOUR FRIEND TO LEAVE.

Seriously? It took every ounce of will power just to come here! She'll have to force me out!

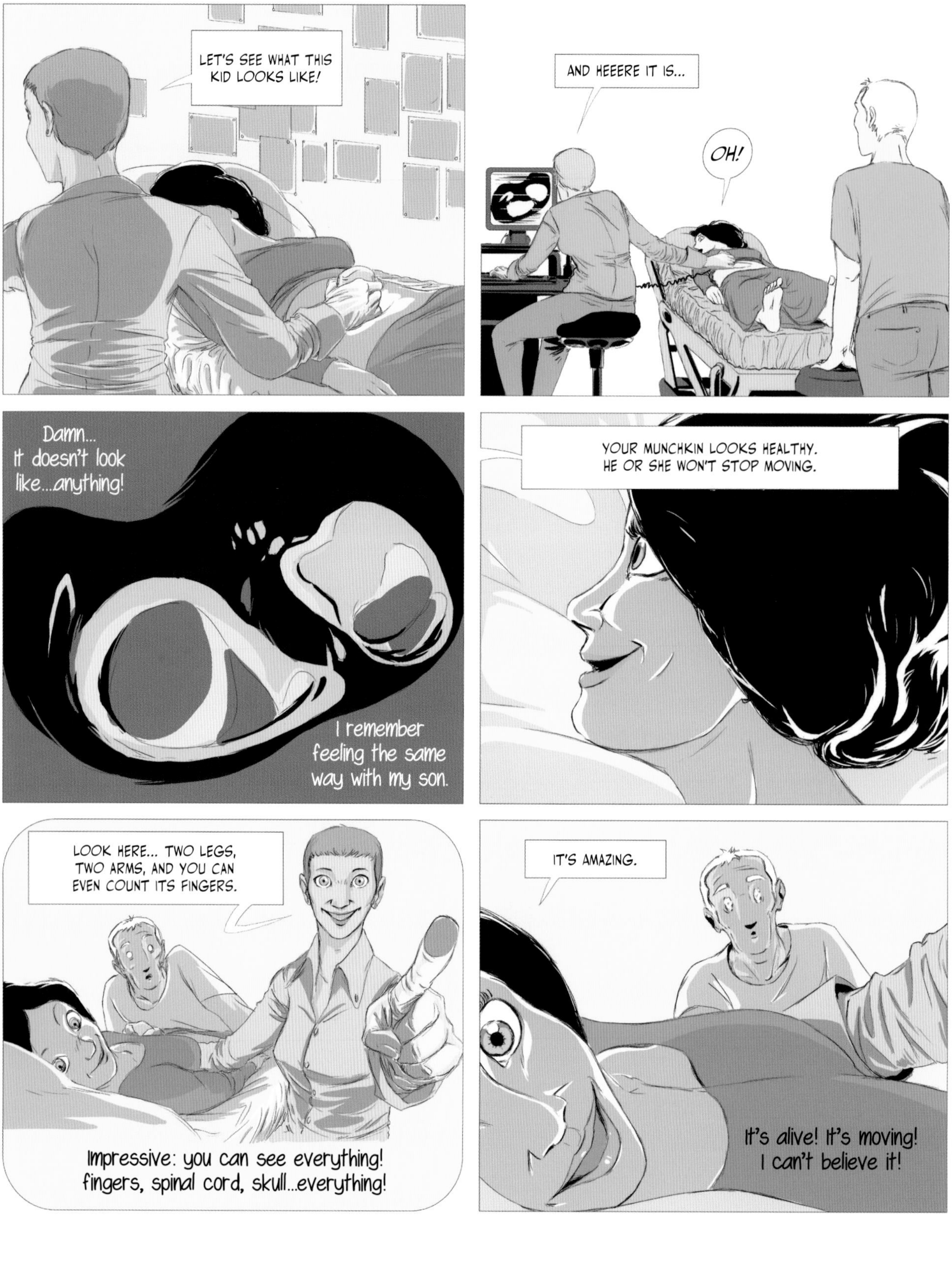
LET'S SEE WHAT THIS KID LOOKS LIKE!
AND HEEERE IT IS...
OH!
Damn... It doesn't look like...anything!
I remember feeling the same way with my son.
YOUR MUNCHKIN LOOKS HEALTHY. HE OR SHE WON'T STOP MOVING.
LOOK HERE... TWO LEGS, TWO ARMS, AND YOU CAN EVEN COUNT ITS FINGERS.
Impressive: you can see everything! fingers, spinal cord, skull...everything!
IT'S AMAZING.
It's alive! It's moving! I can't believe it!

NOW FOR THE NUCHAL TRANSLUCENCY...

YOU NEED TO STOP MOVING, LITTLE ONE...

THERE! 1.1!

ALL GOOD?

I HEARD THAT THE FATHER'S AGE CAN BE A FACTOR...FOR DOWN SYNDROME...

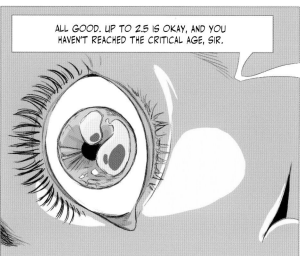

ALL GOOD. UP TO 2.5 IS OKAY, AND YOU HAVEN'T REACHED THE CRITICAL AGE, SIR.

"SO. THE LITTLE ONE IS OVER 2 INCHES LONG FROM HEAD TO BUTT, AND 2 MORE WITH THE LEGS."

The baby's right here. Before my eyes. Becoming a reality.

I can finally let go.

Try to forget everything else.

How could I not be happy to see her glowing like that?

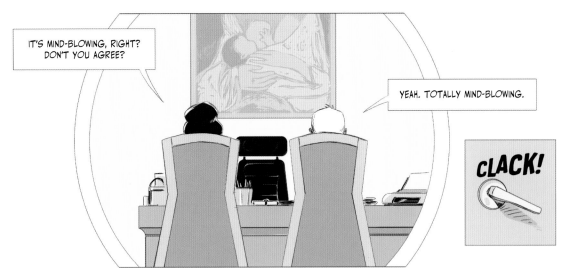

IT'S MIND-BLOWING, RIGHT? DON'T YOU AGREE?

YEAH. TOTALLY MIND-BLOWING.

CLACK!

HERE ARE THE PHOTOS.

I ENLARGED THE BEST ONE.

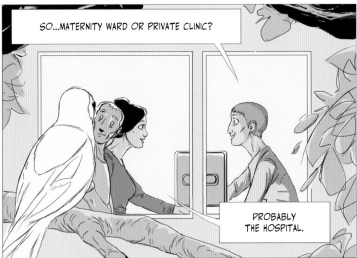

SO...MATERNITY WARD OR PRIVATE CLINIC?

PROBABLY THE HOSPITAL.

WE'LL NEED TO RUN SOME GENETIC TESTS AND SCHEDULE MORE CHECK-UPS. YOU SAID YOU'RE GOING ON VACATION?

I feel like something new is starting between us.

I like it.

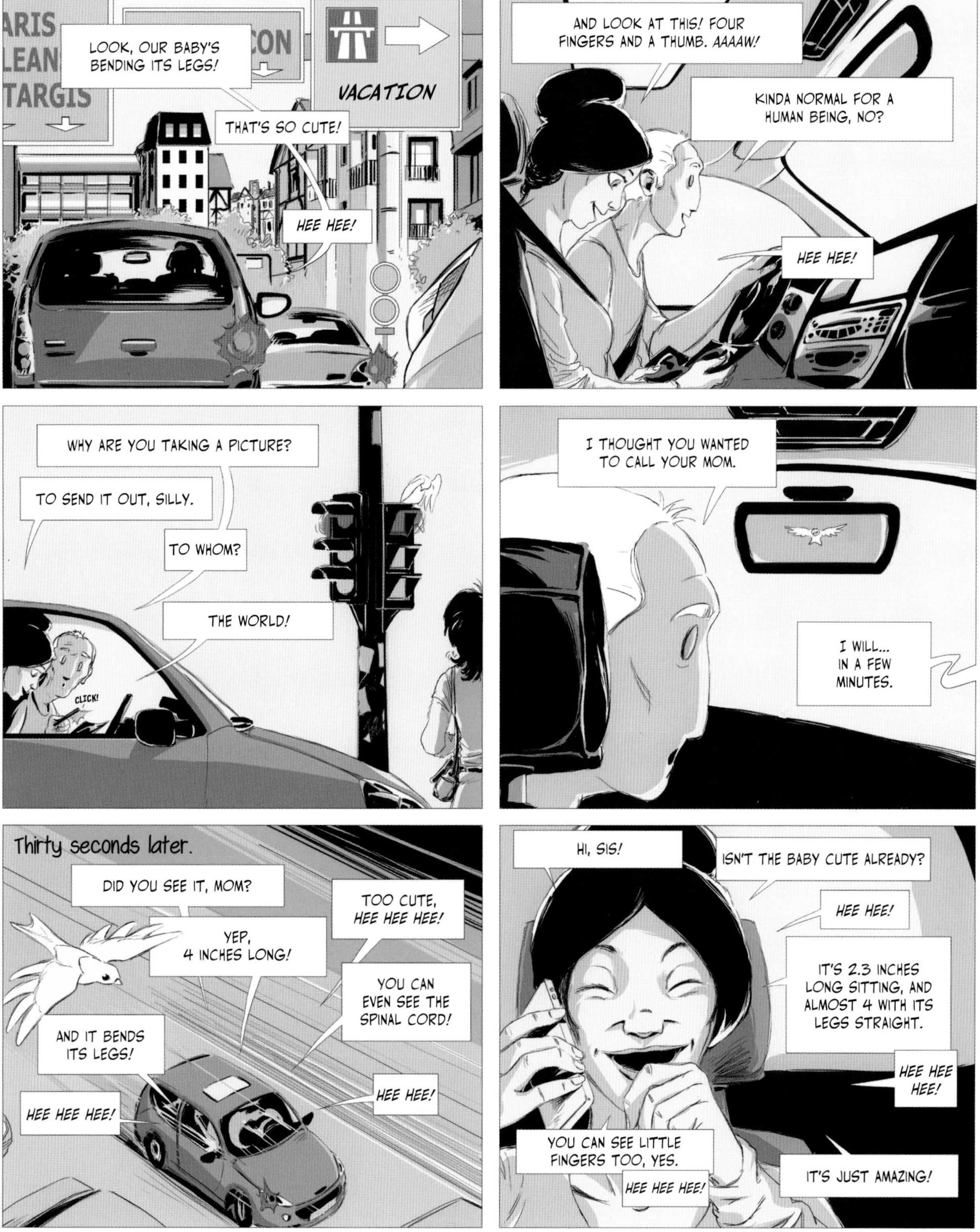
ARIS
LEAN
TARGIS
CON
VACATION
LOOK, OUR BABY'S BENDING ITS LEGS!
THAT'S SO CUTE!
HEE HEE!
AND LOOK AT THIS! FOUR FINGERS AND A THUMB. AAAAW!
KINDA NORMAL FOR A HUMAN BEING, NO?
HEE HEE!
WHY ARE YOU TAKING A PICTURE?
TO SEND IT OUT, SILLY.
TO WHOM?
THE WORLD!
CLICK!
I THOUGHT YOU WANTED TO CALL YOUR MOM.
I WILL... IN A FEW MINUTES.
Thirty seconds later.
DID YOU SEE IT, MOM?
YEP, 4 INCHES LONG!
TOO CUTE, HEE HEE HEE!
YOU CAN EVEN SEE THE SPINAL CORD!
AND IT BENDS ITS LEGS!
HEE HEE HEE!
HEE HEE!
HI, SIS!
ISN'T THE BABY CUTE ALREADY?
HEE HEE!
IT'S 2.3 INCHES LONG SITTING, AND ALMOST 4 WITH ITS LEGS STRAIGHT.
HEE HEE HEE!
YOU CAN SEE LITTLE FINGERS TOO, YES.
HEE HEE HEE!
IT'S JUST AMAZING!

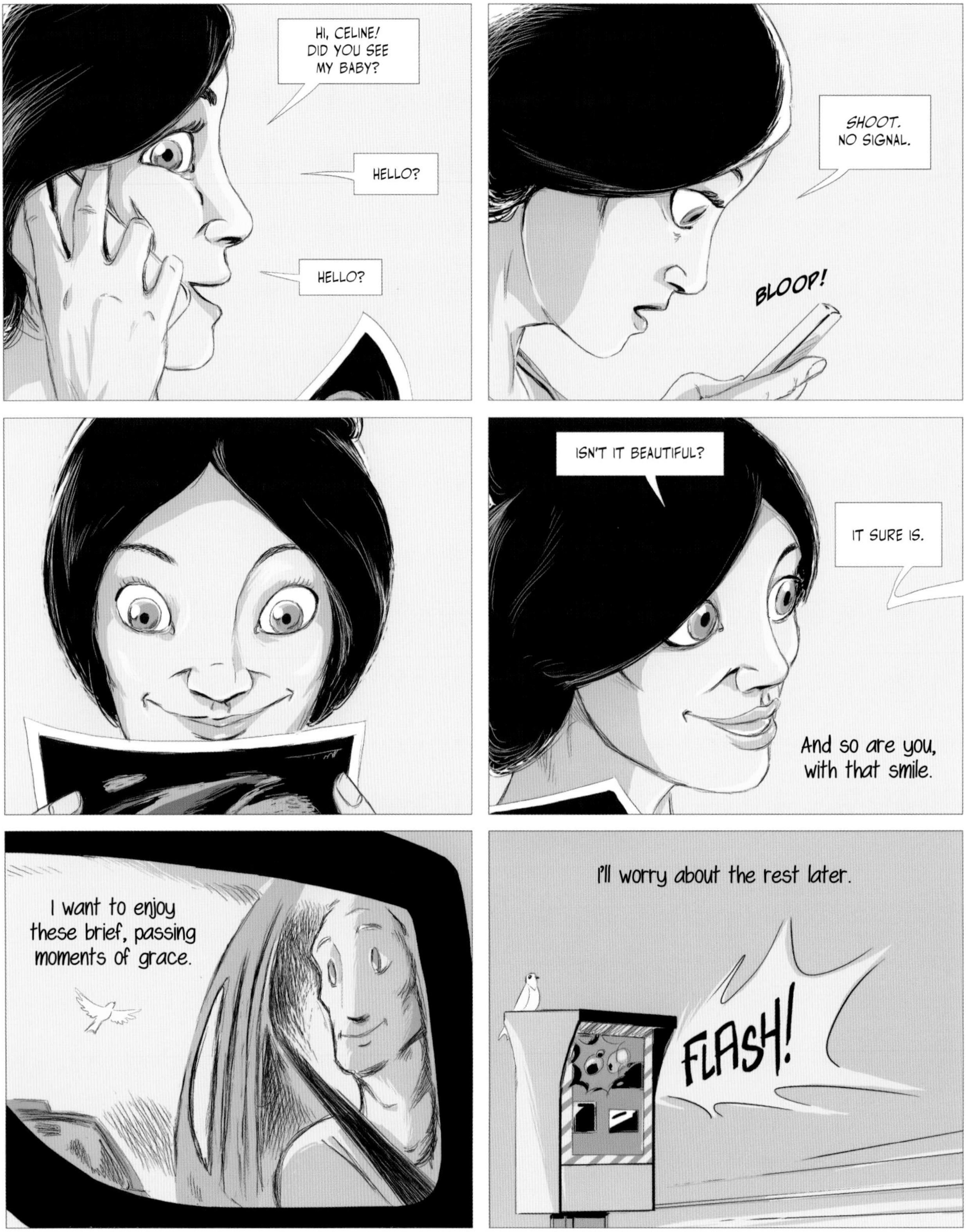

HI, CELINE! DID YOU SEE MY BABY?
HELLO?
HELLO?
SHOOT. NO SIGNAL.
BLOOP!
ISN'T IT BEAUTIFUL?
IT SURE IS.
And so are you, with that smile.
I want to enjoy these brief, passing moments of grace.
I'll worry about the rest later.
FLASH!

AUGUST

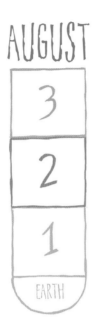

3

2

1

EARTH

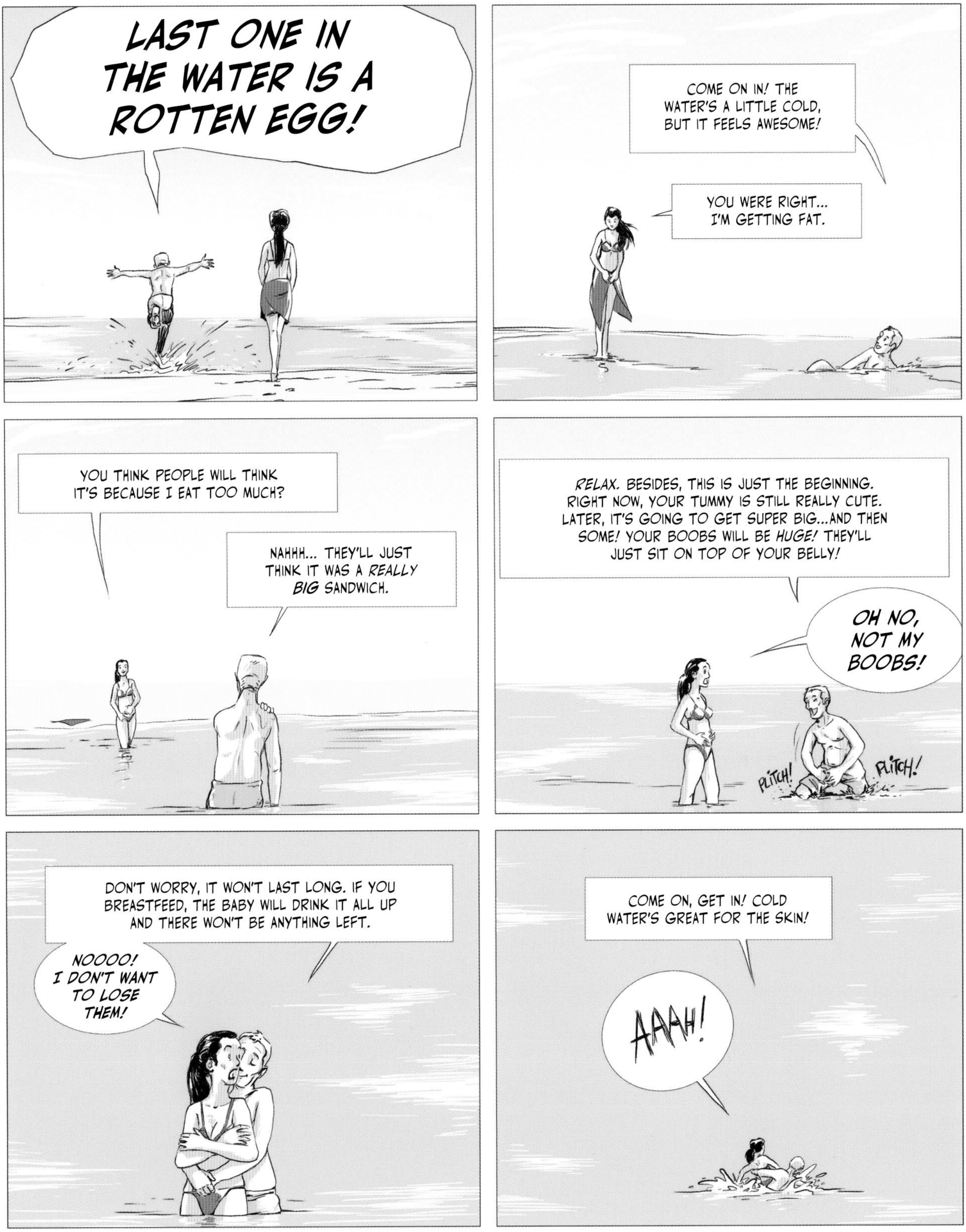
LAST ONE IN THE WATER IS A ROTTEN EGG!
COME ON IN! THE WATER'S A LITTLE COLD, BUT IT FEELS AWESOME!
YOU WERE RIGHT... I'M GETTING FAT.
YOU THINK PEOPLE WILL THINK IT'S BECAUSE I EAT TOO MUCH?
NAHHH... THEY'LL JUST THINK IT WAS A *REALLY BIG* SANDWICH.
RELAX. BESIDES, THIS IS JUST THE BEGINNING. RIGHT NOW, YOUR TUMMY IS STILL REALLY CUTE. LATER, IT'S GOING TO GET SUPER BIG...AND THEN SOME! YOUR BOOBS WILL BE *HUGE!* THEY'LL JUST SIT ON TOP OF YOUR BELLY!
OH NO, NOT MY BOOBS!
PLITCH!
PLITCH!
DON'T WORRY, IT WON'T LAST LONG. IF YOU BREASTFEED, THE BABY WILL DRINK IT ALL UP AND THERE WON'T BE ANYTHING LEFT.
NOOOO! I DON'T WANT TO LOSE THEM!
COME ON, GET IN! COLD WATER'S GREAT FOR THE SKIN!
AAAH!

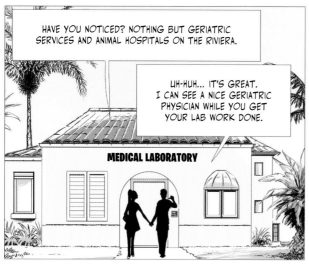

HAVE YOU NOTICED? NOTHING BUT GERIATRIC SERVICES AND ANIMAL HOSPITALS ON THE RIVIERA.

UH-HUH... IT'S GREAT. I CAN SEE A NICE GERIATRIC PHYSICIAN WHILE YOU GET YOUR LAB WORK DONE.

MEDICAL LABORATORY

I REALLY HOPE THEY DON'T MAKE A MISTAKE.

SILLY BOY...

HOW ABOUT BREAKFAST ON THE PATIO?

OH, GREAT IDEA.

CROISSANT OR CHOCOLATE BRIOCHE?

BOTH. I NEED ENERGY, AFTER ALL THE BLOOD THEY JUST TOOK.

I WASN'T AWARE OF THOSE "SERIC MARKERS." I DON'T THINK THEY HAD THEM WHEN MY SON WAS BORN.

MEH, IT'S JUST A PRECAUTION.

A PRECAUTION? LOOK, I TRUST YOUR DOCTOR AND ALL, BUT I'M STILL WORRIED, GIVEN MY AGE.

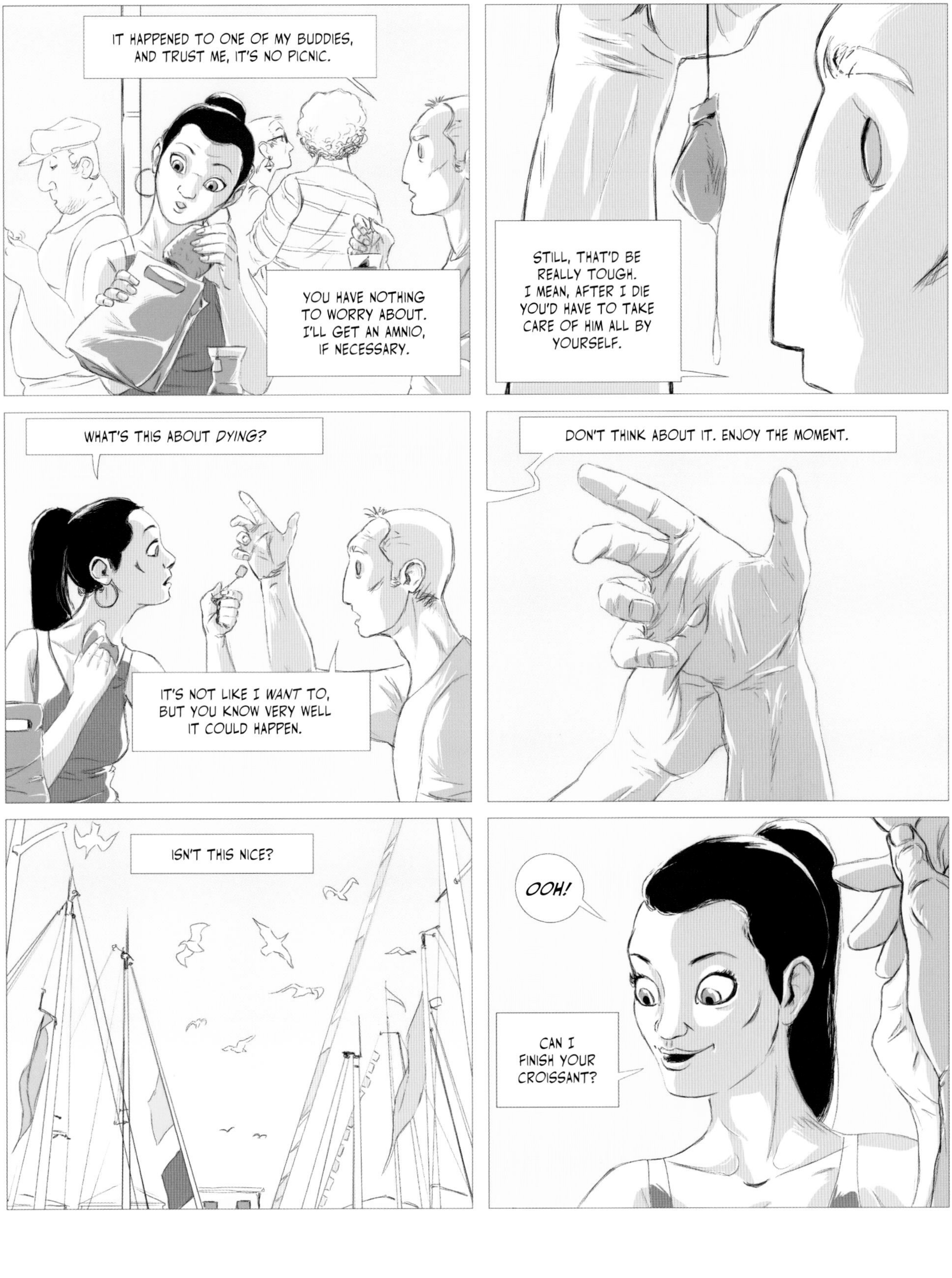
IT HAPPENED TO ONE OF MY BUDDIES, AND TRUST ME, IT'S NO PICNIC.
YOU HAVE NOTHING TO WORRY ABOUT. I'LL GET AN AMNIO, IF NECESSARY.
STILL, THAT'D BE REALLY TOUGH. I MEAN, AFTER I DIE YOU'D HAVE TO TAKE CARE OF HIM ALL BY YOURSELF.
WHAT'S THIS ABOUT *DYING?*
IT'S NOT LIKE I *WANT* TO, BUT YOU KNOW VERY WELL IT COULD HAPPEN.
DON'T THINK ABOUT IT. ENJOY THE MOMENT.
ISN'T THIS NICE?
OOH!
CAN I FINISH YOUR CROISSANT?

HAVE YOU SEEN MY SWIMSUIT?

HEY, HAVE YOU SEEN--

WHAT ARE YOU DOING?

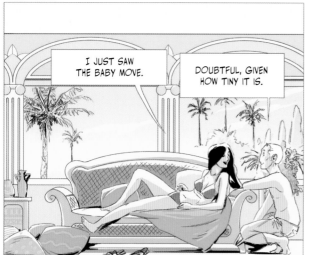

I JUST SAW THE BABY MOVE.

DOUBTFUL, GIVEN HOW TINY IT IS.

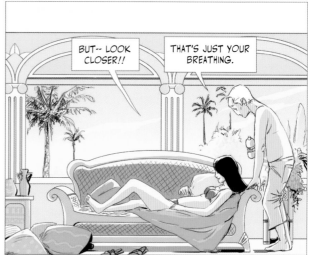

BUT-- LOOK CLOSER!!

THAT'S JUST YOUR BREATHING.

ARE YOU SURE? ...I DON'T KNOW, I'M PRETTY SURE IT WAS OUR BABY!

DON'T WORRY, YOU'LL HAVE PLENTY OF TIME TO SEE IT MOVE LATER.

Be patient.

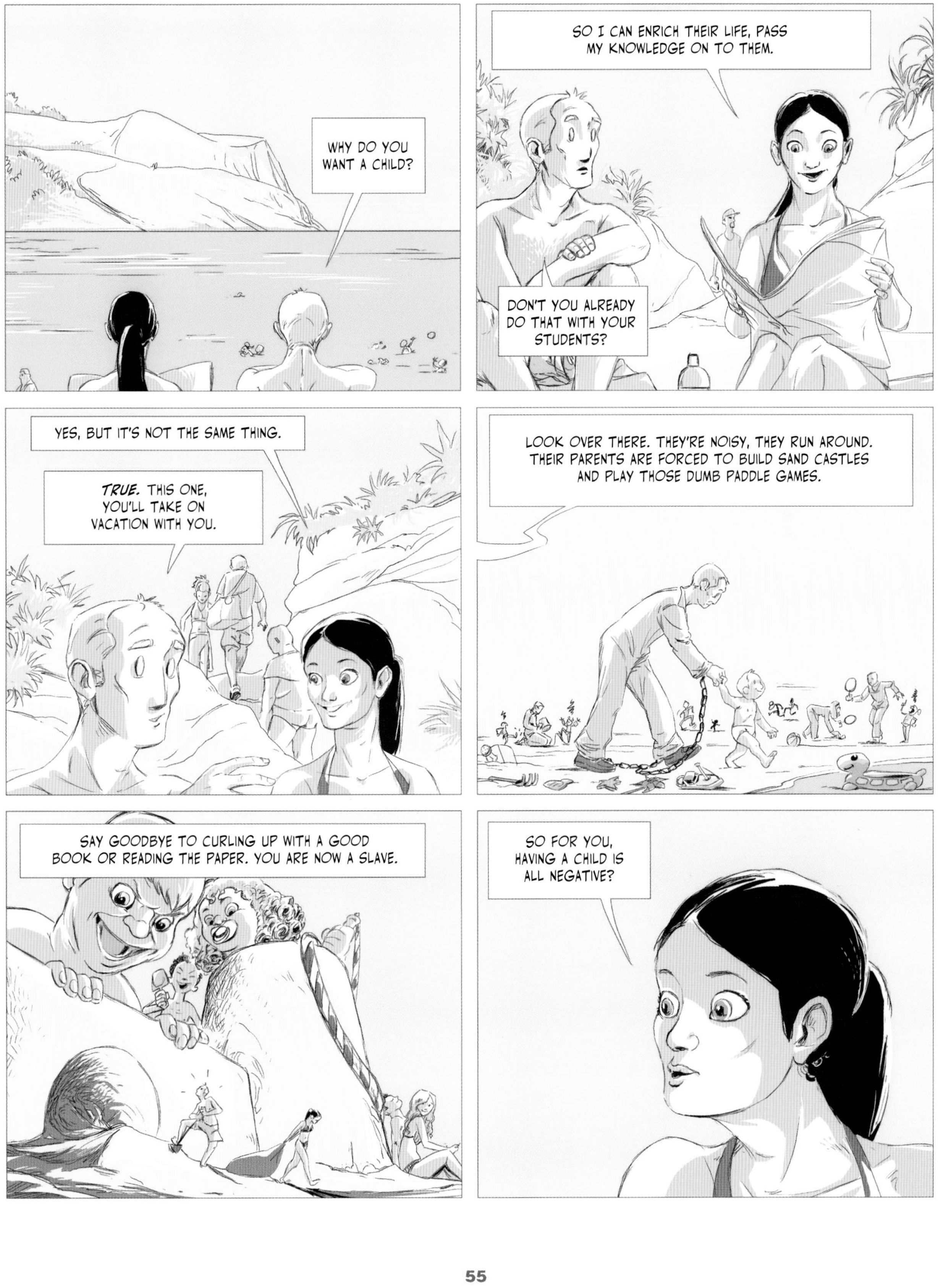
WHY DO YOU WANT A CHILD?
SO I CAN ENRICH THEIR LIFE, PASS MY KNOWLEDGE ON TO THEM.
DON'T YOU ALREADY DO THAT WITH YOUR STUDENTS?
YES, BUT IT'S NOT THE SAME THING.
TRUE. THIS ONE, YOU'LL TAKE ON VACATION WITH YOU.
LOOK OVER THERE. THEY'RE NOISY, THEY RUN AROUND. THEIR PARENTS ARE FORCED TO BUILD SAND CASTLES AND PLAY THOSE DUMB PADDLE GAMES.
SAY GOODBYE TO CURLING UP WITH A GOOD BOOK OR READING THE PAPER. YOU ARE NOW A SLAVE.
SO FOR YOU, HAVING A CHILD IS ALL NEGATIVE?

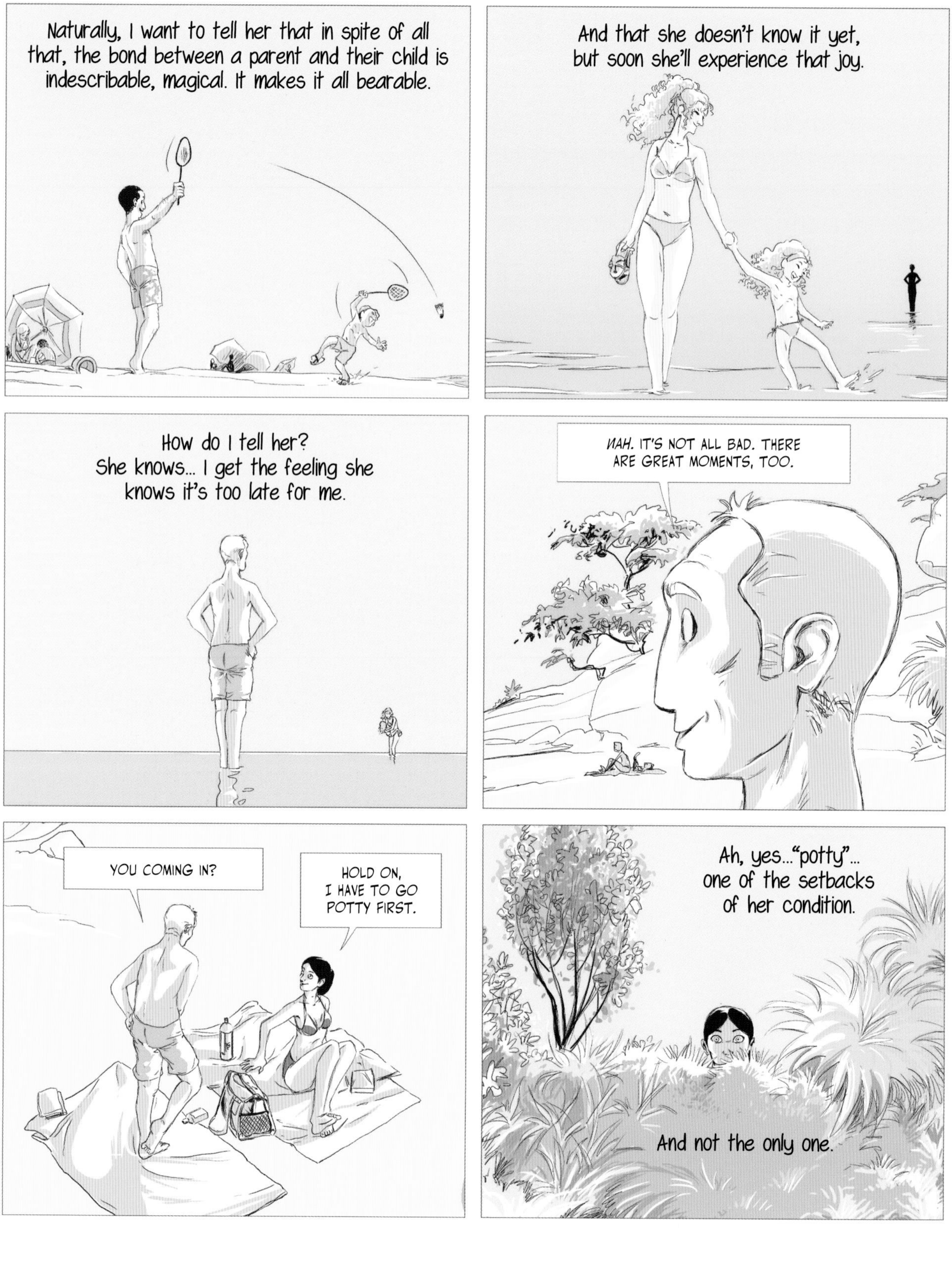
Naturally, I want to tell her that in spite of all that, the bond between a parent and their child is indescribable, magical. It makes it all bearable.
And that she doesn't know it yet, but soon she'll experience that joy.
How do I tell her? She knows... I get the feeling she knows it's too late for me.
NAH. IT'S NOT ALL BAD. THERE ARE GREAT MOMENTS, TOO.
YOU COMING IN?
HOLD ON, I HAVE TO GO POTTY FIRST.
Ah, yes..."potty"... one of the setbacks of her condition.
And not the only one.

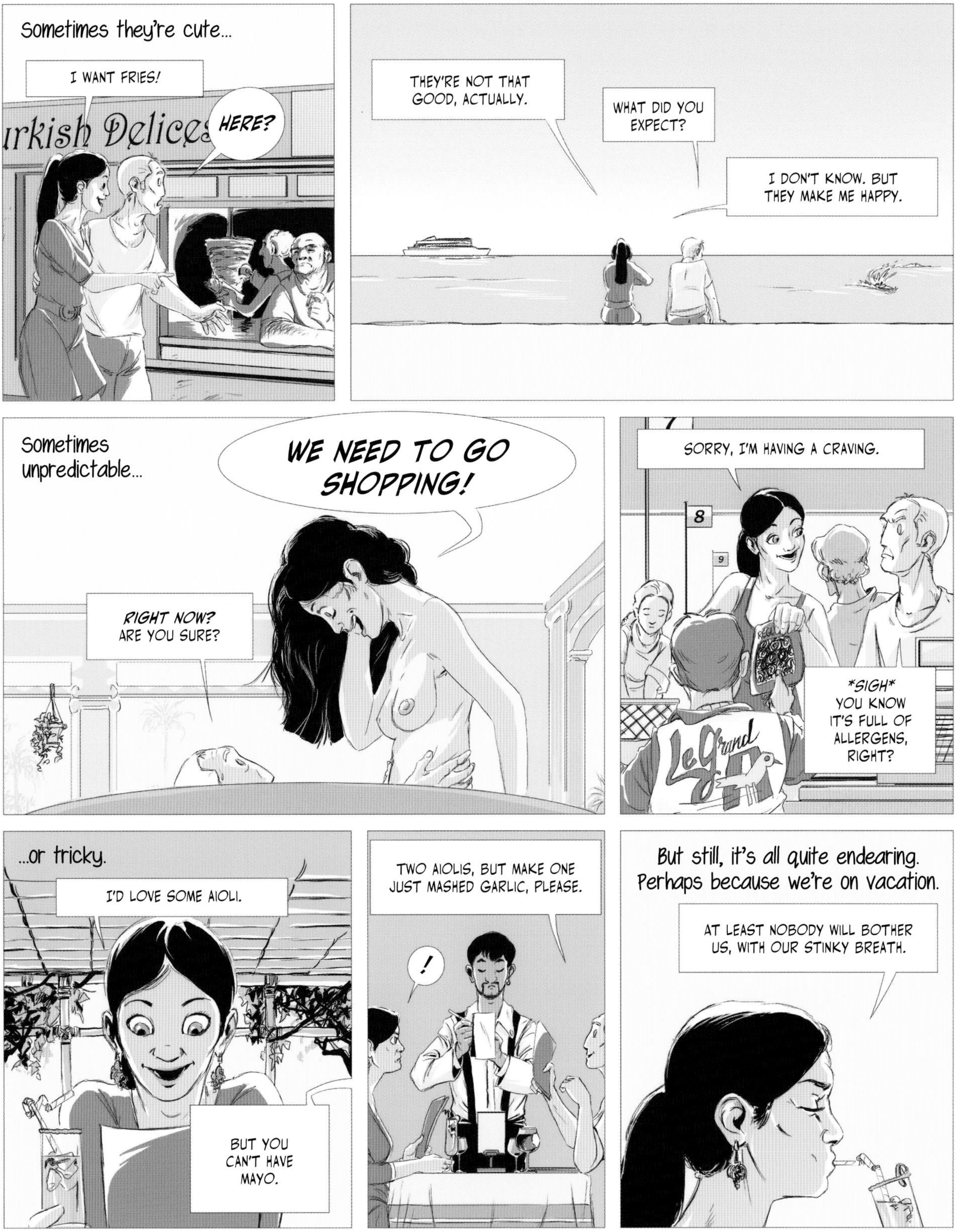
Sometimes they're cute...
I WANT FRIES!
HERE?
THEY'RE NOT THAT GOOD, ACTUALLY.
WHAT DID YOU EXPECT?
I DON'T KNOW. BUT THEY MAKE ME HAPPY.
Sometimes unpredictable...
WE NEED TO GO SHOPPING!
RIGHT NOW? ARE YOU SURE?
SORRY, I'M HAVING A CRAVING.
SIGH YOU KNOW IT'S FULL OF ALLERGENS, RIGHT?
...or tricky.
I'D LOVE SOME AIOLI.
BUT YOU CAN'T HAVE MAYO.
TWO AIOLIS, BUT MAKE ONE JUST MASHED GARLIC, PLEASE.
!
But still, it's all quite endearing. Perhaps because we're on vacation.
AT LEAST NOBODY WILL BOTHER US, WITH OUR STINKY BREATH.

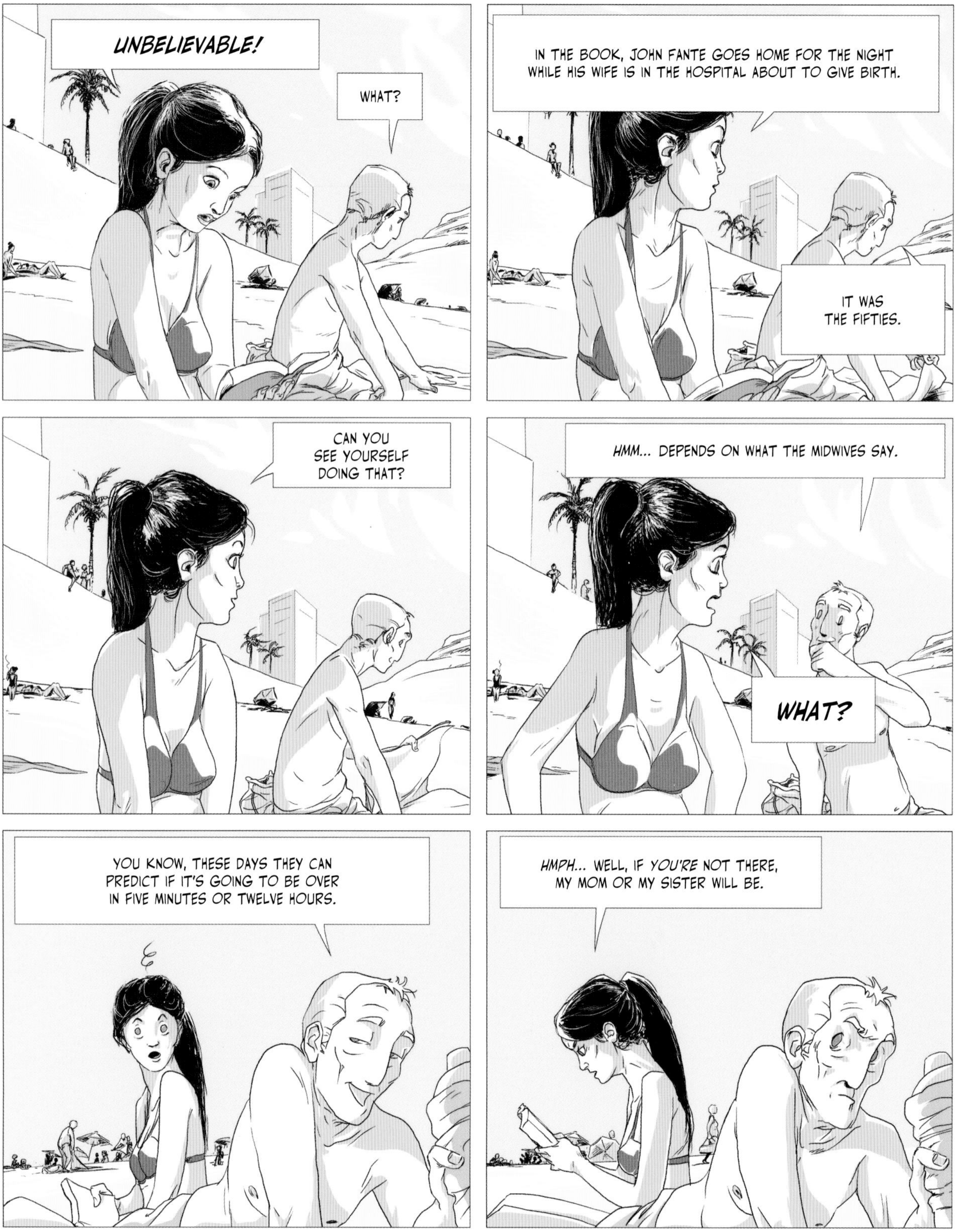
UNBELIEVABLE!
WHAT?
IN THE BOOK, JOHN FANTE GOES HOME FOR THE NIGHT WHILE HIS WIFE IS IN THE HOSPITAL ABOUT TO GIVE BIRTH.
IT WAS THE FIFTIES.
CAN YOU SEE YOURSELF DOING THAT?
HMM... DEPENDS ON WHAT THE MIDWIVES SAY.
WHAT?
YOU KNOW, THESE DAYS THEY CAN PREDICT IF IT'S GOING TO BE OVER IN FIVE MINUTES OR TWELVE HOURS.
HMPH... WELL, IF YOU'RE NOT THERE, MY MOM OR MY SISTER WILL BE.

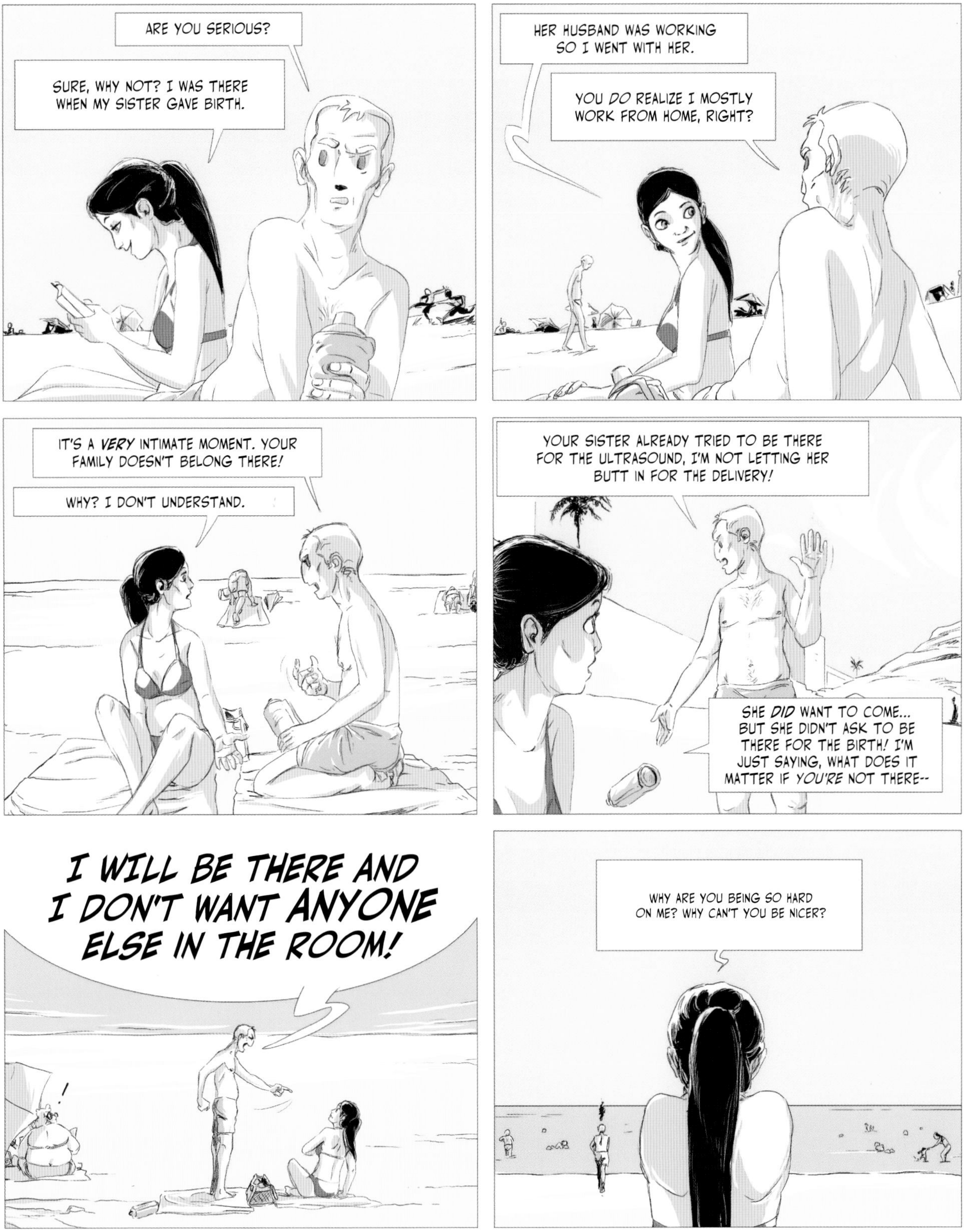
ARE YOU SERIOUS?
SURE, WHY NOT? I WAS THERE WHEN MY SISTER GAVE BIRTH.
HER HUSBAND WAS WORKING SO I WENT WITH HER.
YOU DO REALIZE I MOSTLY WORK FROM HOME, RIGHT?
IT'S A VERY INTIMATE MOMENT. YOUR FAMILY DOESN'T BELONG THERE!
WHY? I DON'T UNDERSTAND.
YOUR SISTER ALREADY TRIED TO BE THERE FOR THE ULTRASOUND, I'M NOT LETTING HER BUTT IN FOR THE DELIVERY!
SHE DID WANT TO COME... BUT SHE DIDN'T ASK TO BE THERE FOR THE BIRTH! I'M JUST SAYING, WHAT DOES IT MATTER IF YOU'RE NOT THERE--
I WILL BE THERE AND I DON'T WANT ANYONE ELSE IN THE ROOM!
!
WHY ARE YOU BEING SO HARD ON ME? WHY CAN'T YOU BE NICER?

We took our last dip early in the morning before leaving. It was a pretty zen moment despite the melancholy of the summer being over and the looming difficulty of the months ahead.

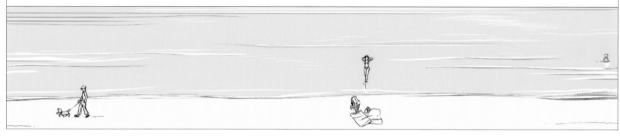

I savored the moment, knowing it would never come again. I was nostalgic already and I wanted to stop time.

Next year? I'd rather not think about it.

It sounds strange, but I spent a lot of time watching kids play on the beach...walk in the street...buy ice cream cones...

And I still don't know if any of that makes me want it, or if I'm ready to accept that life.

DO WE REALLY HAVE TO GO?

THAT'S NOT VERY ORIGINAL.

This baby isn't even born yet... and it's already very present.

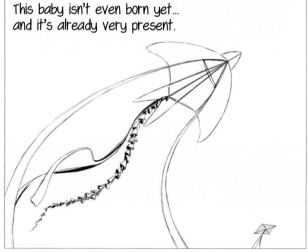

SEPTEMBER

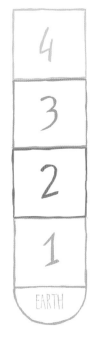

4

3

2

1

EARTH

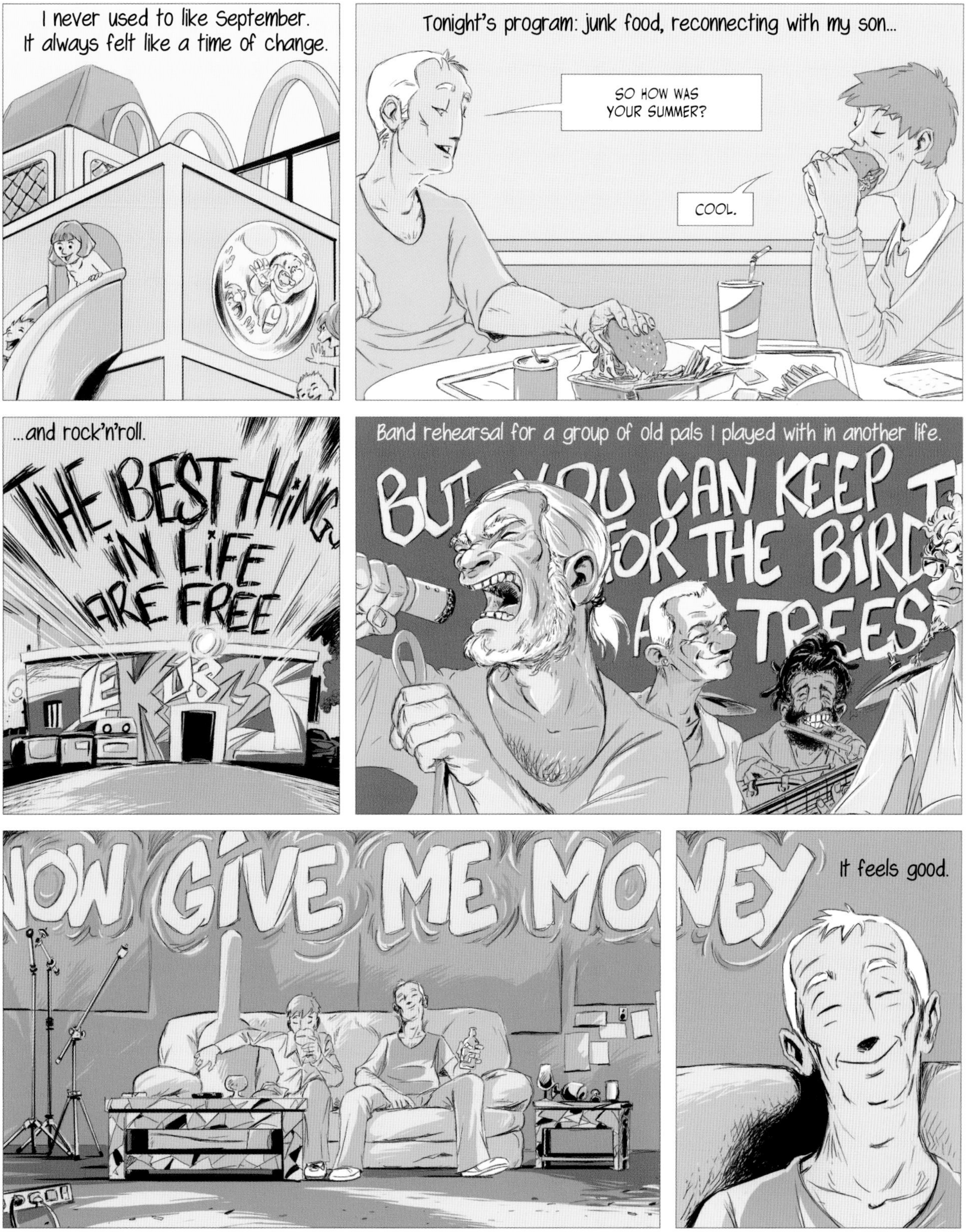

I never used to like September.
It always felt like a time of change.
Tonight's program: junk food, reconnecting with my son...
SO HOW WAS YOUR SUMMER?
COOL.
...and rock'n'roll.
THE BEST THINGS IN LIFE ARE FREE
Band rehearsal for a group of old pals I played with in another life.
BUT YOU CAN KEEP THEM FOR THE BIRDS AND TREES
NOW GIVE ME MONEY
It feels good.

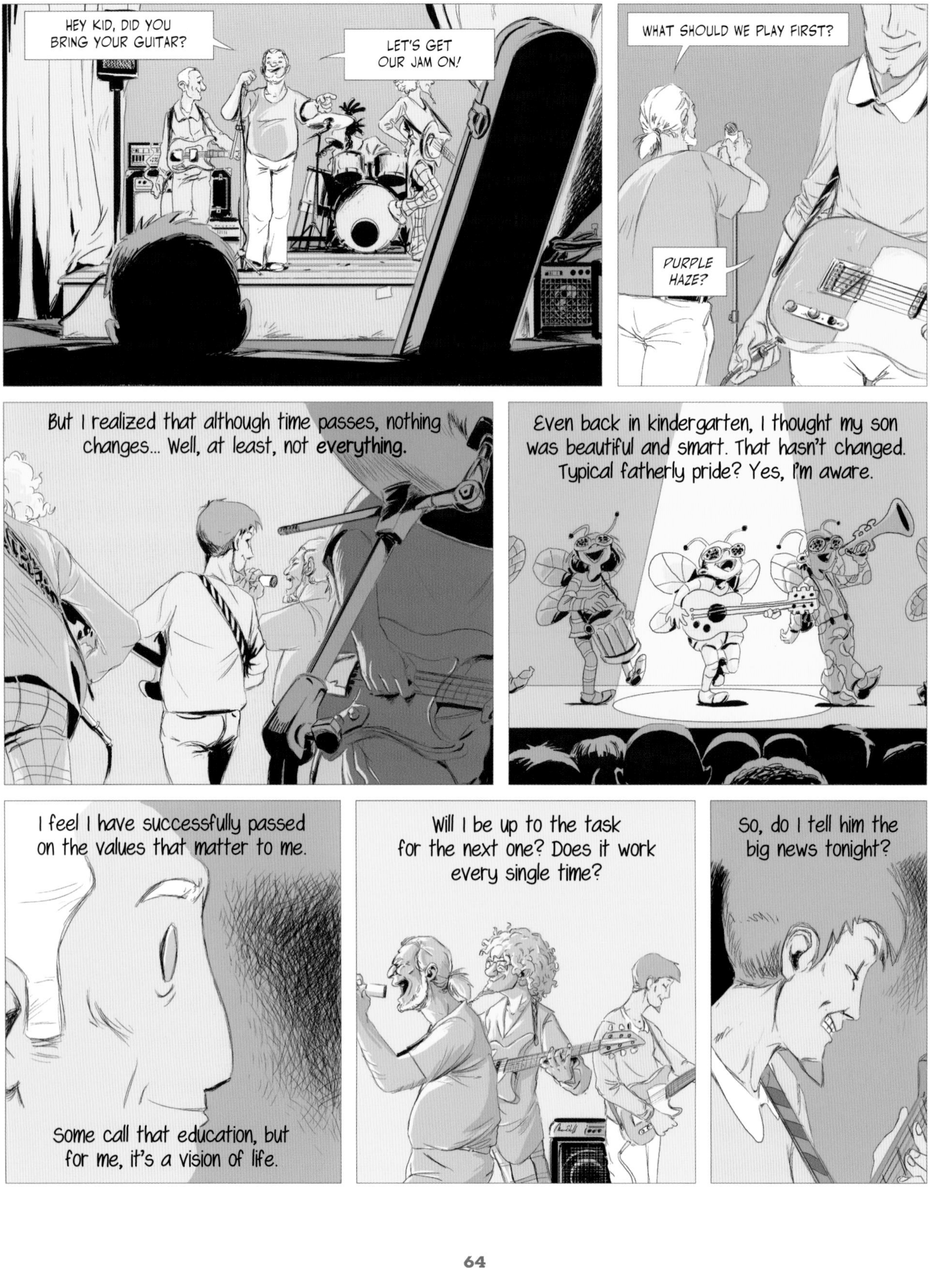
HEY KID, DID YOU BRING YOUR GUITAR?
LET'S GET OUR JAM ON!
WHAT SHOULD WE PLAY FIRST?
PURPLE HAZE?
But I realized that although time passes, nothing changes... Well, at least, not everything.
Even back in kindergarten, I thought my son was beautiful and smart. That hasn't changed. Typical fatherly pride? Yes, I'm aware.
I feel I have successfully passed on the values that matter to me.
Some call that education, but for me, it's a vision of life.
Will I be up to the task for the next one? Does it work every single time?
So, do I tell him the big news tonight?

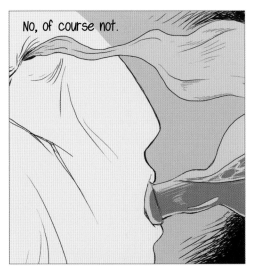

No, of course not.

Just enjoy the moment.

NO HELP ME AW YEAH

Tomorrow's another day.

HEY BRO, HOW'S IT GOING?

SAME OLD, SAME OLD.

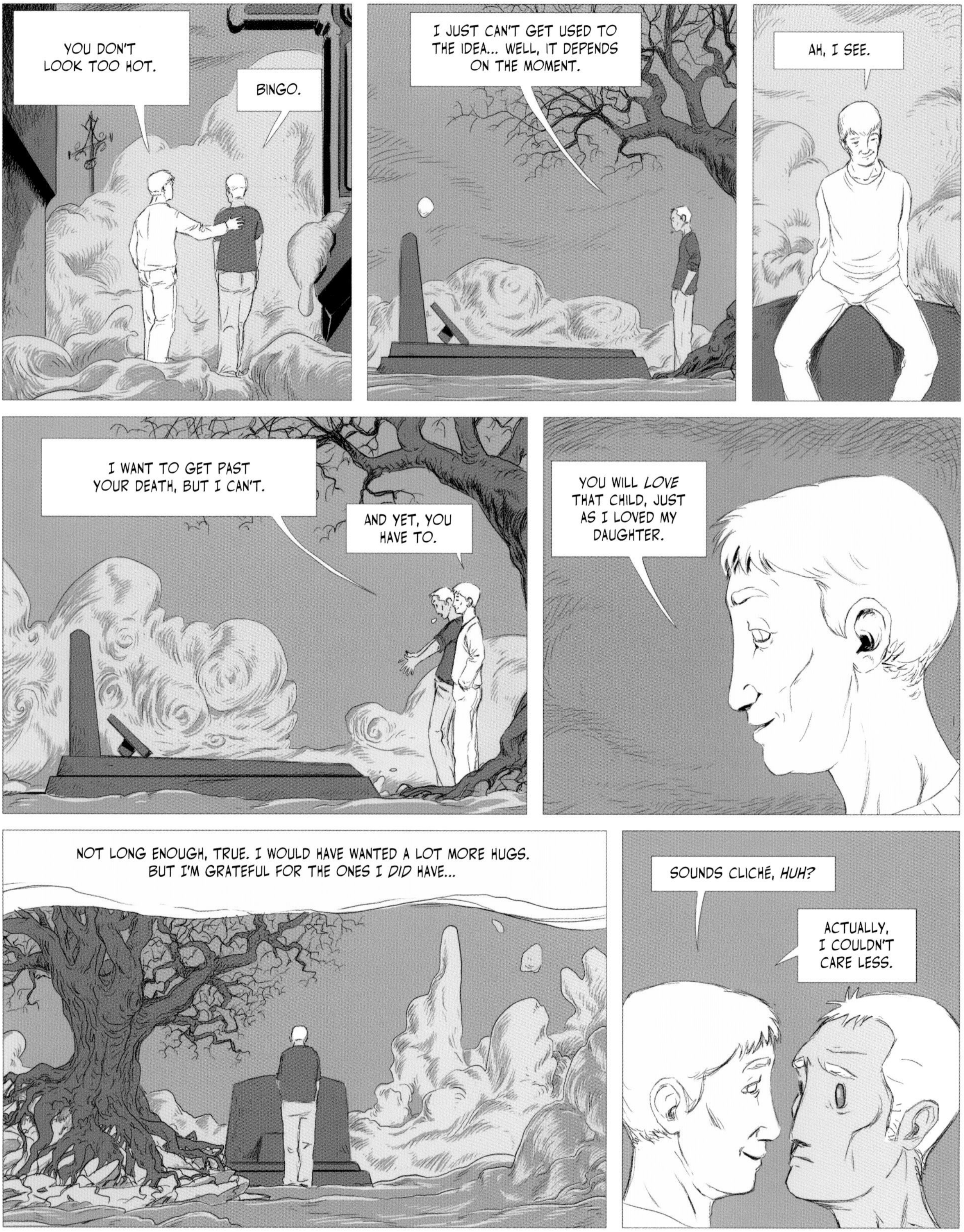
YOU DON'T LOOK TOO HOT.
BINGO.
I JUST CAN'T GET USED TO THE IDEA... WELL, IT DEPENDS ON THE MOMENT.
AH, I SEE.
I WANT TO GET PAST YOUR DEATH, BUT I CAN'T.
AND YET, YOU HAVE TO.
YOU WILL *LOVE* THAT CHILD, JUST AS I LOVED MY DAUGHTER.
NOT LONG ENOUGH, TRUE. I WOULD HAVE WANTED A LOT MORE HUGS. BUT I'M GRATEFUL FOR THE ONES I *DID* HAVE...
SOUNDS CLICHÉ, *HUH?*
ACTUALLY, I COULDN'T CARE LESS.

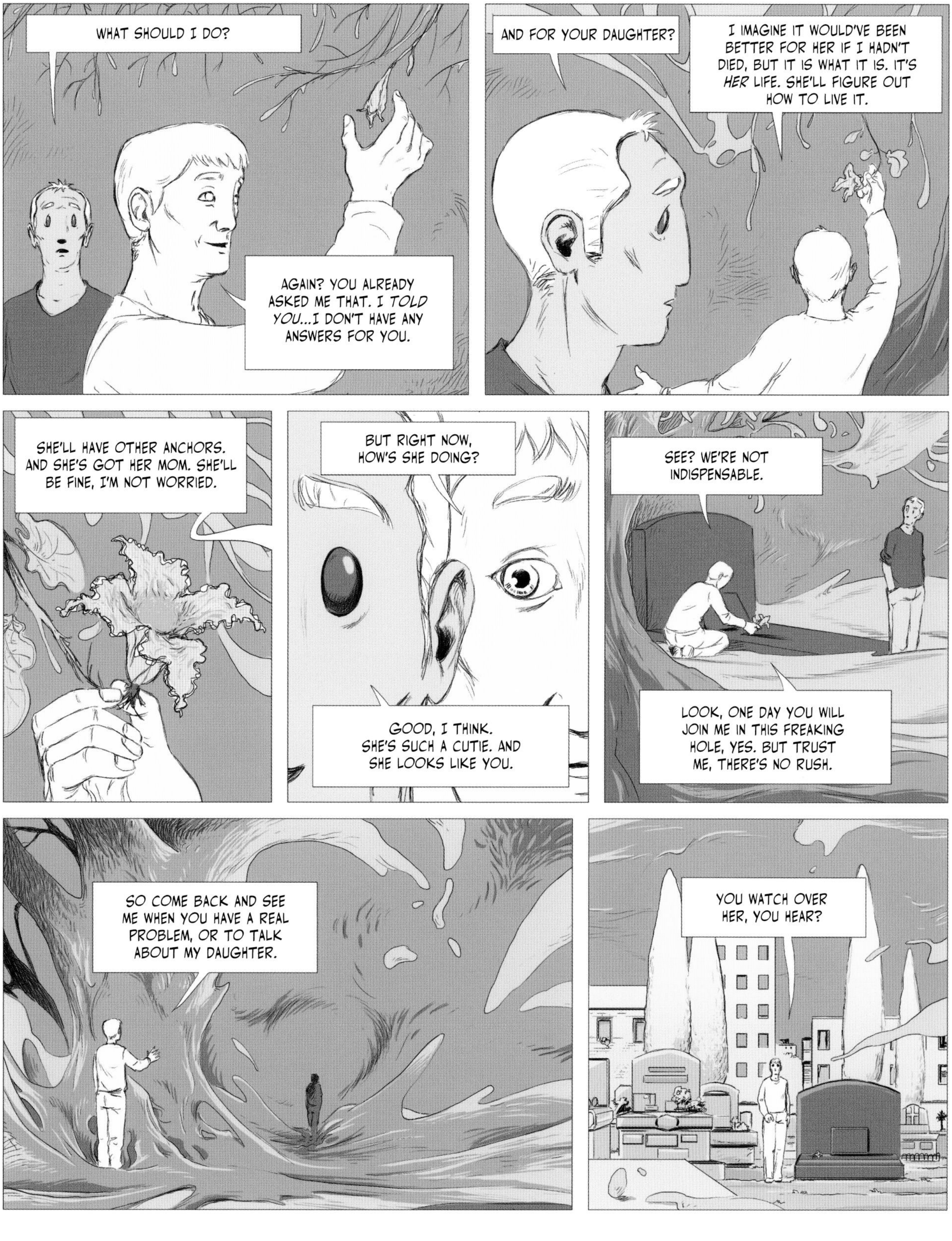
WHAT SHOULD I DO?
AGAIN? YOU ALREADY ASKED ME THAT. I *TOLD YOU*...I DON'T HAVE ANY ANSWERS FOR YOU.
AND FOR YOUR DAUGHTER?
I IMAGINE IT WOULD'VE BEEN BETTER FOR HER IF I HADN'T DIED, BUT IT IS WHAT IT IS. IT'S *HER* LIFE. SHE'LL FIGURE OUT HOW TO LIVE IT.
SHE'LL HAVE OTHER ANCHORS. AND SHE'S GOT HER MOM. SHE'LL BE FINE, I'M NOT WORRIED.
BUT RIGHT NOW, HOW'S SHE DOING?
GOOD, I THINK. SHE'S SUCH A CUTIE. AND SHE LOOKS LIKE YOU.
SEE? WE'RE NOT INDISPENSABLE.
LOOK, ONE DAY YOU WILL JOIN ME IN THIS FREAKING HOLE, YES. BUT TRUST ME, THERE'S NO RUSH.
SO COME BACK AND SEE ME WHEN YOU HAVE A REAL PROBLEM, OR TO TALK ABOUT MY DAUGHTER.
YOU WATCH OVER HER, YOU HEAR?

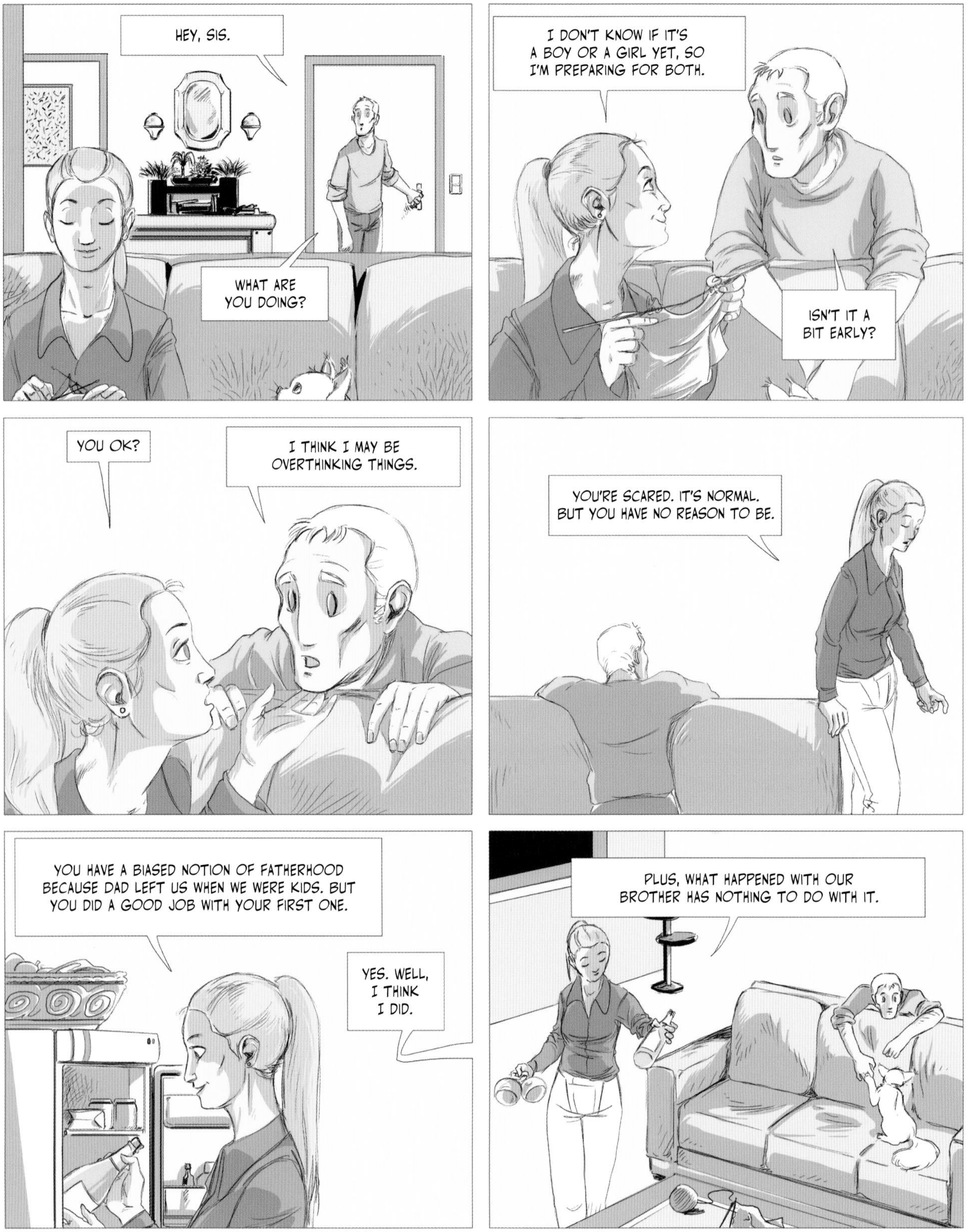
HEY, SIS.
WHAT ARE YOU DOING?
I DON'T KNOW IF IT'S A BOY OR A GIRL YET, SO I'M PREPARING FOR BOTH.
ISN'T IT A BIT EARLY?
YOU OK?
I THINK I MAY BE OVERTHINKING THINGS.
YOU'RE SCARED. IT'S NORMAL. BUT YOU HAVE NO REASON TO BE.
YOU HAVE A BIASED NOTION OF FATHERHOOD BECAUSE DAD LEFT US WHEN WE WERE KIDS. BUT YOU DID A GOOD JOB WITH YOUR FIRST ONE.
YES. WELL, I THINK I DID.
PLUS, WHAT HAPPENED WITH OUR BROTHER HAS NOTHING TO DO WITH IT.

GO HOME. TAKE CARE OF LEA...

...BUT FIRST, GRAB US A COUPLE OF BEERS.

"WHEN'S THE DUE DATE?"

"MID-FEBRUARY."

"GOOD THING, TOO. I HAVE A LOT OF WORK UP NORTH IN JANUARY."

"SEE? THINGS ARE WORKING OUT."

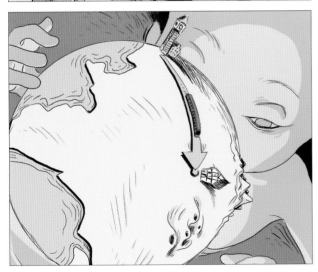

Wednesday the 26th

DID YOU FORGET WHAT WE'RE DOING TODAY?

?

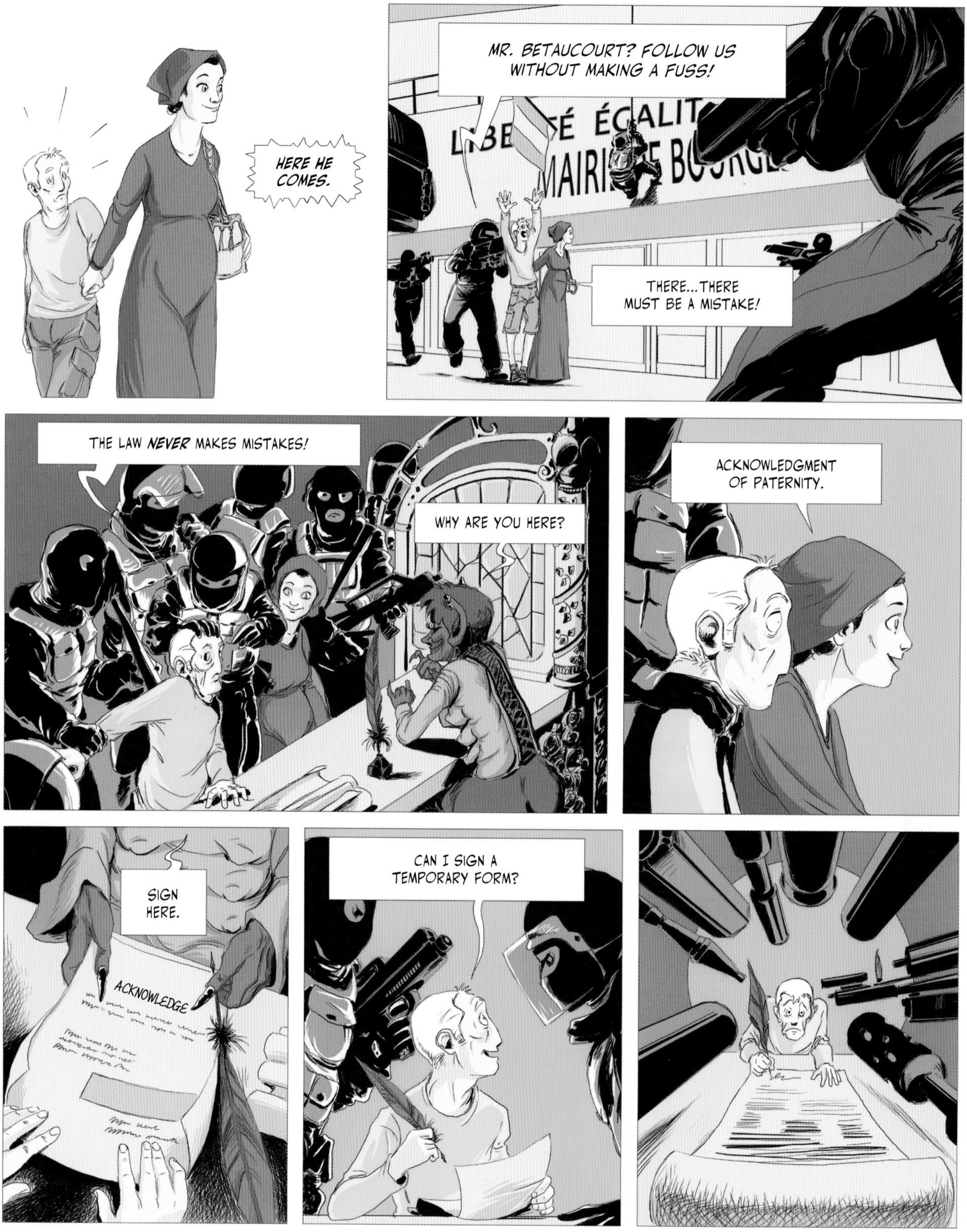
HERE HE COMES.
MR. BETAUCOURT? FOLLOW US WITHOUT MAKING A FUSS!
THERE...THERE MUST BE A MISTAKE!
THE LAW NEVER MAKES MISTAKES!
WHY ARE YOU HERE?
ACKNOWLEDGMENT OF PATERNITY.
SIGN HERE.
ACKNOWLEDGE
CAN I SIGN A TEMPORARY FORM?

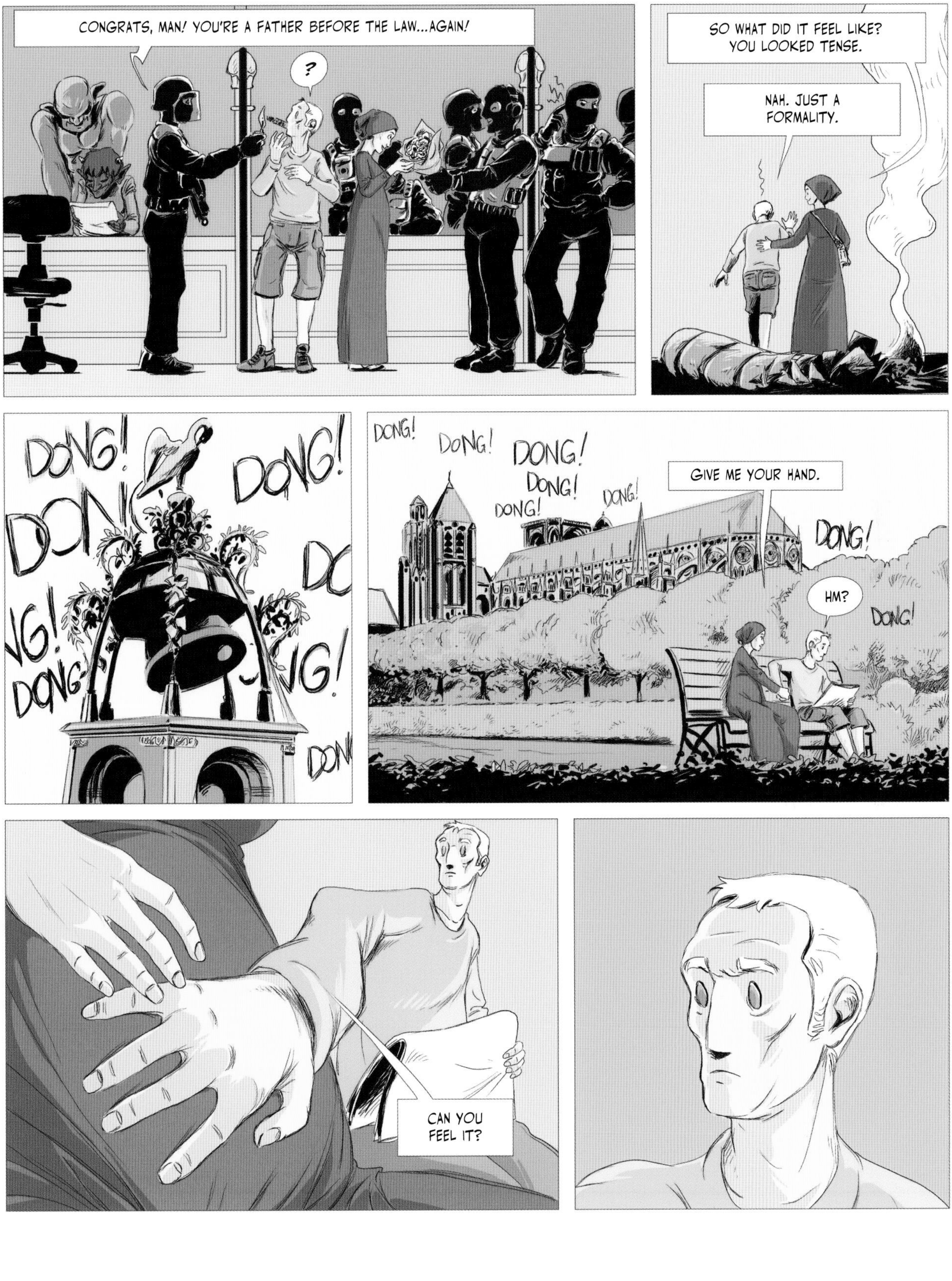
CONGRATS, MAN! YOU'RE A FATHER BEFORE THE LAW...AGAIN!
?
SO WHAT DID IT FEEL LIKE? YOU LOOKED TENSE.
NAH. JUST A FORMALITY.
DONG! DONG! DONG! DONG! DONG!
DONG! DONG! DONG! DONG! DONG! DONG! DONG!
GIVE ME YOUR HAND.
HM?
CAN YOU FEEL IT?

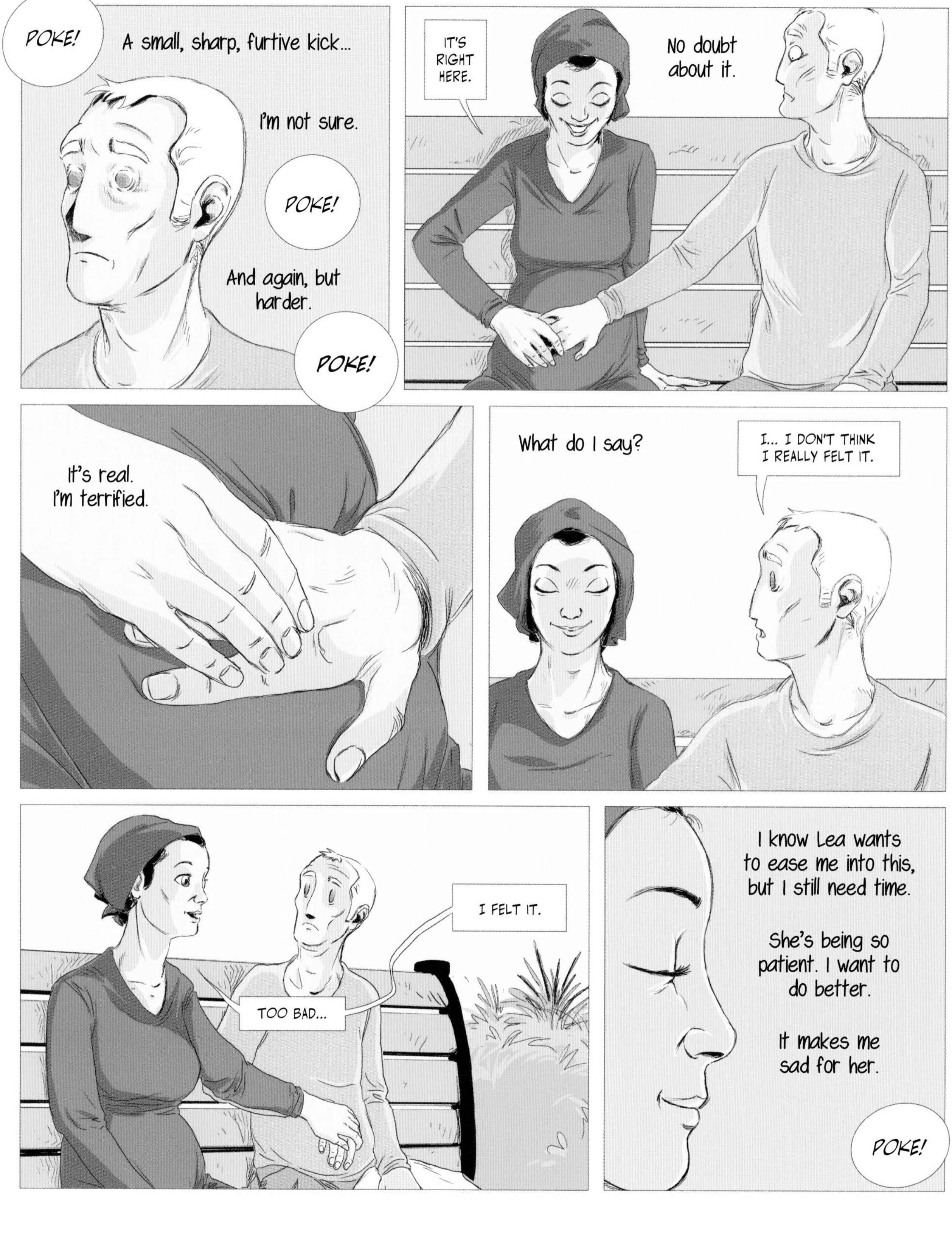
POKE!
A small, sharp, furtive kick...
I'm not sure.
POKE!
And again, but harder.
POKE!
IT'S RIGHT HERE.
No doubt about it.
It's real. I'm terrified.
What do I say?
I... I DON'T THINK I REALLY FELT IT.
I FELT IT.
TOO BAD...
I know Lea wants to ease me into this, but I still need time.
She's being so patient. I want to do better.
It makes me sad for her.
POKE!

OCTOBER

4
5
3
2
1
EARTH

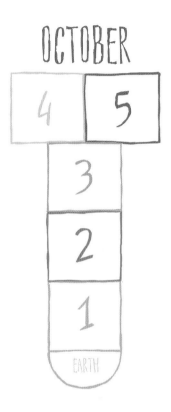

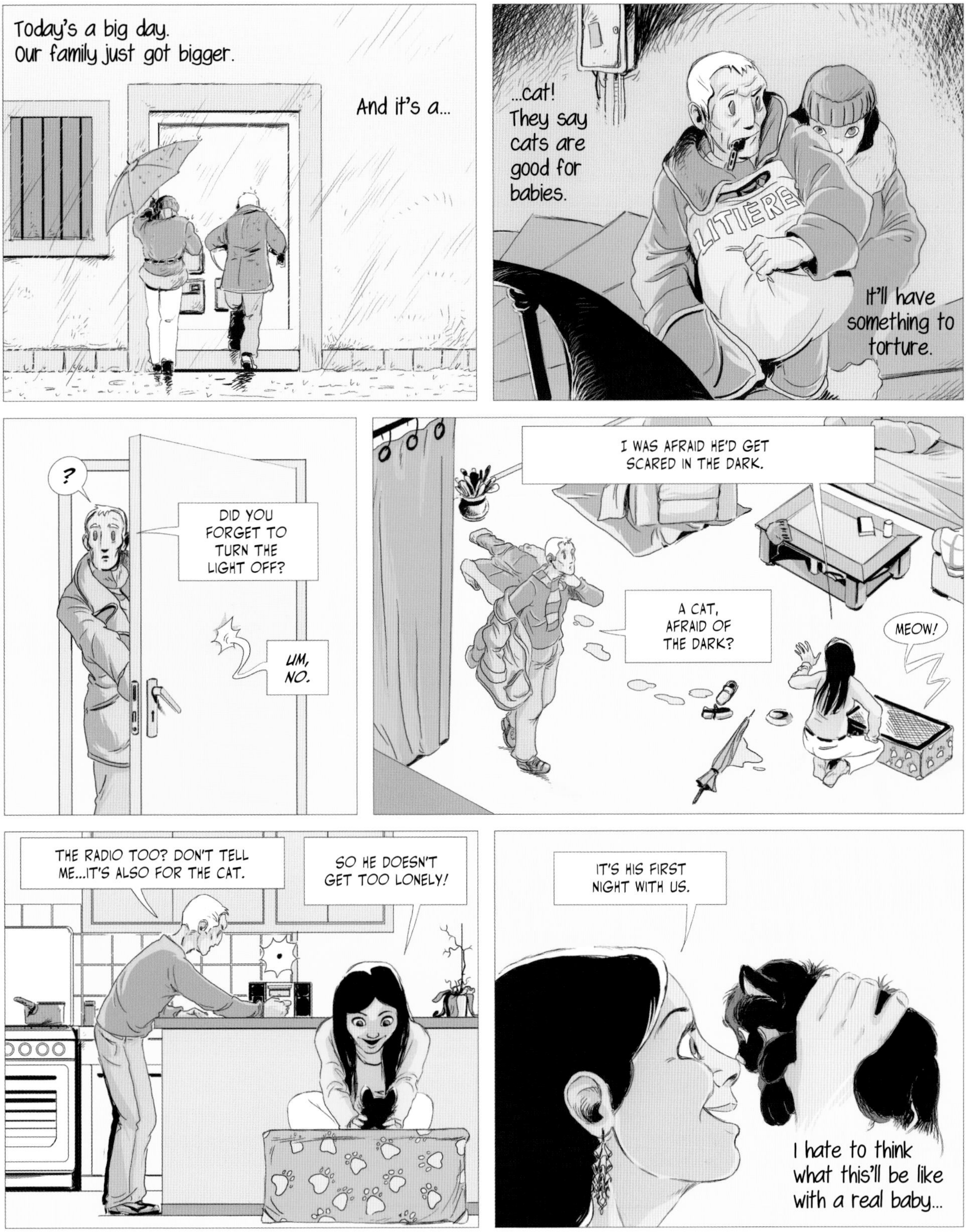

Today's a big day.
Our family just got bigger.
And it's a...
...cat! They say cats are good for babies.
LITIÈRE
It'll have something to torture.
?
DID YOU FORGET TO TURN THE LIGHT OFF?
UM, NO.
I WAS AFRAID HE'D GET SCARED IN THE DARK.
A CAT, AFRAID OF THE DARK?
MEOW!
THE RADIO TOO? DON'T TELL ME...IT'S ALSO FOR THE CAT.
SO HE DOESN'T GET TOO LONELY!
IT'S HIS FIRST NIGHT WITH US.
I hate to think what this'll be like with a real baby...

Saturday the 6th

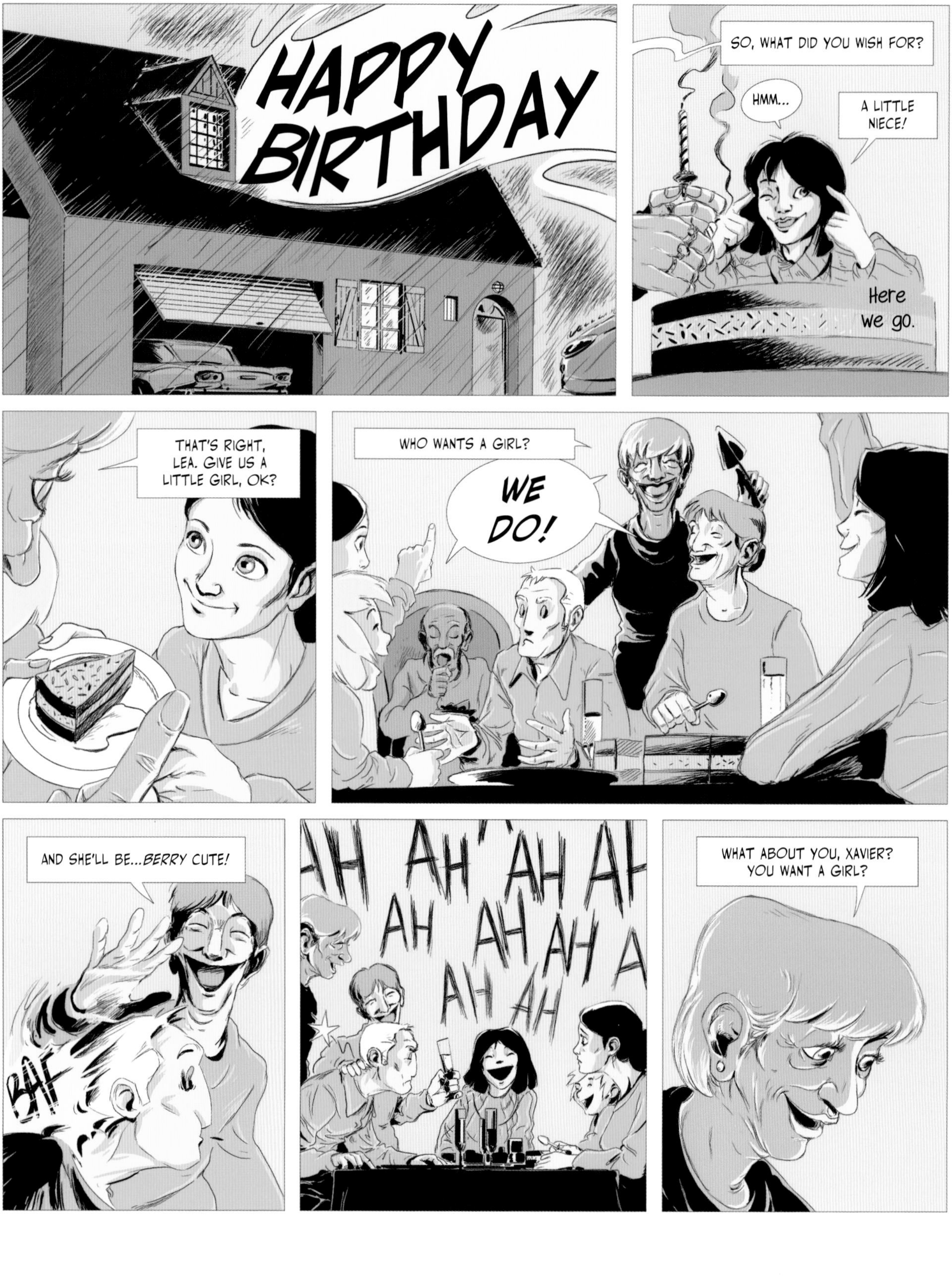
HAPPY BIRTHDAY
SO, WHAT DID YOU WISH FOR?
HMM...
A LITTLE NIECE!
Here we go.
THAT'S RIGHT, LEA. GIVE US A LITTLE GIRL, OK?
WHO WANTS A GIRL?
WE DO!
AND SHE'LL BE...*BERRY* CUTE!
BAF
AH AH AH AH AH AH AH AH AH AH
WHAT ABOUT YOU, XAVIER? YOU WANT A GIRL?

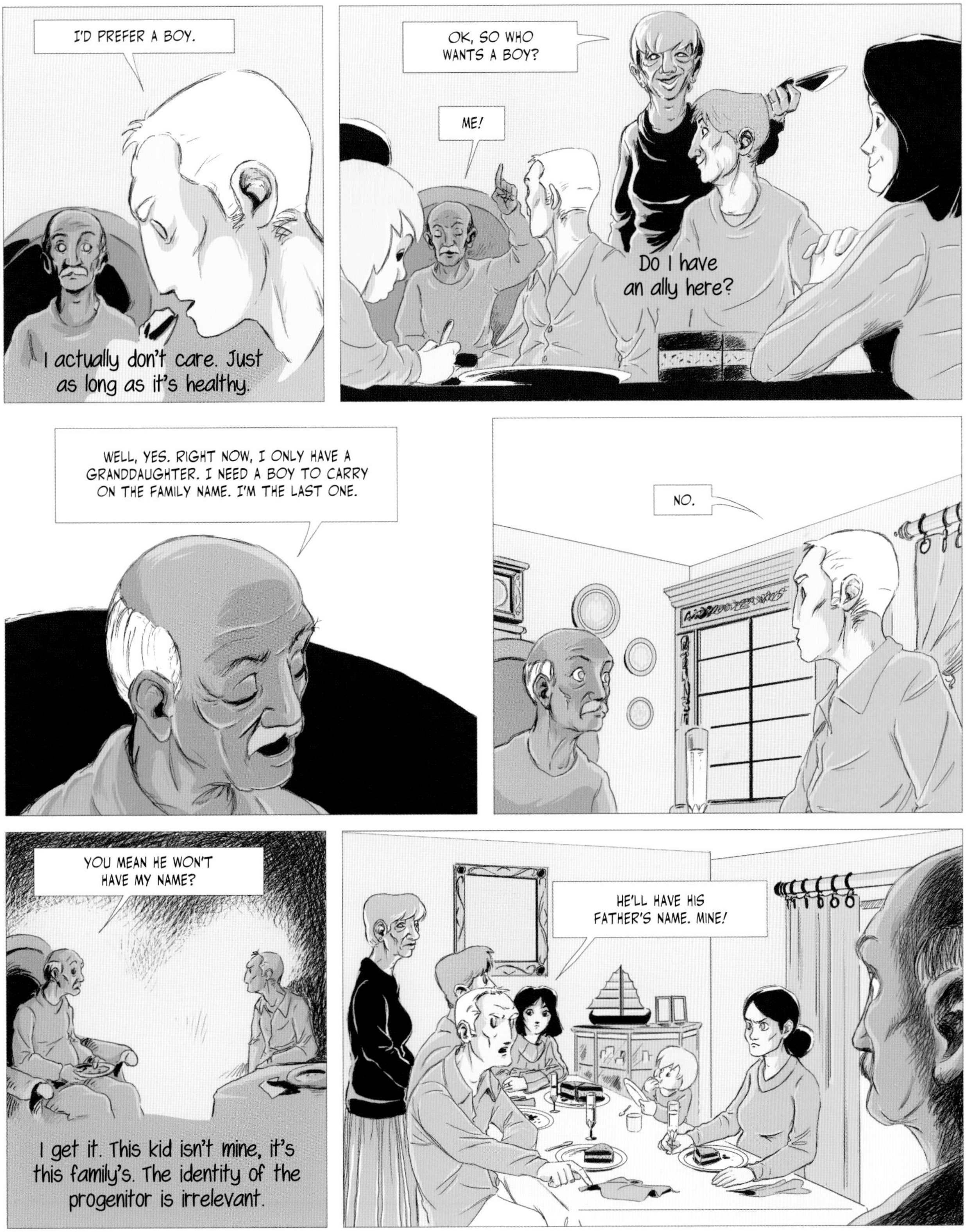
I'D PREFER A BOY.
I actually don't care. Just as long as it's healthy.
OK, SO WHO WANTS A BOY?
ME!
Do I have an ally here?
WELL, YES. RIGHT NOW, I ONLY HAVE A GRANDDAUGHTER. I NEED A BOY TO CARRY ON THE FAMILY NAME. I'M THE LAST ONE.
NO.
YOU MEAN HE WON'T HAVE MY NAME?
I get it. This kid isn't mine, it's this family's. The identity of the progenitor is irrelevant.
HE'LL HAVE HIS FATHER'S NAME. MINE!

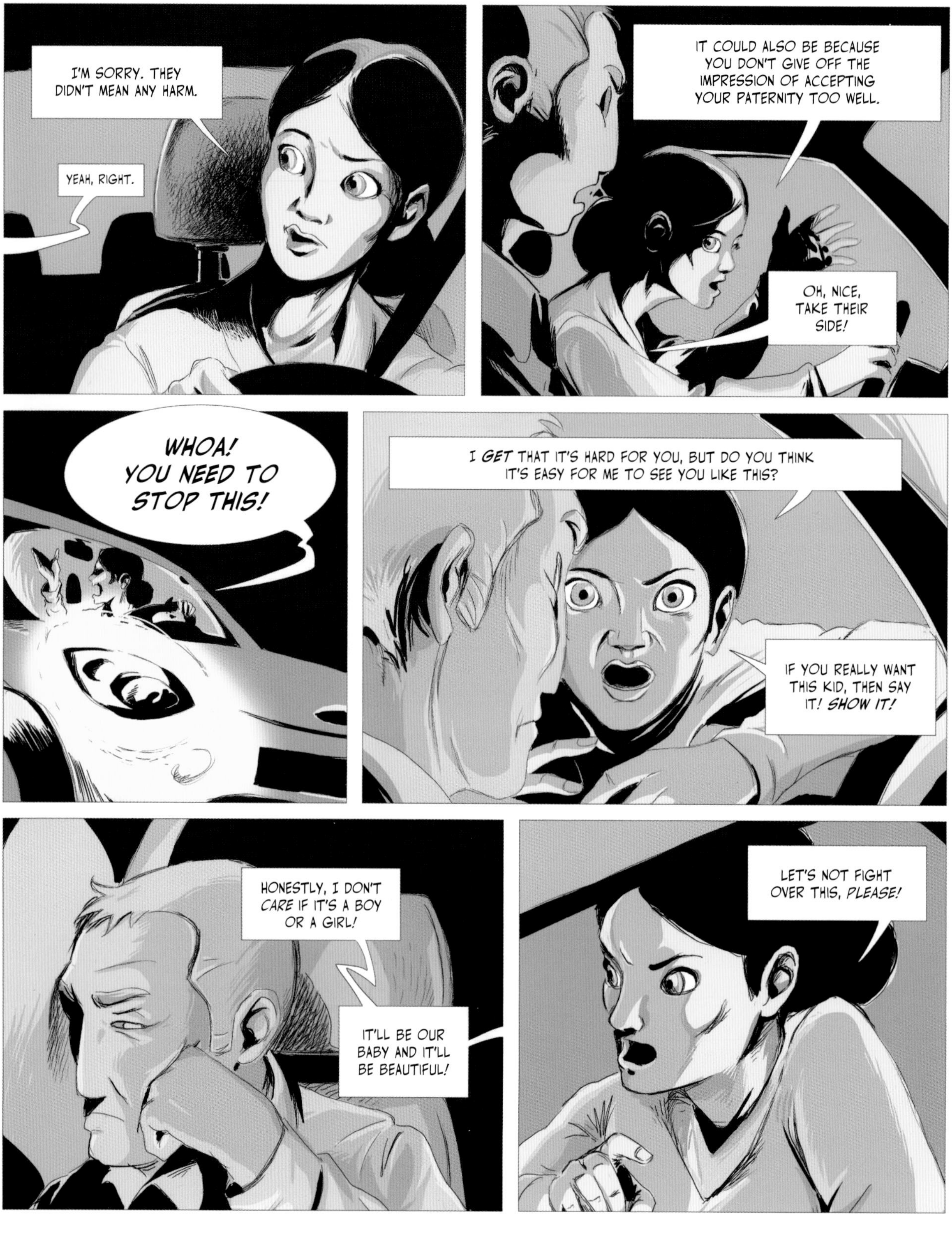
I'M SORRY. THEY DIDN'T MEAN ANY HARM.
YEAH, RIGHT.
IT COULD ALSO BE BECAUSE YOU DON'T GIVE OFF THE IMPRESSION OF ACCEPTING YOUR PATERNITY TOO WELL.
OH, NICE, TAKE THEIR SIDE!
WHOA! YOU NEED TO STOP THIS!
I *GET* THAT IT'S HARD FOR YOU, BUT DO YOU THINK IT'S EASY FOR ME TO SEE YOU LIKE THIS?
IF YOU REALLY WANT THIS KID, THEN SAY IT! *SHOW IT!*
HONESTLY, I DON'T *CARE* IF IT'S A BOY OR A GIRL!
IT'LL BE OUR BABY AND IT'LL BE BEAUTIFUL!
LET'S NOT FIGHT OVER THIS, *PLEASE!*

ALL THE ORGANS ARE WHERE THEY SHOULD BE...

11.4 INCHES, 1.25 POUNDS, THE BODY OF A LITTLE MODEL... JUST *PERFECT!*

DO YOU WANT TO KNOW THE SEX?

YES!

YOU SEE THAT COFFEE BEAN THERE? THAT MEANS IT'S A...

She knows... it's a boy!

...A GIRL!

A GIRL?

A girl...

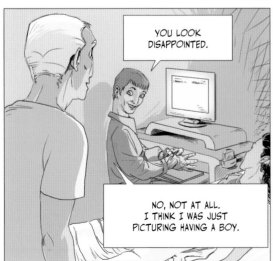

YOU LOOK DISAPPOINTED.

NO, NOT AT ALL. I THINK I WAS JUST PICTURING HAVING A BOY.

But a little girl's great too.

DADDY!

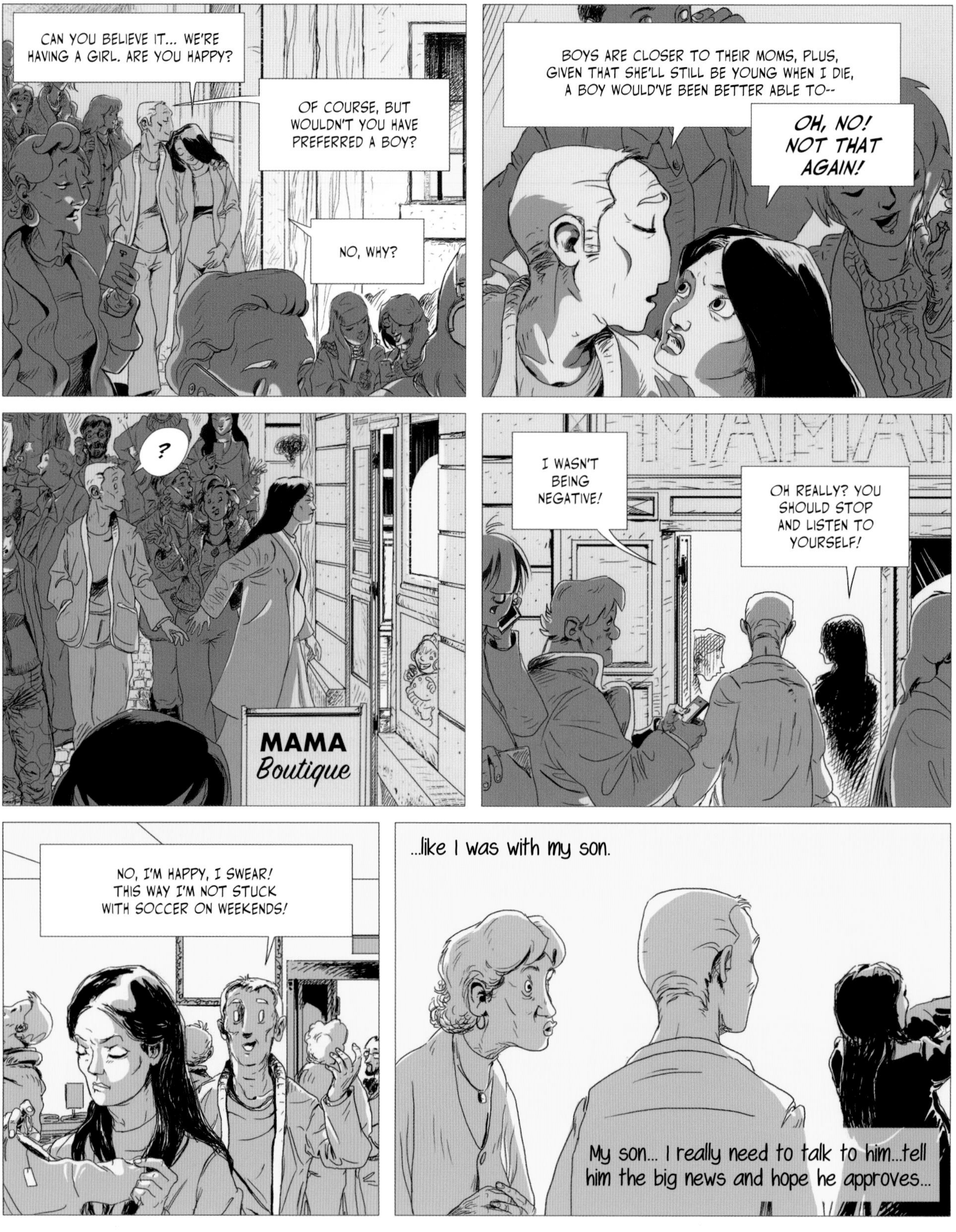
CAN YOU BELIEVE IT... WE'RE HAVING A GIRL. ARE YOU HAPPY?
OF COURSE, BUT WOULDN'T YOU HAVE PREFERRED A BOY?
NO, WHY?
BOYS ARE CLOSER TO THEIR MOMS, PLUS, GIVEN THAT SHE'LL STILL BE YOUNG WHEN I DIE, A BOY WOULD'VE BEEN BETTER ABLE TO--
OH, NO! NOT THAT AGAIN!
?
MAMA Boutique
MAMA
I WASN'T BEING NEGATIVE!
OH REALLY? YOU SHOULD STOP AND LISTEN TO YOURSELF!
NO, I'M HAPPY, I SWEAR! THIS WAY I'M NOT STUCK WITH SOCCER ON WEEKENDS!
...like I was with my son.
My son... I really need to talk to him...tell him the big news and hope he approves...

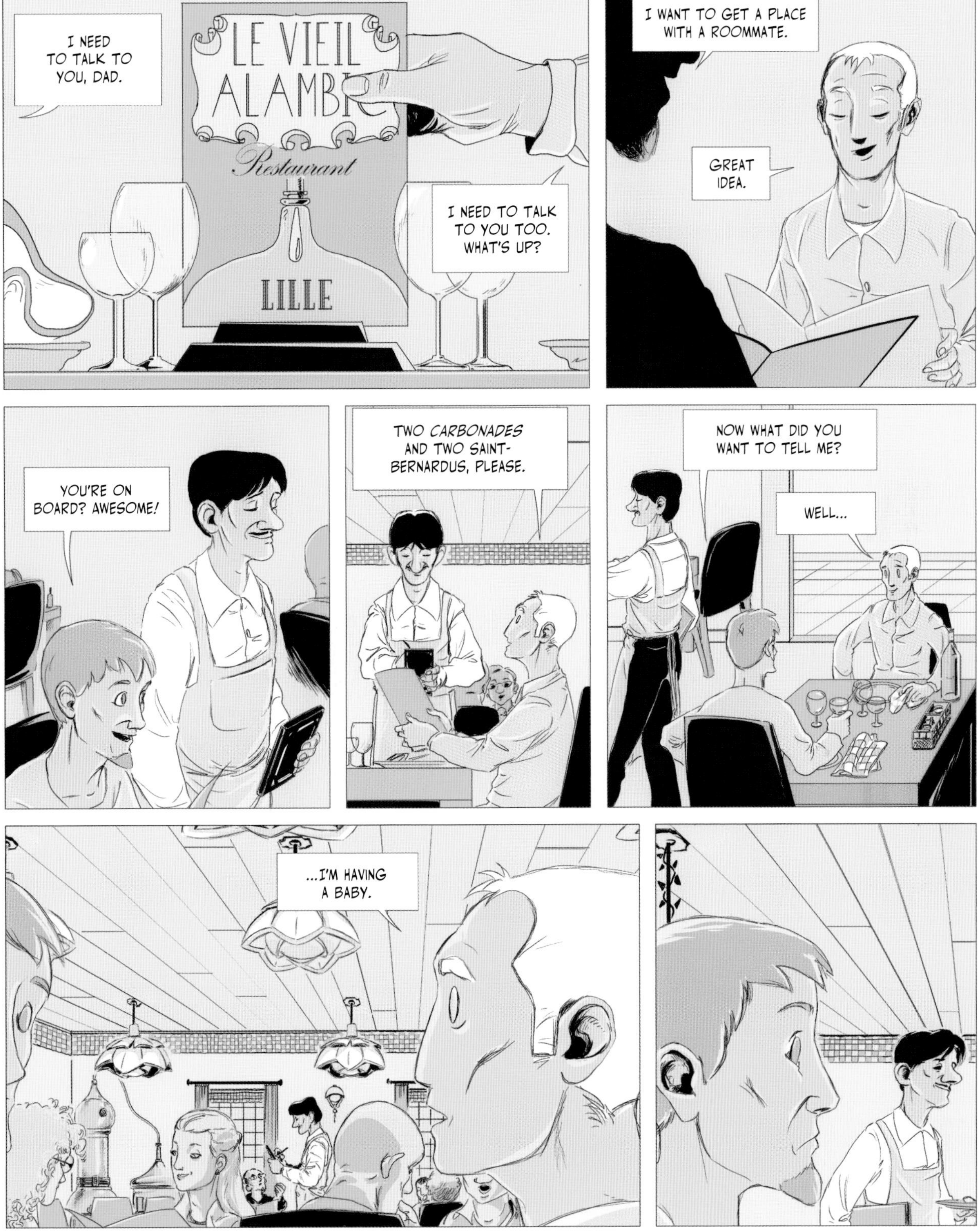
I NEED TO TALK TO YOU, DAD.
LE VIEIL ALAMBIC
Restaurant
LILLE
I NEED TO TALK TO YOU TOO. WHAT'S UP?
I WANT TO GET A PLACE WITH A ROOMMATE.
GREAT IDEA.
YOU'RE ON BOARD? AWESOME!
TWO *CARBONADES* AND TWO SAINT-BERNARDUS, PLEASE.
NOW WHAT DID YOU WANT TO TELL ME?
WELL...
...I'M HAVING A BABY.

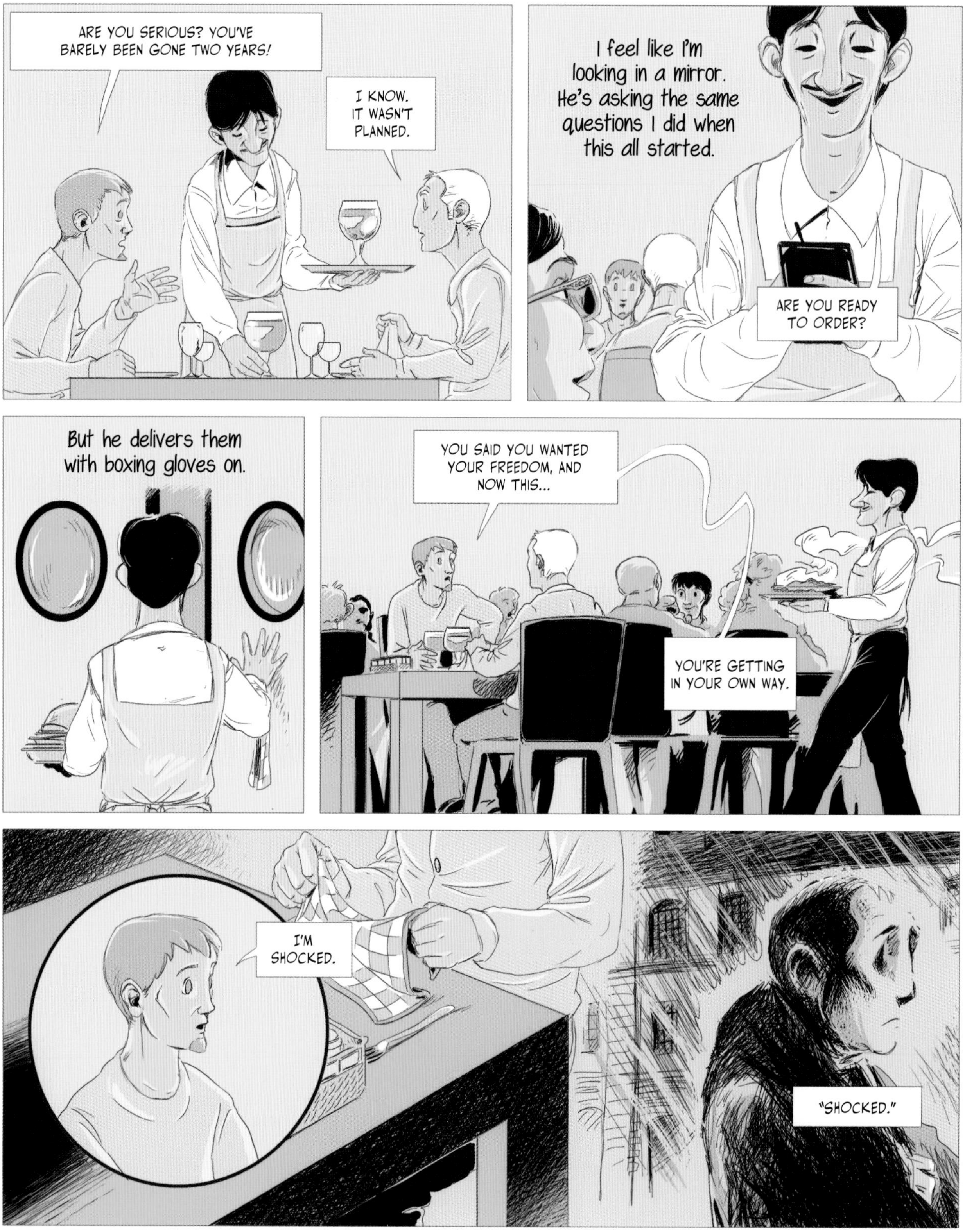
ARE YOU SERIOUS? YOU'VE BARELY BEEN GONE TWO YEARS!
I KNOW. IT WASN'T PLANNED.
I feel like I'm looking in a mirror. He's asking the same questions I did when this all started.
ARE YOU READY TO ORDER?
But he delivers them with boxing gloves on.
YOU SAID YOU WANTED YOUR FREEDOM, AND NOW THIS...
YOU'RE GETTING IN YOUR OWN WAY.
I'M SHOCKED.
"SHOCKED."

NOVEMBER

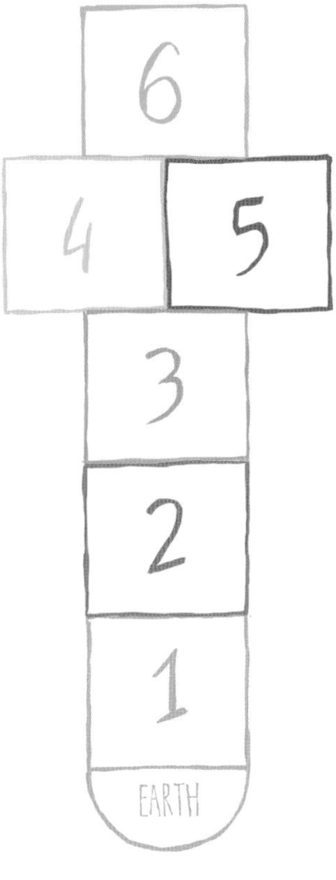
6
4
5
3
2
1
EARTH

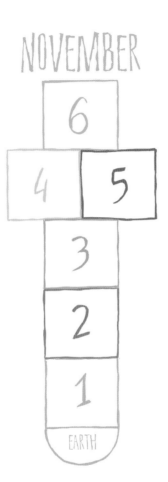

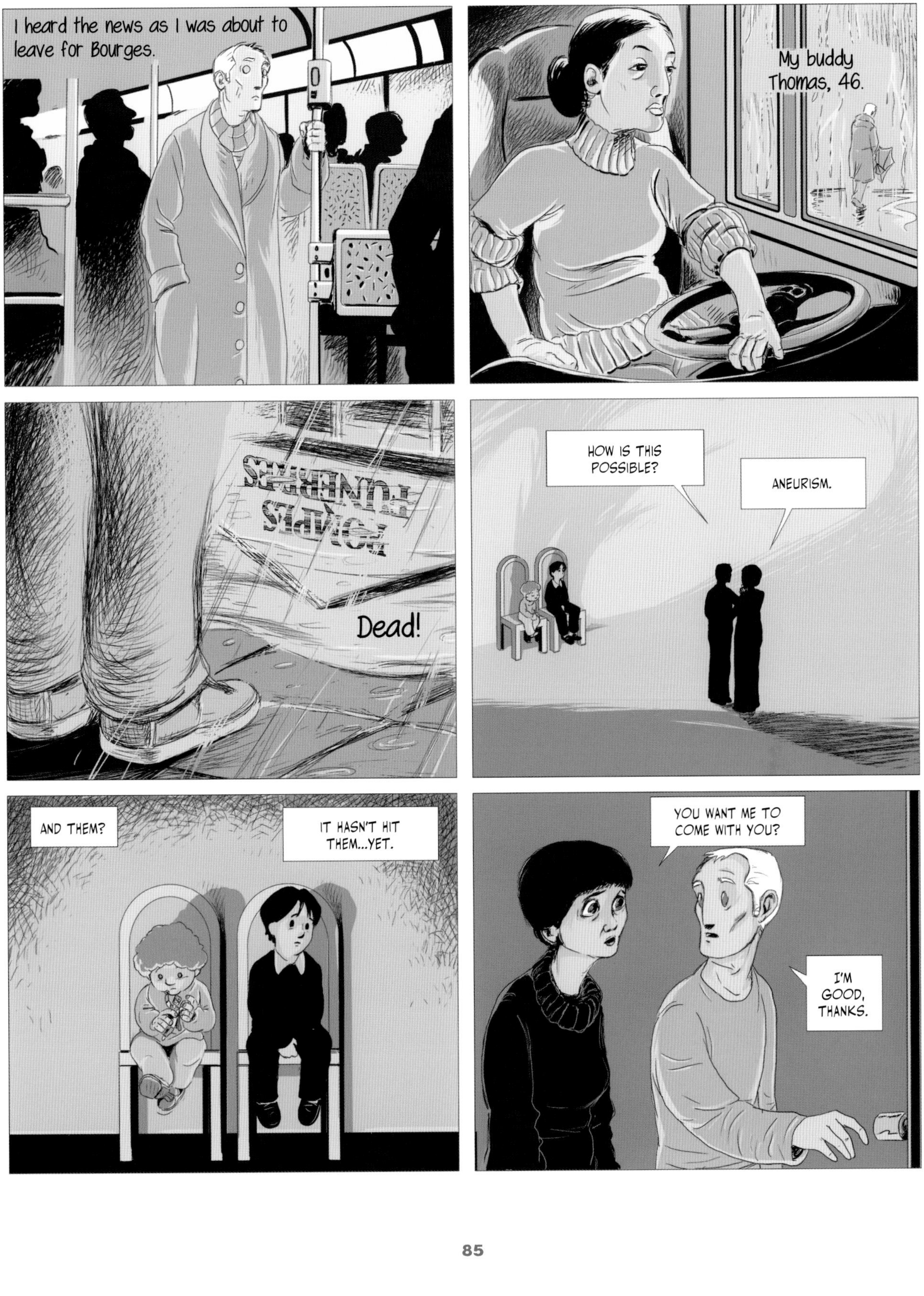
I heard the news as I was about to leave for Bourges.
My buddy Thomas, 46.
Dead!
HOW IS THIS POSSIBLE?
ANEURISM.
AND THEM?
IT HASN'T HIT THEM...YET.
YOU WANT ME TO COME WITH YOU?
I'M GOOD, THANKS.

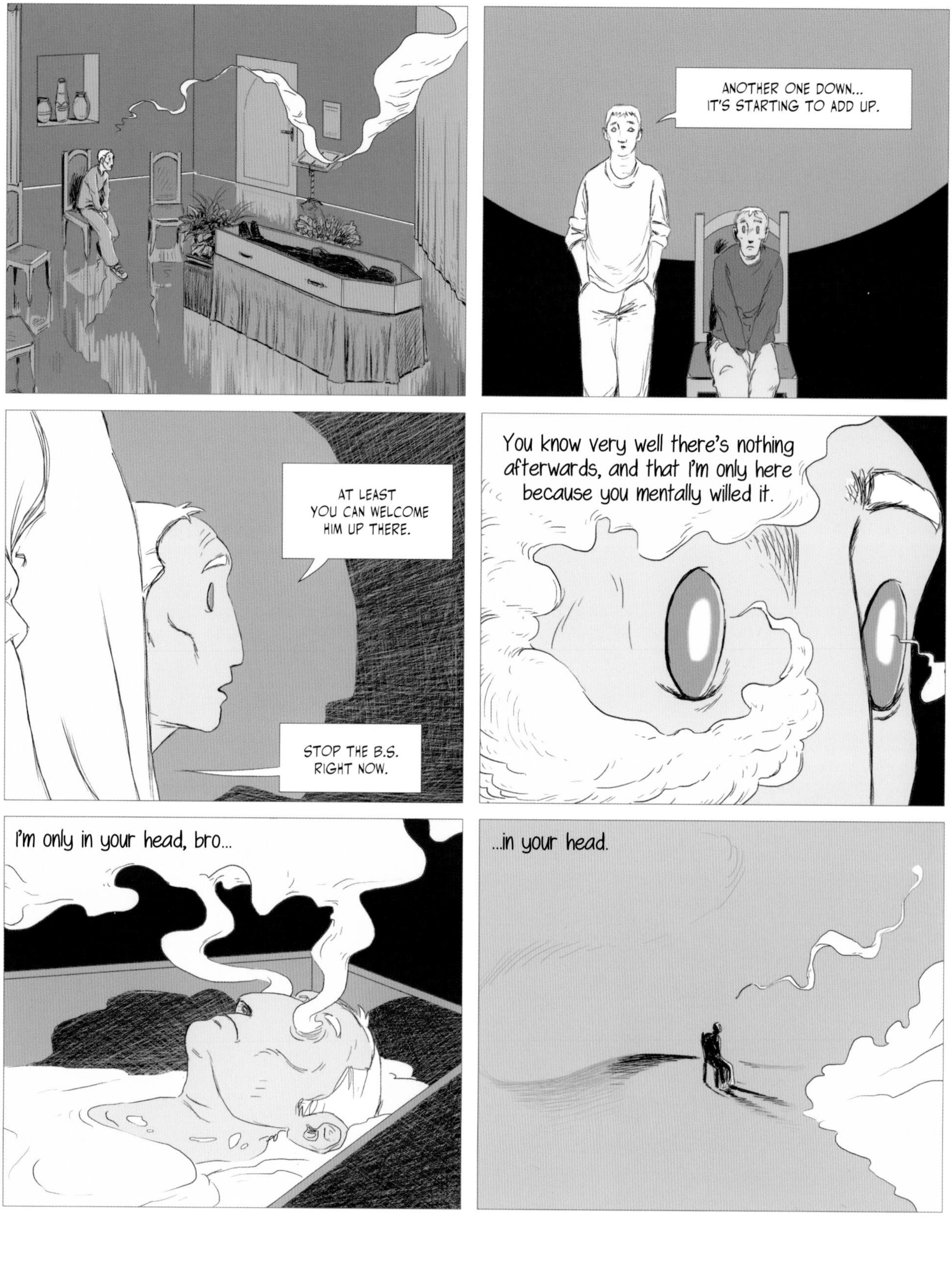
ANOTHER ONE DOWN... IT'S STARTING TO ADD UP.
AT LEAST YOU CAN WELCOME HIM UP THERE.
STOP THE B.S. RIGHT NOW.
You know very well there's nothing afterwards, and that I'm only here because you mentally willed it.
I'm only in your head, bro...
...in your head.

Wednesday the 7th

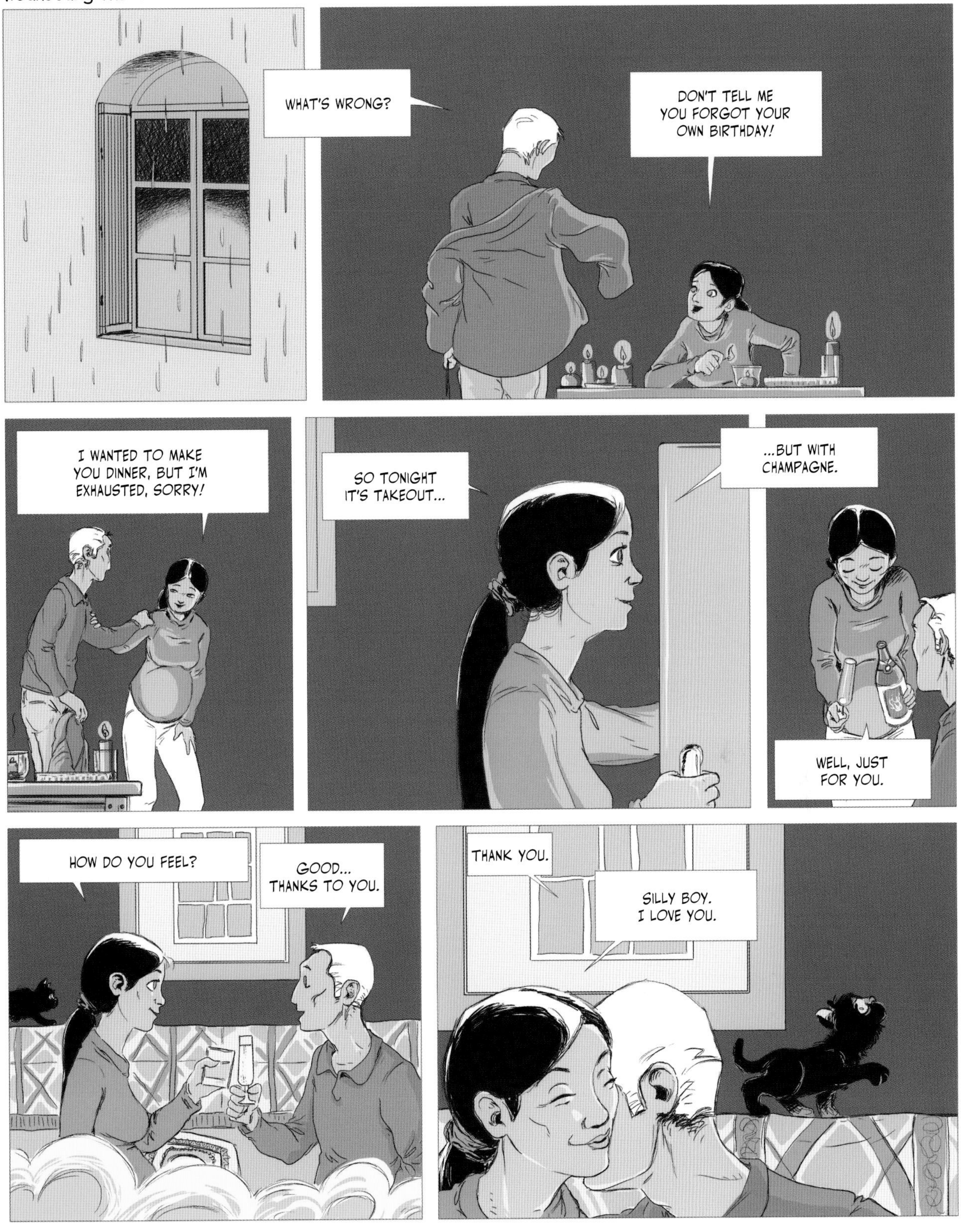
WHAT'S WRONG?
DON'T TELL ME YOU FORGOT YOUR OWN BIRTHDAY!
I WANTED TO MAKE YOU DINNER, BUT I'M EXHAUSTED, SORRY!
SO TONIGHT IT'S TAKEOUT...
...BUT WITH CHAMPAGNE.
WELL, JUST FOR YOU.
HOW DO YOU FEEL?
GOOD... THANKS TO YOU.
THANK YOU.
SILLY BOY. I LOVE YOU.

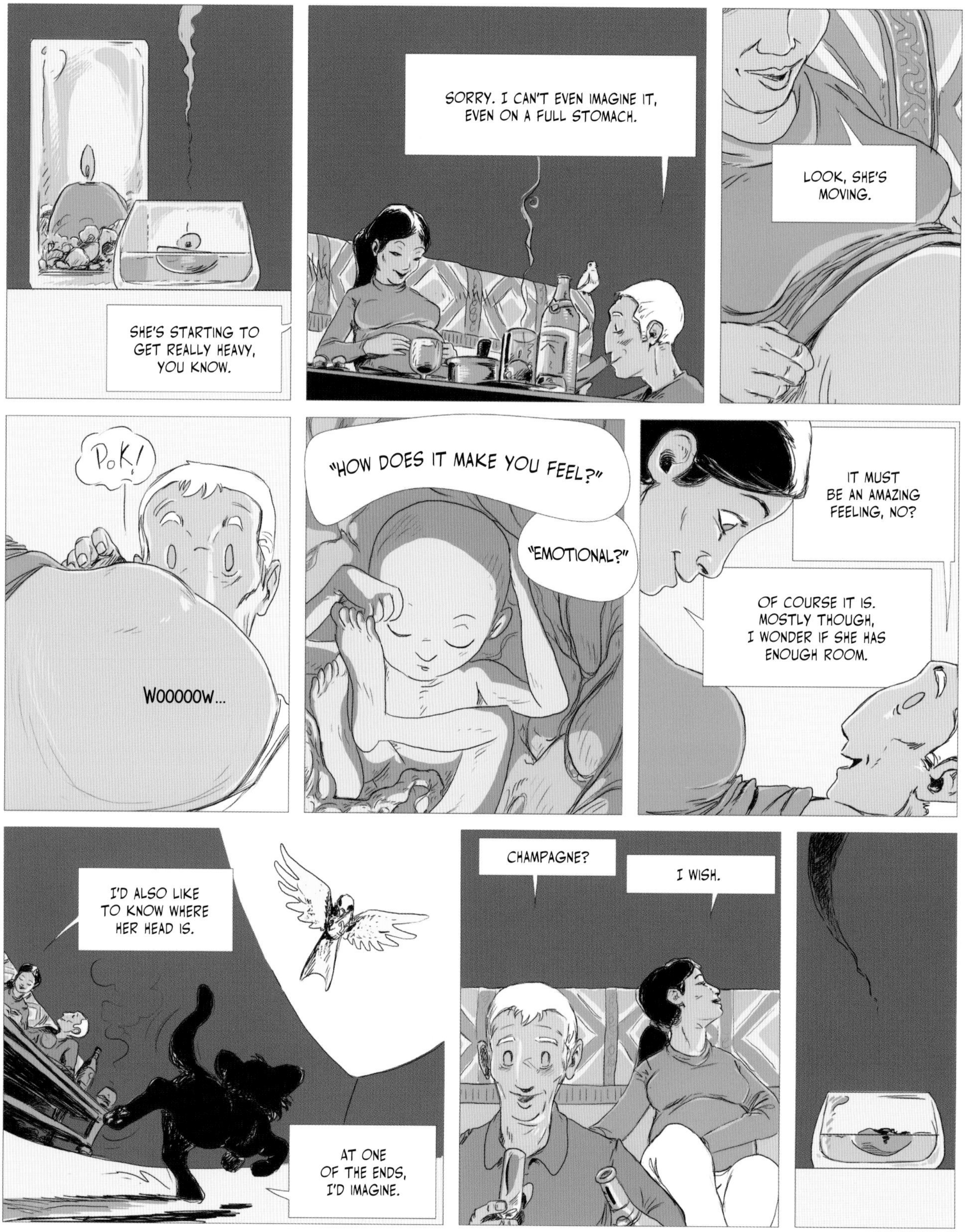
SHE'S STARTING TO GET REALLY HEAVY, YOU KNOW.
SORRY. I CAN'T EVEN IMAGINE IT, EVEN ON A FULL STOMACH.
LOOK, SHE'S MOVING.
PoK!
WOOOOOW...
"HOW DOES IT MAKE YOU FEEL?"
"EMOTIONAL?"
IT MUST BE AN AMAZING FEELING, NO?
OF COURSE IT IS. MOSTLY THOUGH, I WONDER IF SHE HAS ENOUGH ROOM.
I'D ALSO LIKE TO KNOW WHERE HER HEAD IS.
AT ONE OF THE ENDS, I'D IMAGINE.
CHAMPAGNE?
I WISH.

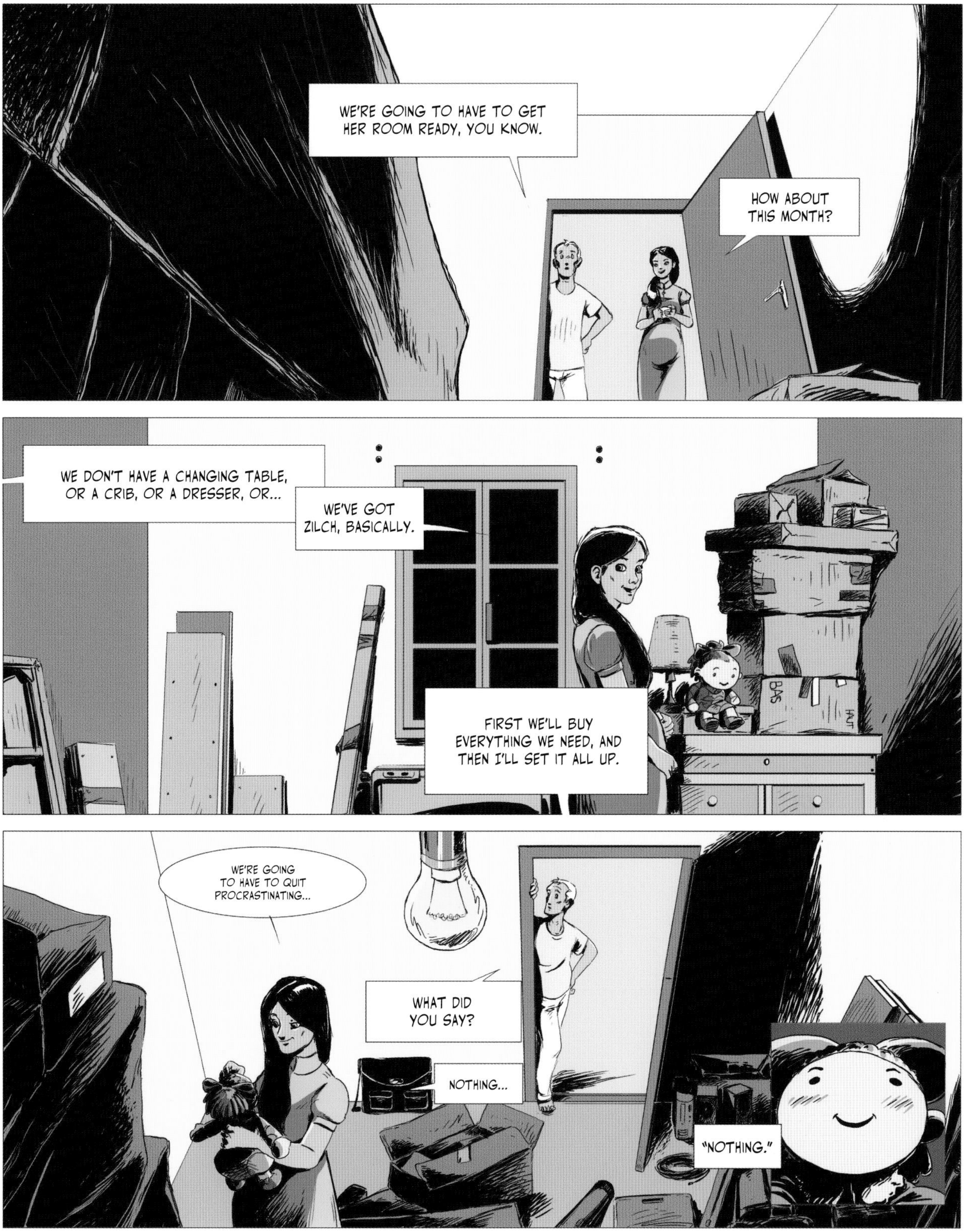
WE'RE GOING TO HAVE TO GET HER ROOM READY, YOU KNOW.
HOW ABOUT THIS MONTH?
WE DON'T HAVE A CHANGING TABLE, OR A CRIB, OR A DRESSER, OR...
WE'VE GOT ZILCH, BASICALLY.
BAS
HAUT
FIRST WE'LL BUY EVERYTHING WE NEED, AND THEN I'LL SET IT ALL UP.
WE'RE GOING TO HAVE TO QUIT PROCRASTINATING...
WHAT DID YOU SAY?
NOTHING...
"NOTHING."

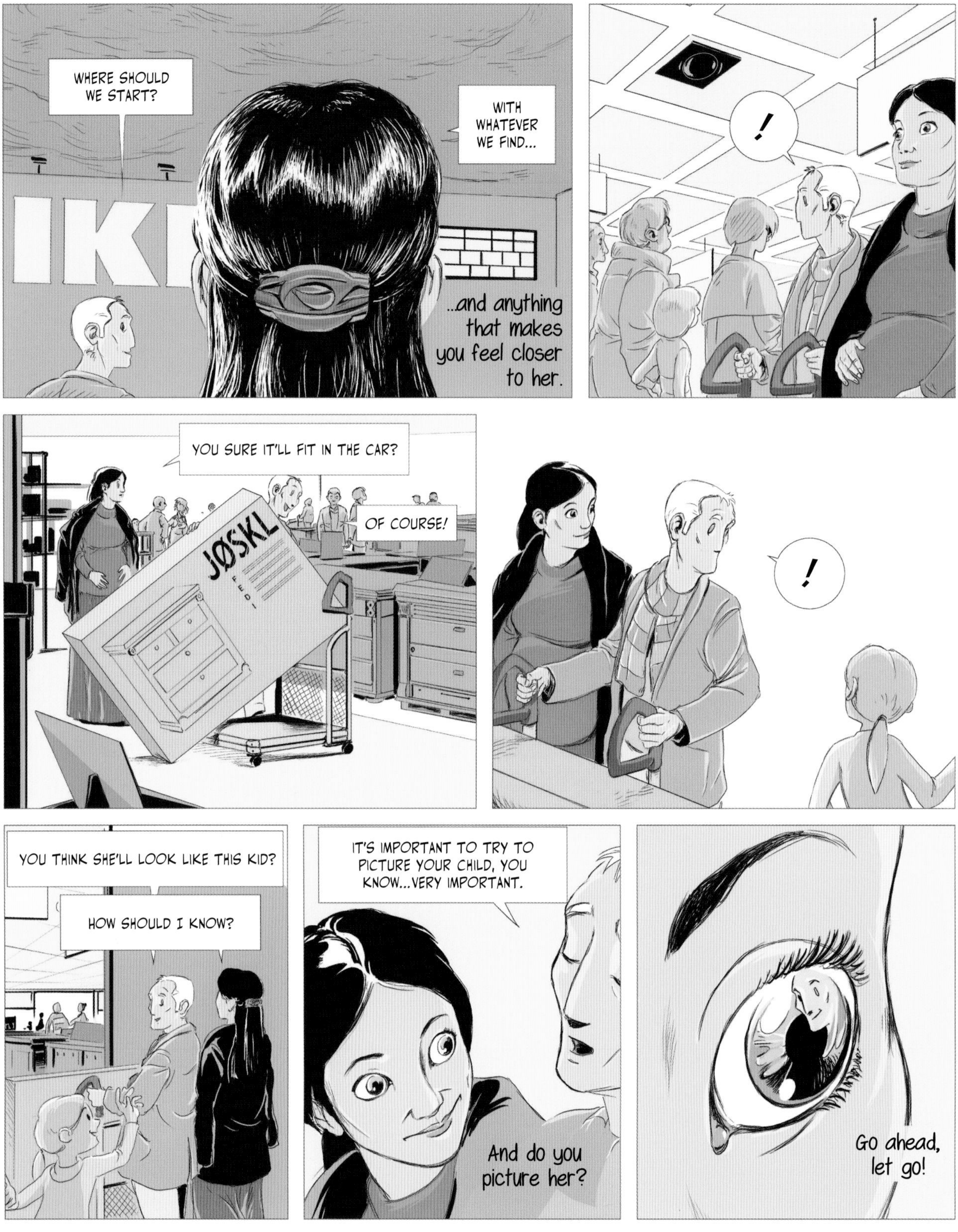
WHERE SHOULD WE START?
WITH WHATEVER WE FIND...
..and anything that makes you feel closer to her.
!
YOU SURE IT'LL FIT IN THE CAR?
OF COURSE!
JØSKL
!
YOU THINK SHE'LL LOOK LIKE THIS KID?
HOW SHOULD I KNOW?
IT'S IMPORTANT TO TRY TO PICTURE YOUR CHILD, YOU KNOW...VERY IMPORTANT.
And do you picture her?
Go ahead, let go!

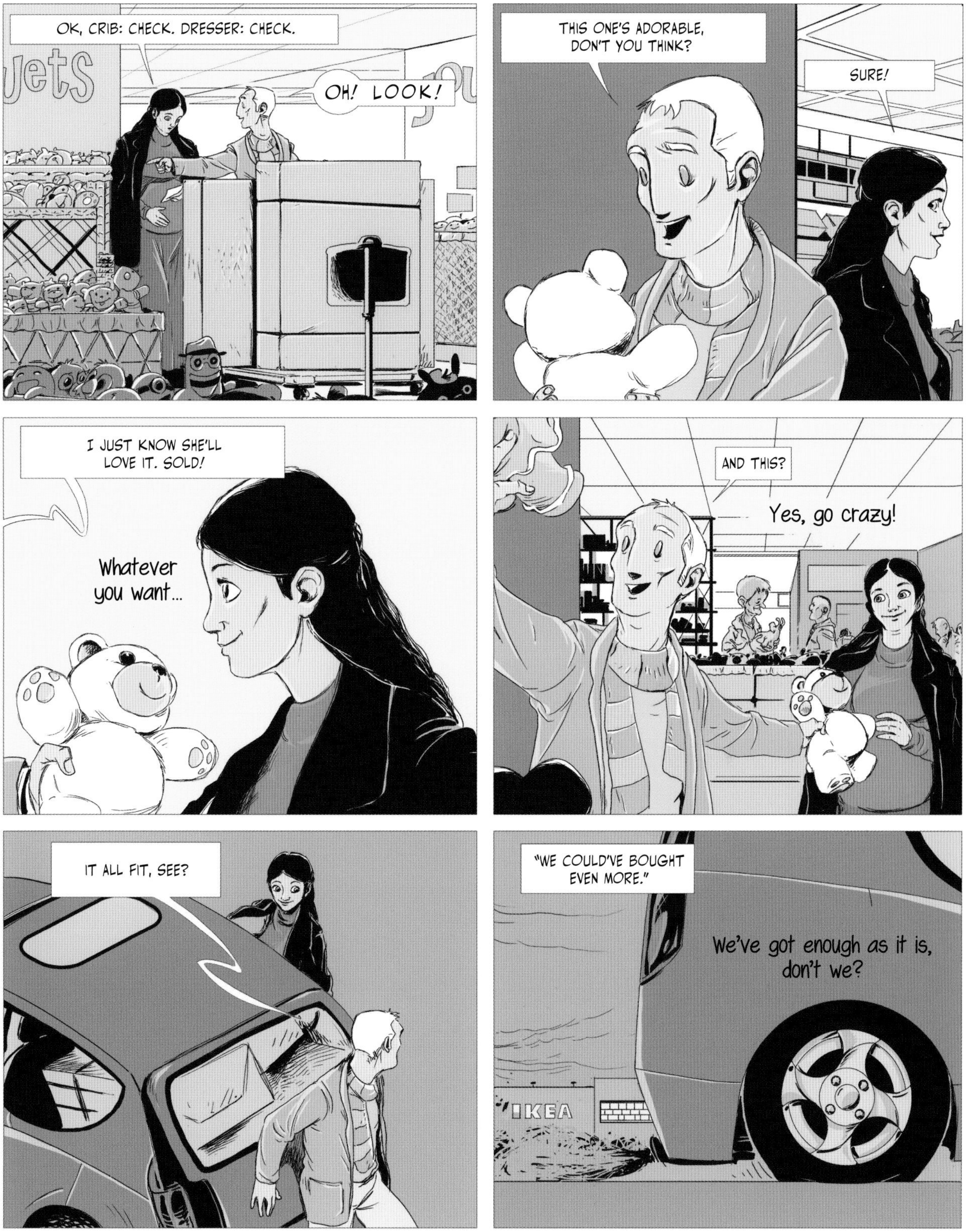
OK, CRIB: CHECK. DRESSER: CHECK.
OH! LOOK!
THIS ONE'S ADORABLE, DON'T YOU THINK?
SURE!
I JUST KNOW SHE'LL LOVE IT. SOLD!
Whatever you want...
AND THIS?
Yes, go crazy!
IT ALL FIT, SEE?
"WE COULD'VE BOUGHT EVEN MORE."
We've got enough as it is, don't we?
IKEA

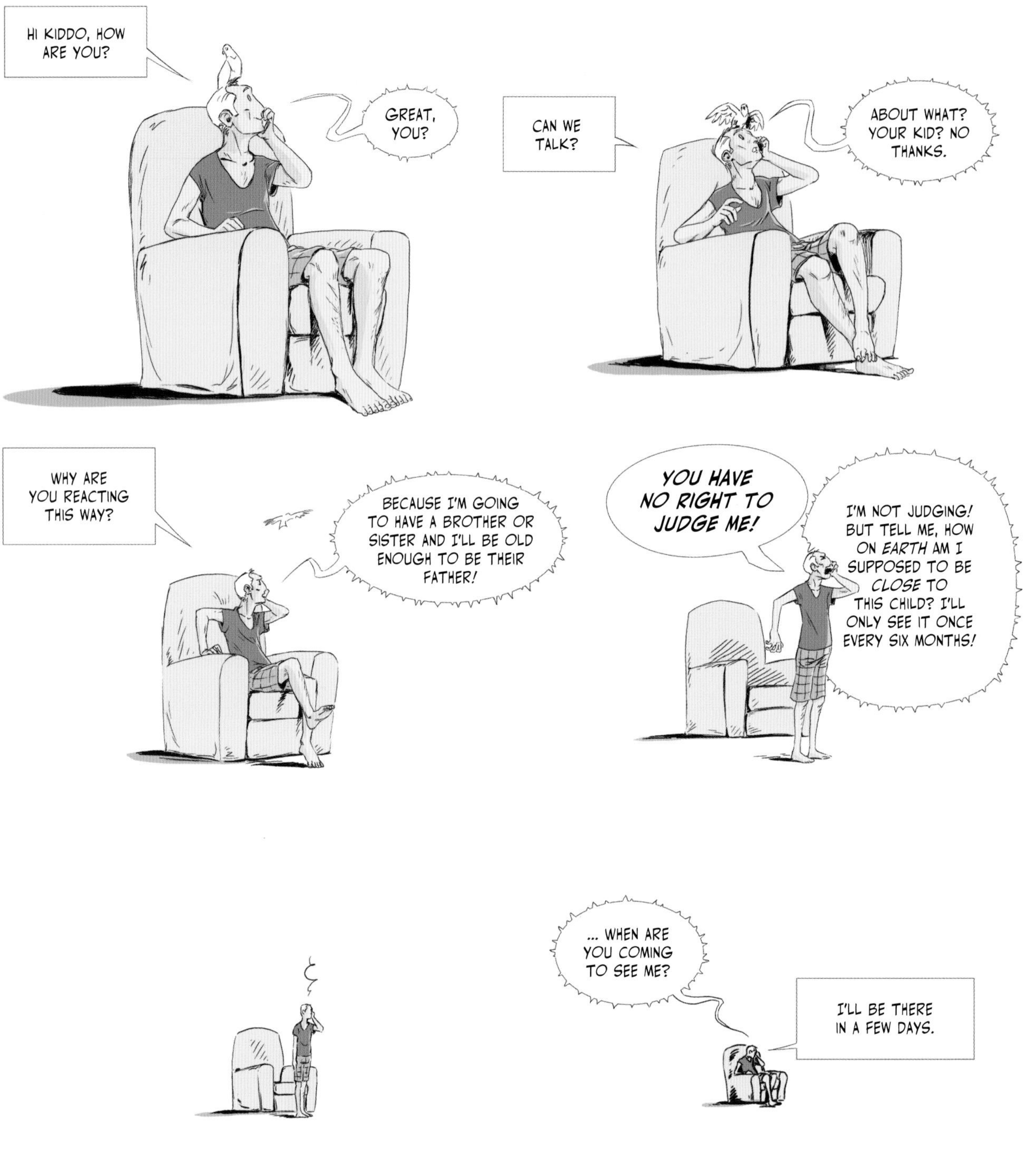
HI KIDDO, HOW ARE YOU?
GREAT, YOU?
CAN WE TALK?
ABOUT WHAT? YOUR KID? NO THANKS.
WHY ARE YOU REACTING THIS WAY?
BECAUSE I'M GOING TO HAVE A BROTHER OR SISTER AND I'LL BE OLD ENOUGH TO BE THEIR FATHER!
YOU HAVE NO RIGHT TO JUDGE ME!
I'M NOT JUDGING! BUT TELL ME, HOW ON EARTH AM I SUPPOSED TO BE CLOSE TO THIS CHILD? I'LL ONLY SEE IT ONCE EVERY SIX MONTHS!
... WHEN ARE YOU COMING TO SEE ME?
I'LL BE THERE IN A FEW DAYS.

DECEMBER

7
6
4
5
3
2
1
EARTH

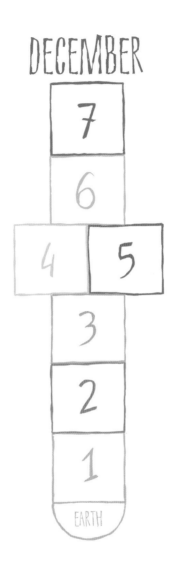

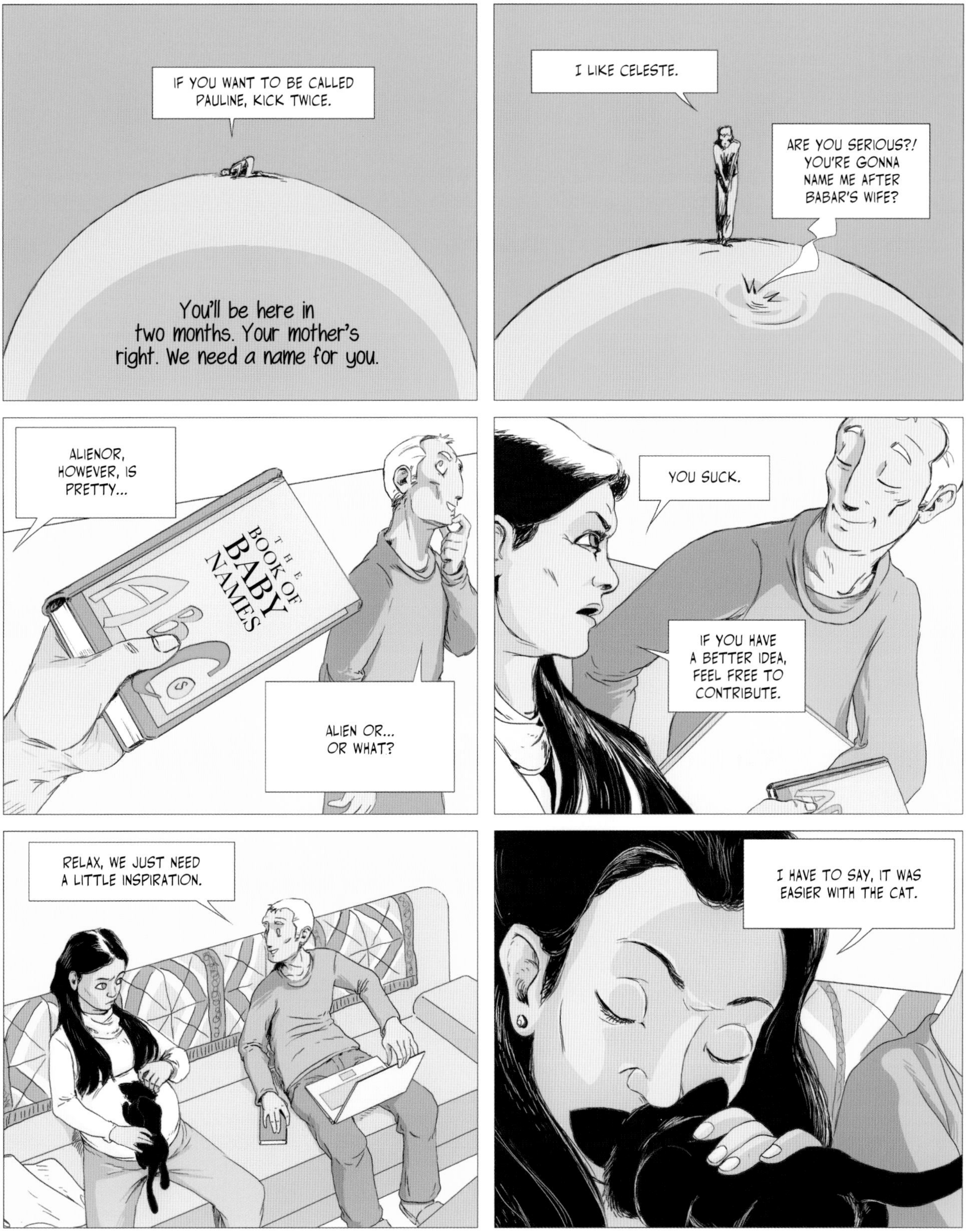
IF YOU WANT TO BE CALLED PAULINE, KICK TWICE.
You'll be here in two months. Your mother's right. We need a name for you.
I LIKE CELESTE.
ARE YOU SERIOUS?! YOU'RE GONNA NAME ME AFTER BABAR'S WIFE?
ALIENOR, HOWEVER, IS PRETTY...
THE BOOK OF BABY NAMES
ALIEN OR... OR WHAT?
YOU SUCK.
IF YOU HAVE A BETTER IDEA, FEEL FREE TO CONTRIBUTE.
RELAX, WE JUST NEED A LITTLE INSPIRATION.
I HAVE TO SAY, IT WAS EASIER WITH THE CAT.

Saturday the 15th

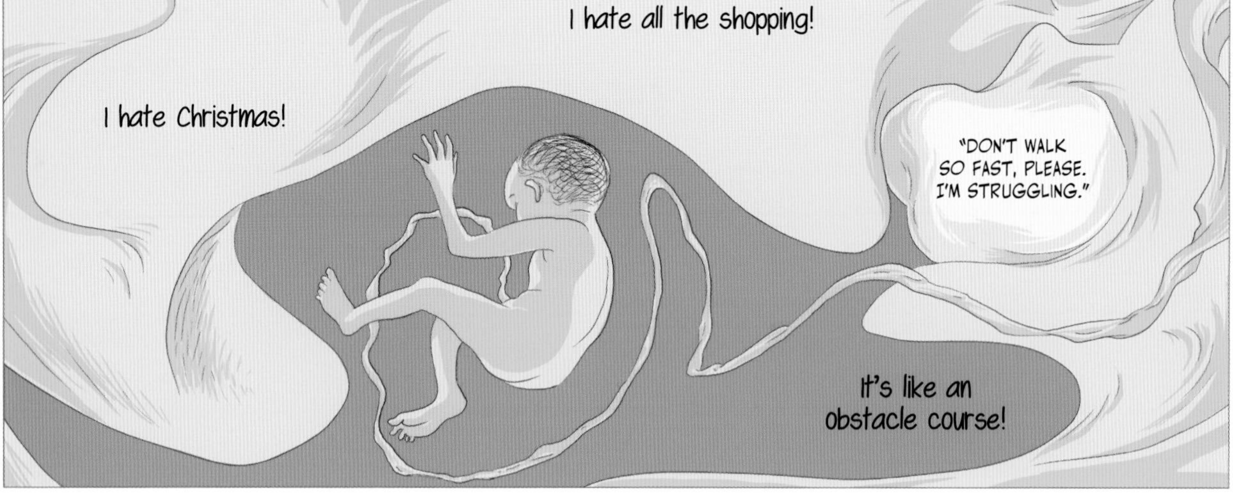
I hate Christmas!
I hate all the shopping!
"DON'T WALK SO FAST, PLEASE. I'M STRUGGLING."
It's like an obstacle course!

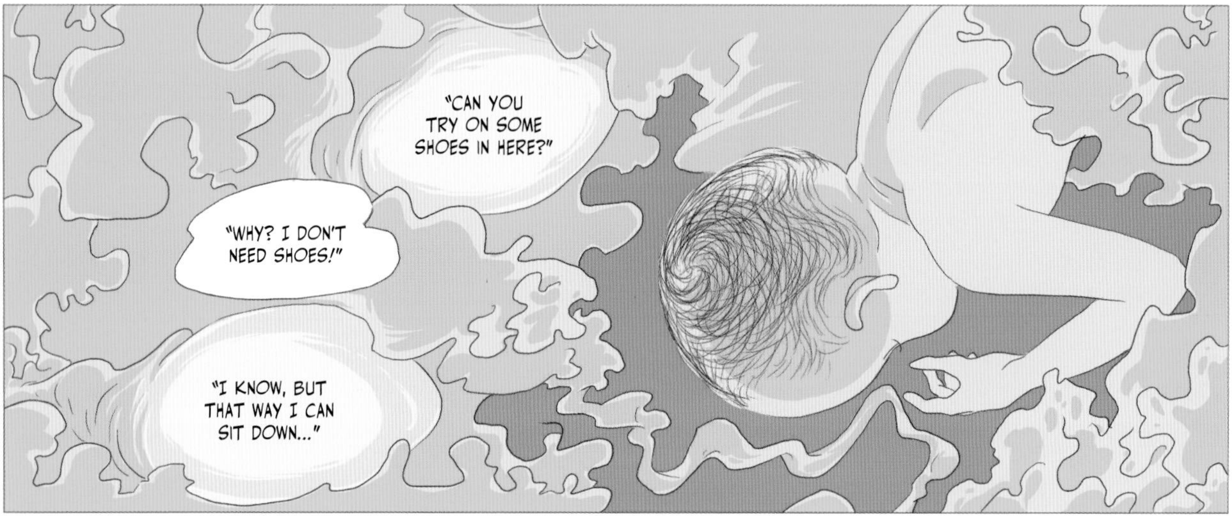
"CAN YOU TRY ON SOME SHOES IN HERE?"
"WHY? I DON'T NEED SHOES!"
"I KNOW, BUT THAT WAY I CAN SIT DOWN..."

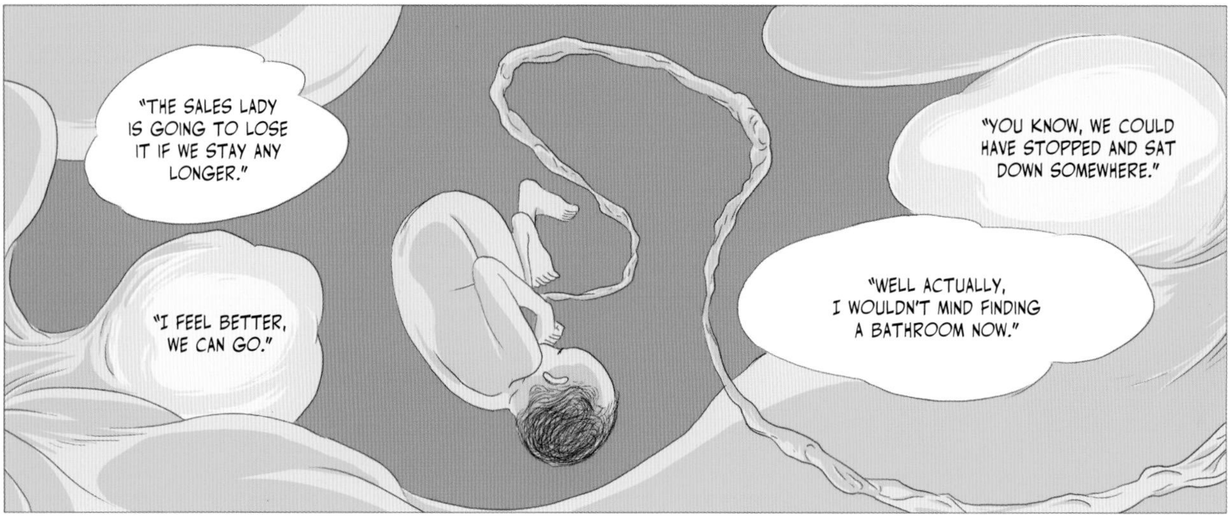
"THE SALES LADY IS GOING TO LOSE IT IF WE STAY ANY LONGER."
"I FEEL BETTER, WE CAN GO."
"YOU KNOW, WE COULD HAVE STOPPED AND SAT DOWN SOMEWHERE."
"WELL ACTUALLY, I WOULDN'T MIND FINDING A BATHROOM NOW."

Monday the 24th

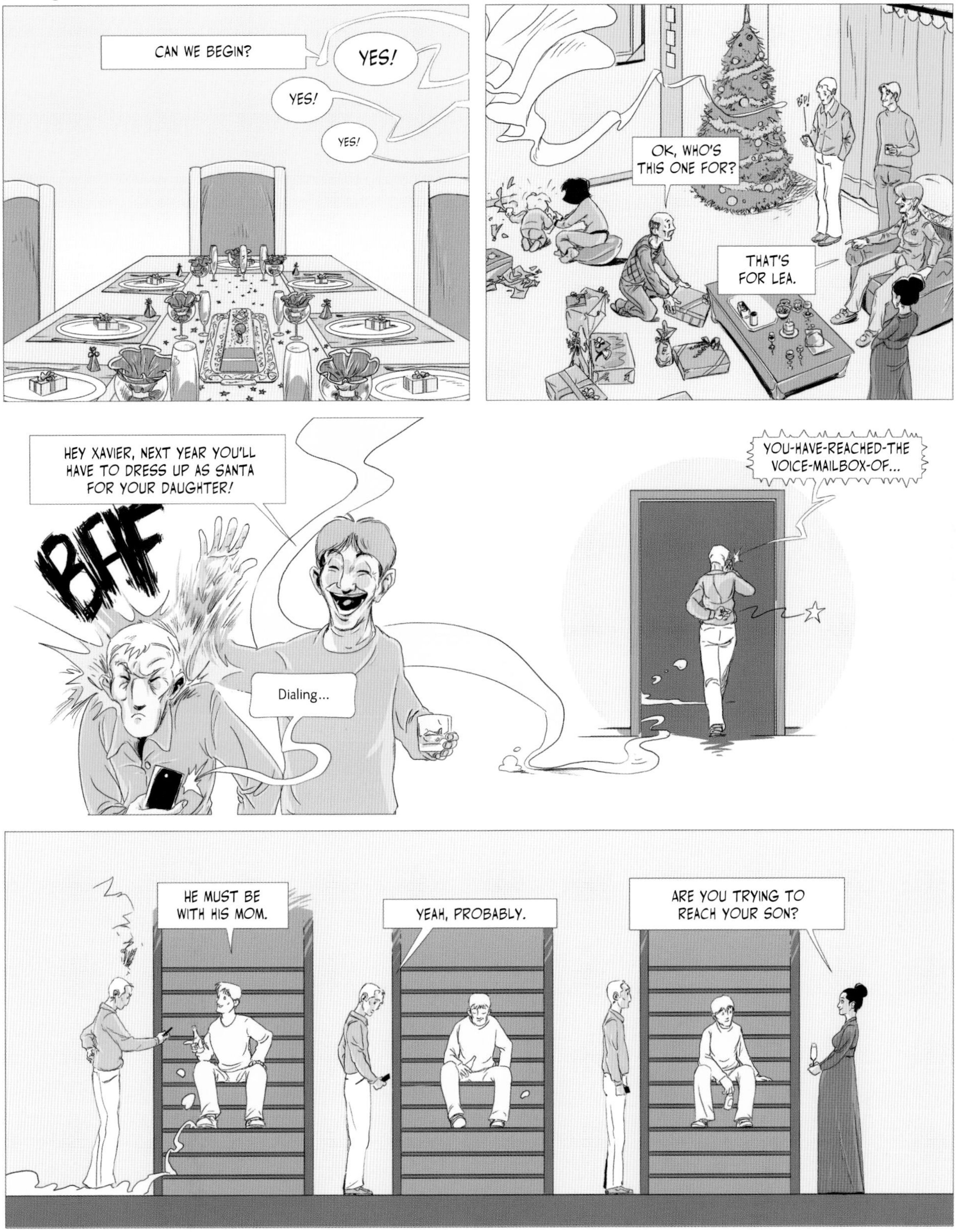

CAN WE BEGIN?
YES!
YES!
YES!
OK, WHO'S THIS ONE FOR?
THAT'S FOR LEA.
HEY XAVIER, NEXT YEAR YOU'LL HAVE TO DRESS UP AS SANTA FOR YOUR DAUGHTER!
BAF
Dialing...
YOU-HAVE-REACHED-THE VOICE-MAILBOX-OF...
HE MUST BE WITH HIS MOM.
YEAH, PROBABLY.
ARE YOU TRYING TO REACH YOUR SON?

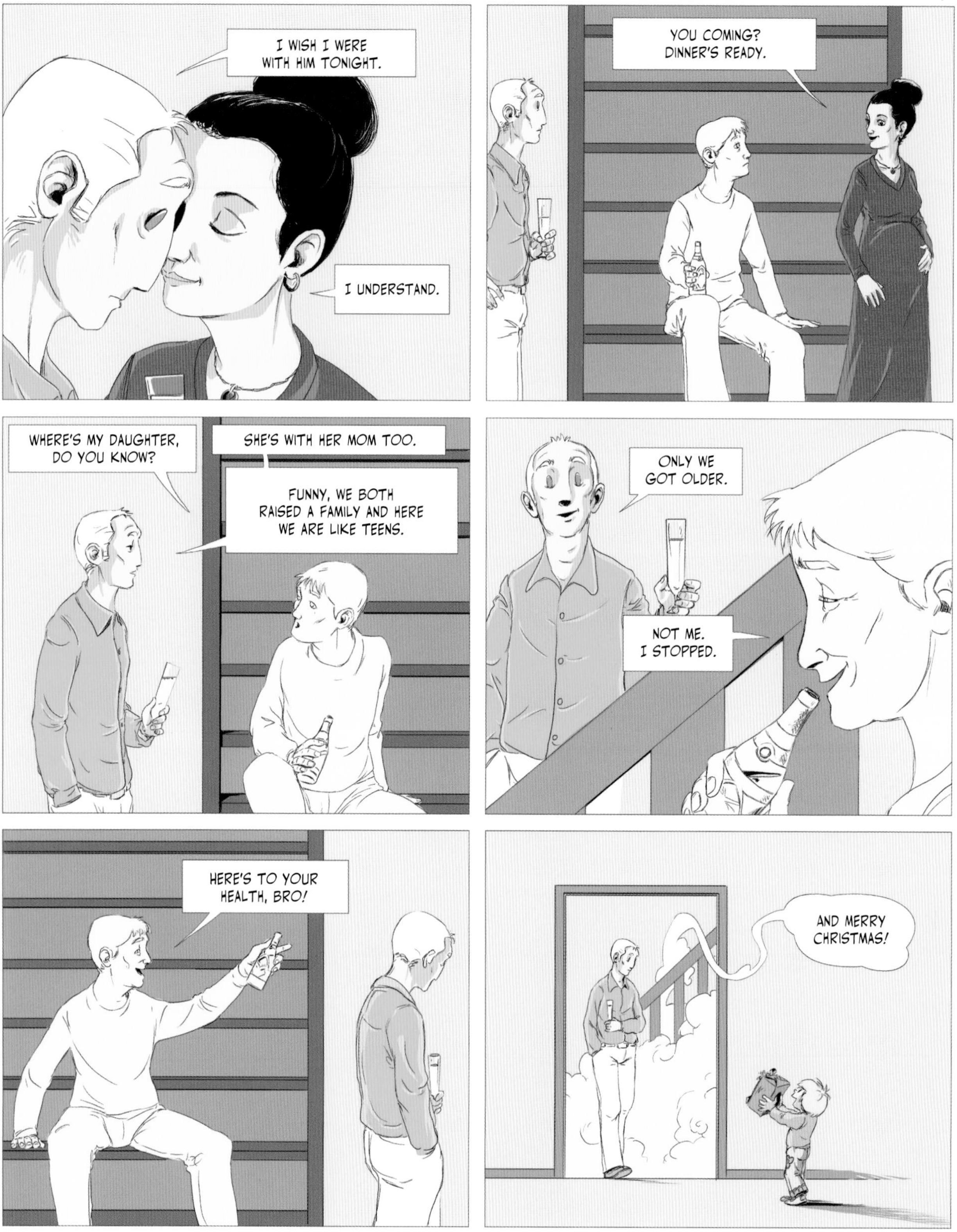
I WISH I WERE WITH HIM TONIGHT.
I UNDERSTAND.
YOU COMING? DINNER'S READY.
WHERE'S MY DAUGHTER, DO YOU KNOW?
SHE'S WITH HER MOM TOO.
FUNNY, WE BOTH RAISED A FAMILY AND HERE WE ARE LIKE TEENS.
ONLY WE GOT OLDER.
NOT ME. I STOPPED.
HERE'S TO YOUR HEALTH, BRO!
AND MERRY CHRISTMAS!

Monday the 31st

Here we are. The last day of this *annus horribilis*. Time to take inventory...

On the menu: a quiet evening with friends. Perfect, given Lea's condition.

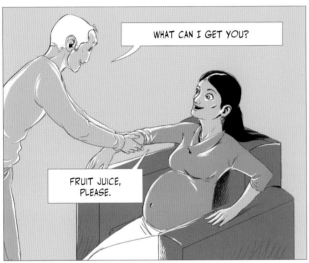

WHAT CAN I GET YOU?

FRUIT JUICE, PLEASE.

A year ago, we were dancing, drinking wine, partying and ready to start something new. How could we ever have imagined...?

HOW DO YOU FEEL?

LIKE AN OLD GRANNY. WHAT ABOUT YOU? NOT TOO BORED?

NAH. I LIKE YOUR FRIENDS AND IT'S A NICE SPREAD.

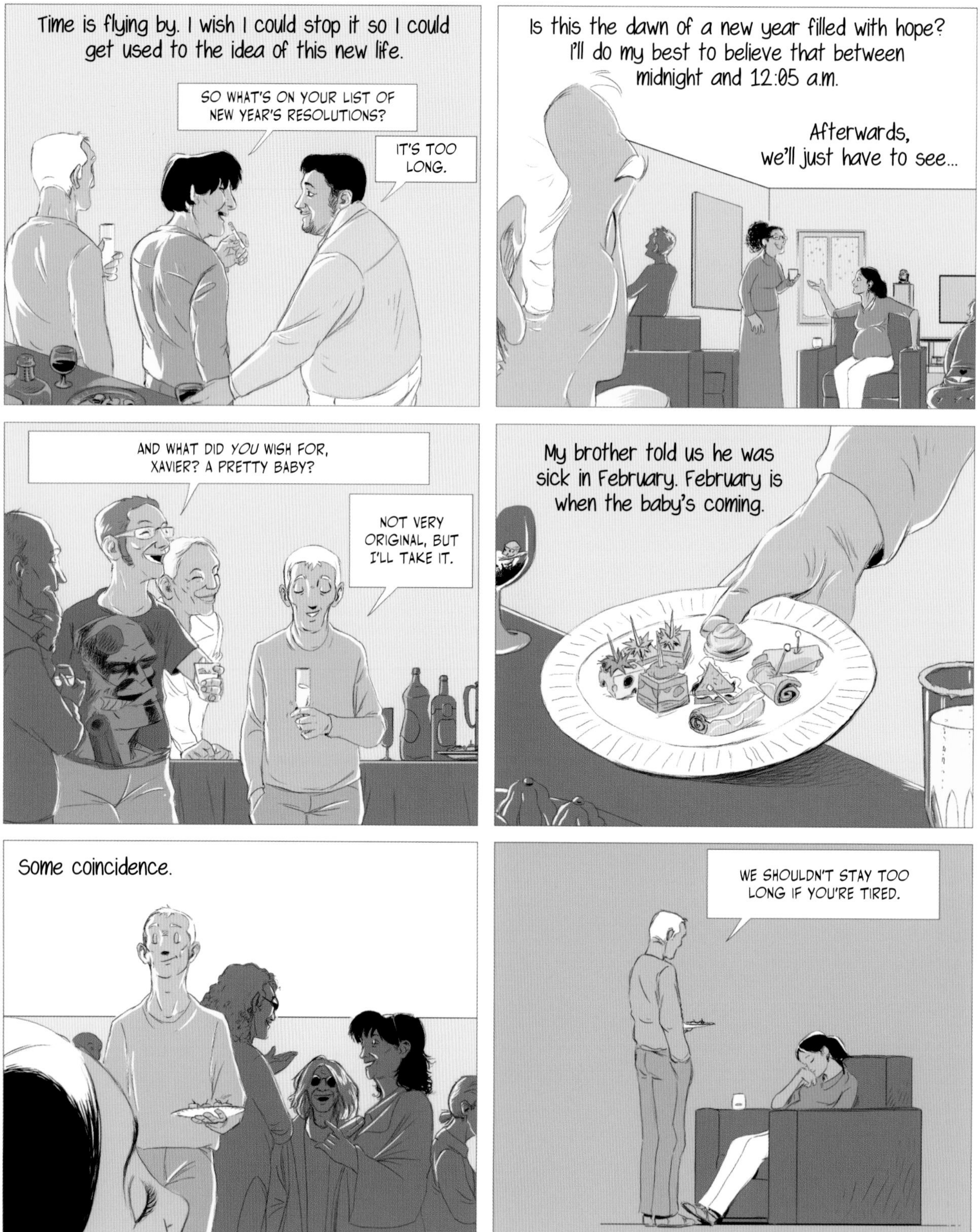
Time is flying by. I wish I could stop it so I could get used to the idea of this new life.
SO WHAT'S ON YOUR LIST OF NEW YEAR'S RESOLUTIONS?
IT'S TOO LONG.
Is this the dawn of a new year filled with hope? I'll do my best to believe that between midnight and 12:05 a.m.
Afterwards, we'll just have to see...
AND WHAT DID YOU WISH FOR, XAVIER? A PRETTY BABY?
NOT VERY ORIGINAL, BUT I'LL TAKE IT.
My brother told us he was sick in February. February is when the baby's coming.
Some coincidence.
WE SHOULDN'T STAY TOO LONG IF YOU'RE TIRED.

JANUARY

7
8
6
4
5
3
2
1
EARTH

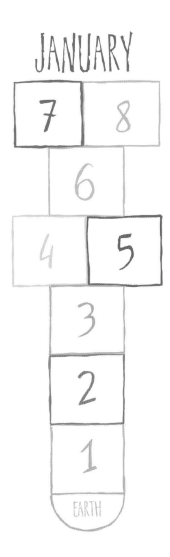

Wednesday the 2nd

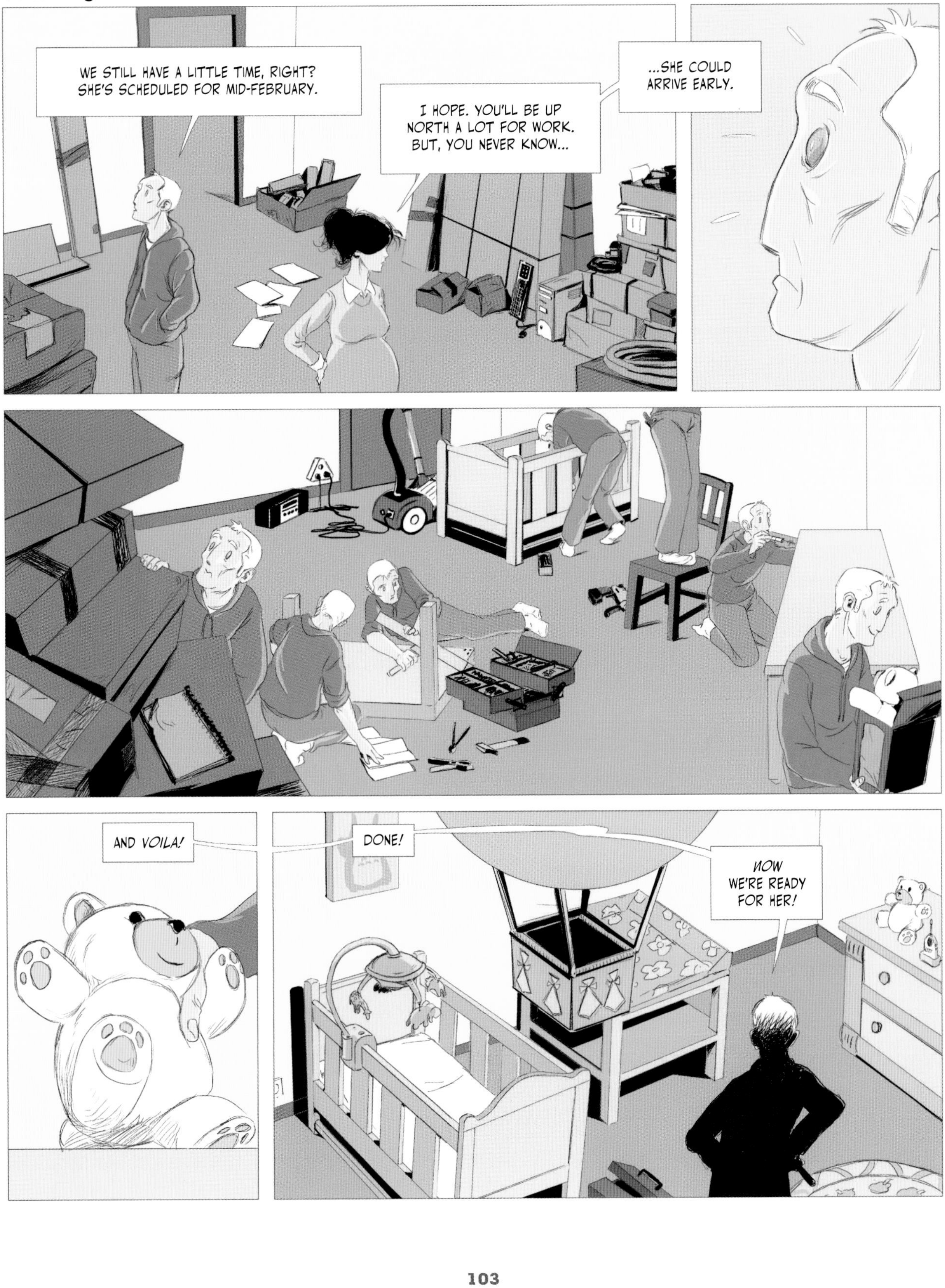
WE STILL HAVE A LITTLE TIME, RIGHT? SHE'S SCHEDULED FOR MID-FEBRUARY.
I HOPE. YOU'LL BE UP NORTH A LOT FOR WORK. BUT, YOU NEVER KNOW...
...SHE COULD ARRIVE EARLY.
AND VOILA!
DONE!
NOW WE'RE READY FOR HER!

Monday the 7th

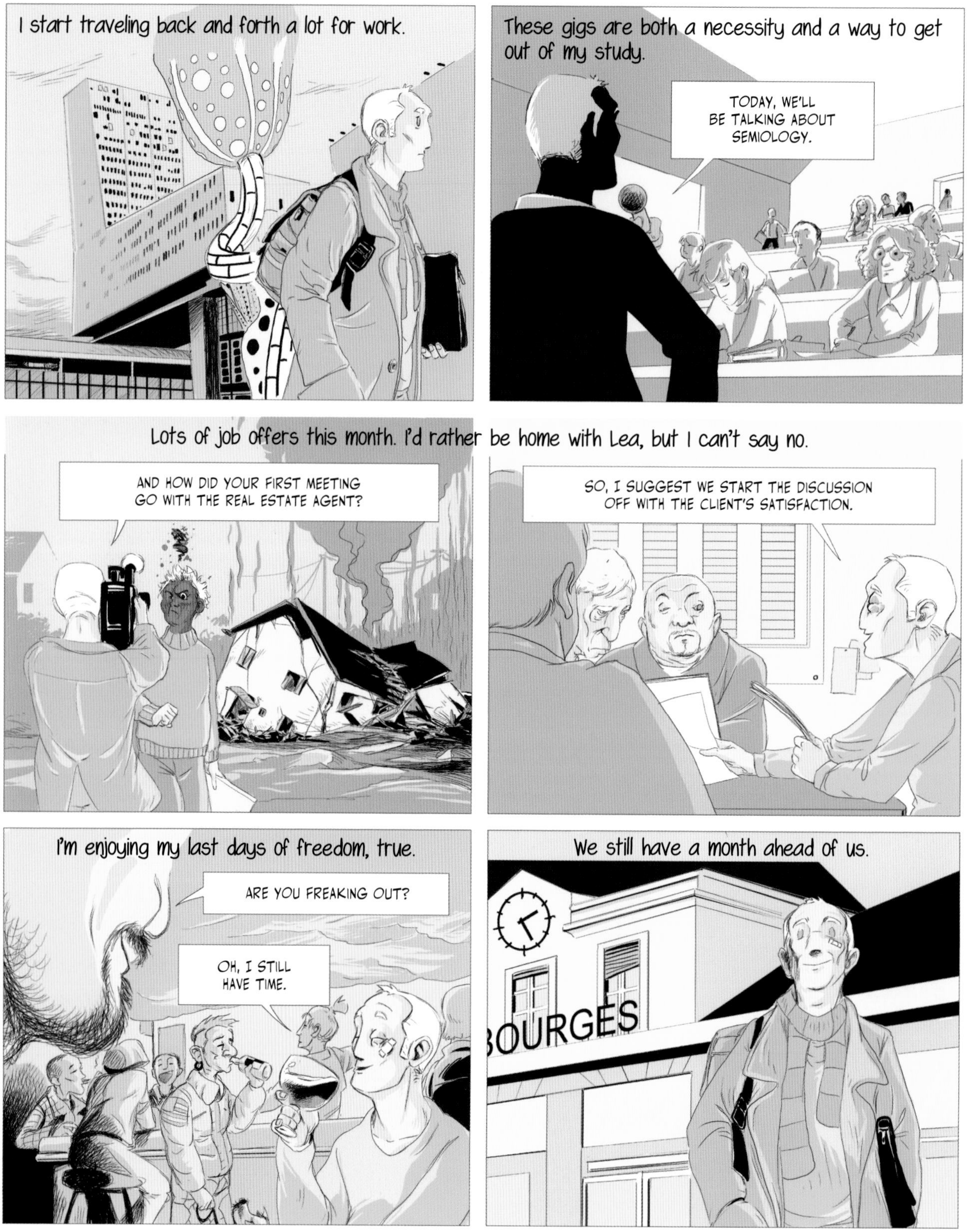
I start traveling back and forth a lot for work.
These gigs are both a necessity and a way to get out of my study.
TODAY, WE'LL BE TALKING ABOUT SEMIOLOGY.
Lots of job offers this month. I'd rather be home with Lea, but I can't say no.
AND HOW DID YOUR FIRST MEETING GO WITH THE REAL ESTATE AGENT?
SO, I SUGGEST WE START THE DISCUSSION OFF WITH THE CLIENT'S SATISFACTION.
I'm enjoying my last days of freedom, true.
ARE YOU FREAKING OUT?
OH, I STILL HAVE TIME.
We still have a month ahead of us.
BOURGES

Saturday the 26th

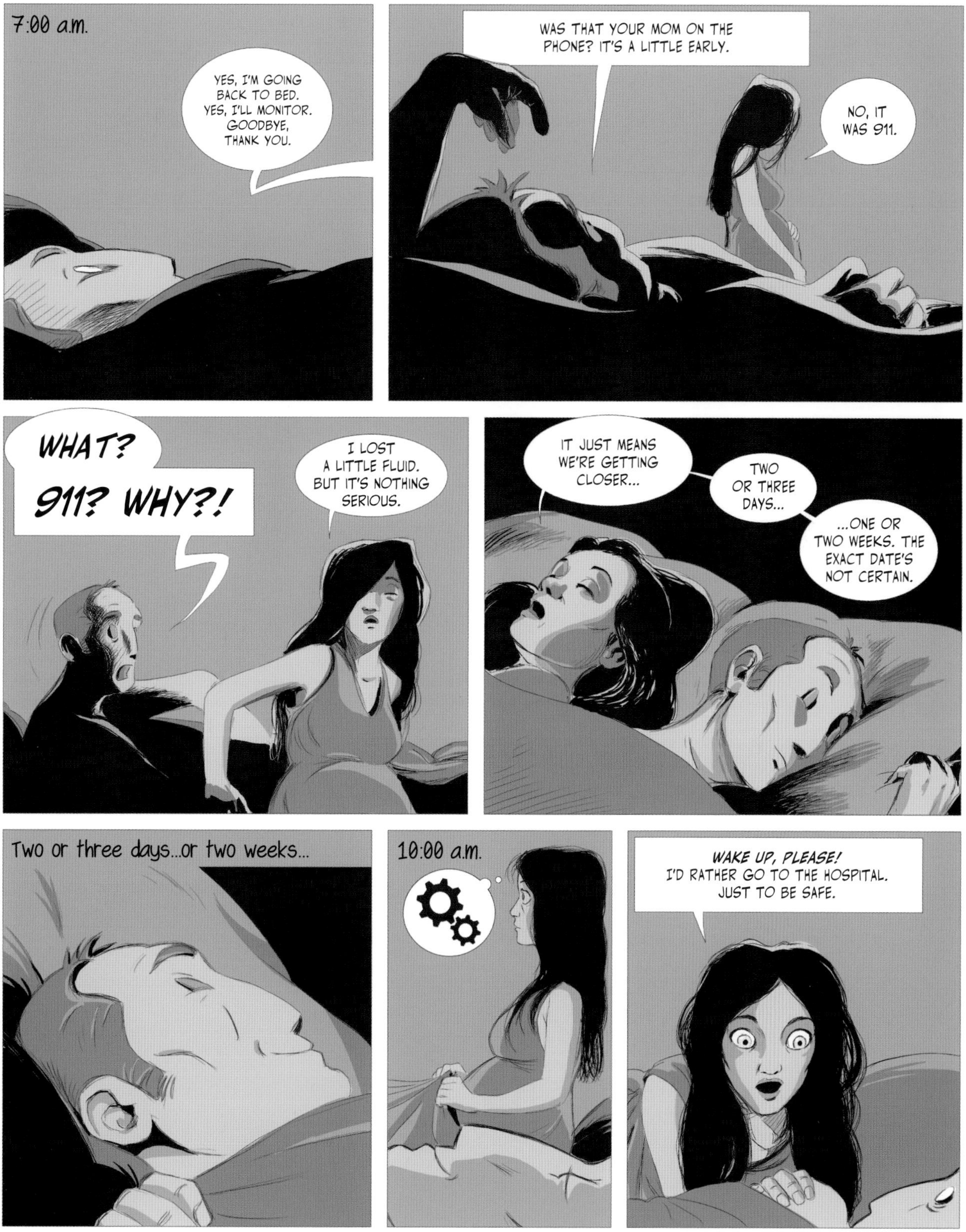
7:00 a.m.
YES, I'M GOING BACK TO BED. YES, I'LL MONITOR. GOODBYE, THANK YOU.
WAS THAT YOUR MOM ON THE PHONE? IT'S A LITTLE EARLY.
NO, IT WAS 911.
WHAT? 911? WHY?!
I LOST A LITTLE FLUID. BUT IT'S NOTHING SERIOUS.
IT JUST MEANS WE'RE GETTING CLOSER...
TWO OR THREE DAYS...
...ONE OR TWO WEEKS. THE EXACT DATE'S NOT CERTAIN.
Two or three days...or two weeks...
10:00 a.m.
WAKE UP, PLEASE! I'D RATHER GO TO THE HOSPITAL. JUST TO BE SAFE.

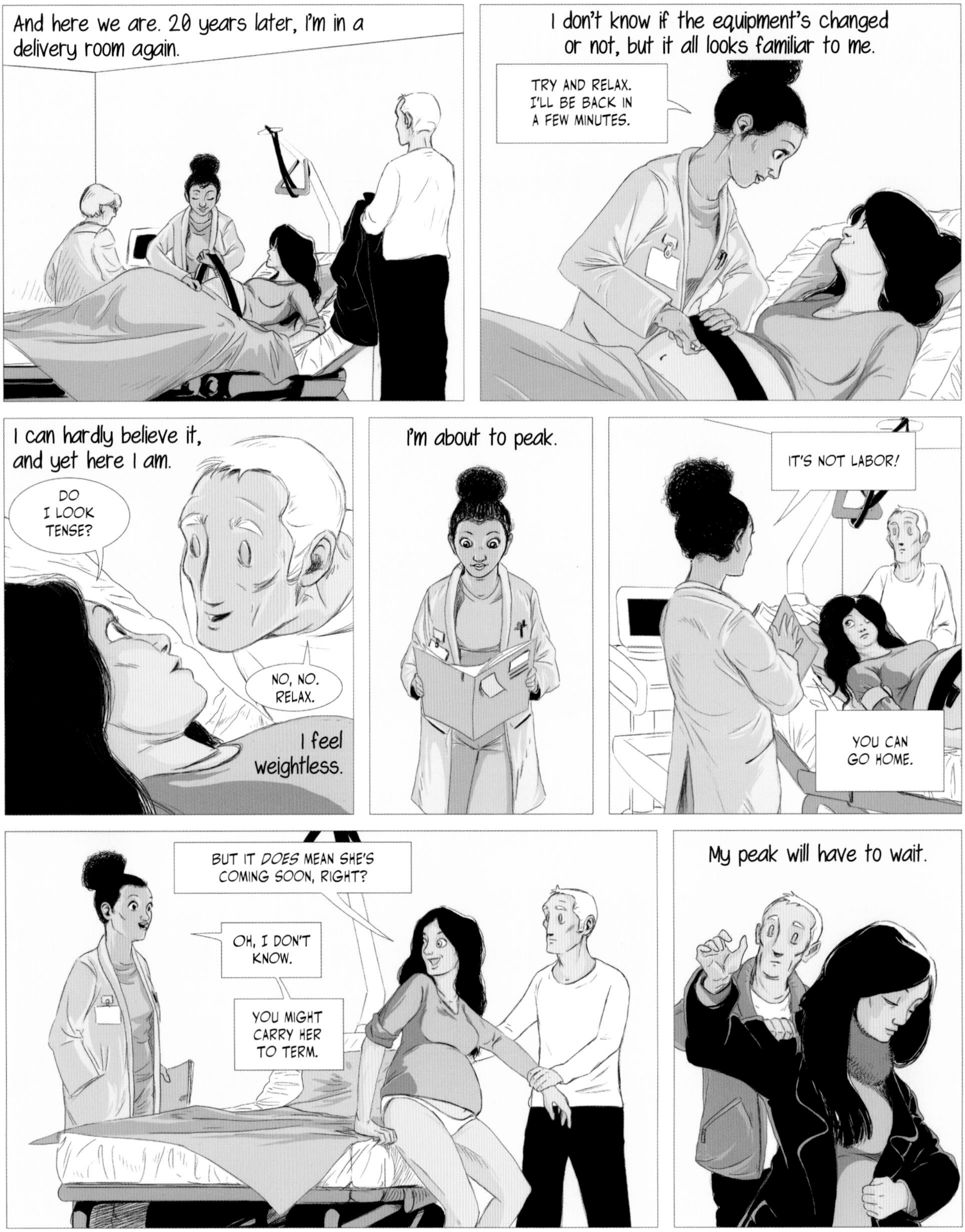
And here we are. 20 years later, I'm in a delivery room again.
I don't know if the equipment's changed or not, but it all looks familiar to me.
TRY AND RELAX. I'LL BE BACK IN A FEW MINUTES.
I can hardly believe it, and yet here I am.
DO I LOOK TENSE?
NO, NO. RELAX.
I feel weightless.
I'm about to peak.
IT'S NOT LABOR!
YOU CAN GO HOME.
BUT IT *DOES* MEAN SHE'S COMING SOON, RIGHT?
OH, I DON'T KNOW.
YOU MIGHT CARRY HER TO TERM.
My peak will have to wait.

Sunday the 27th

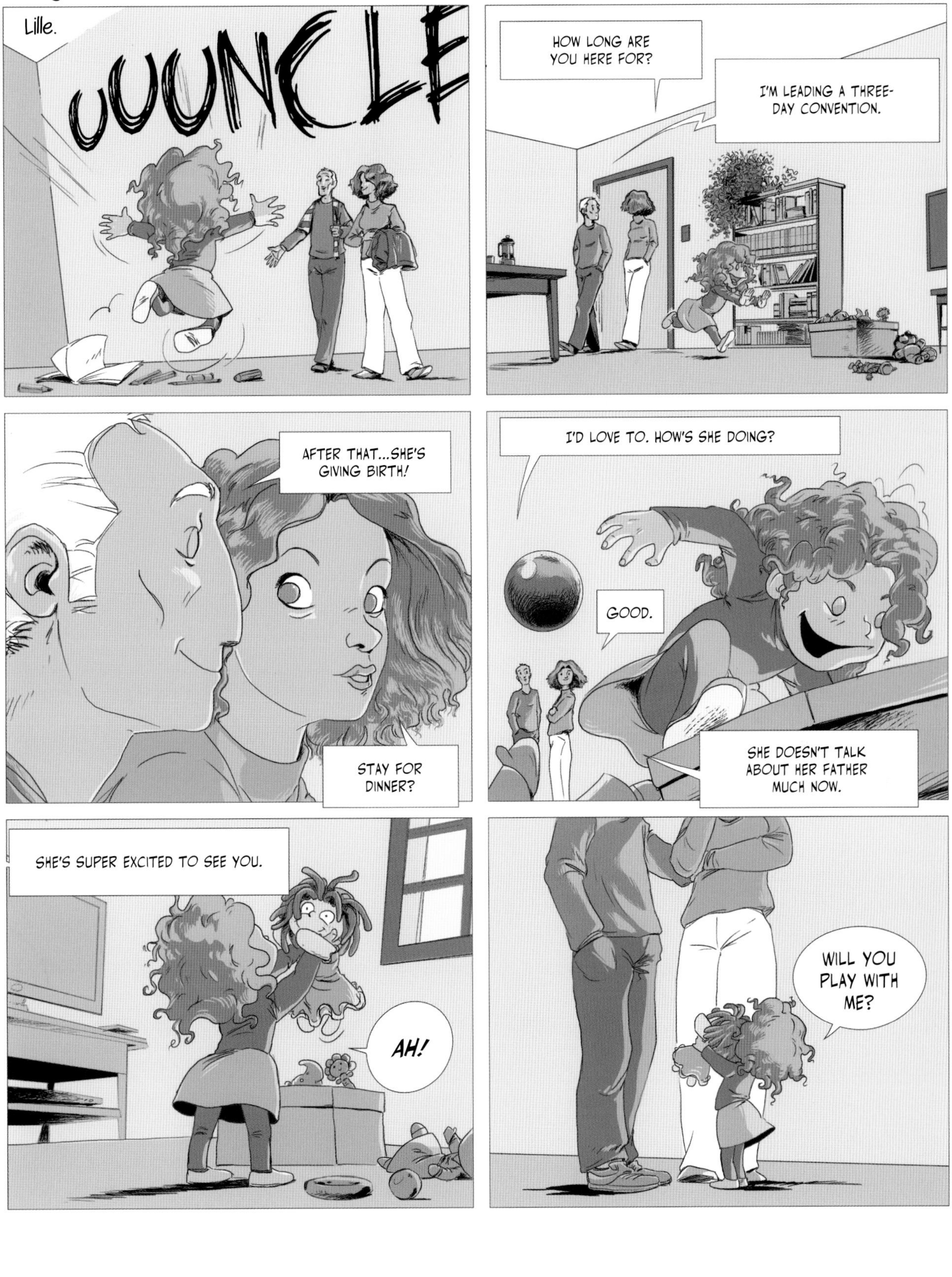
Lille.
UUUNCLE
HOW LONG ARE YOU HERE FOR?
I'M LEADING A THREE-DAY CONVENTION.
AFTER THAT...SHE'S GIVING BIRTH!
STAY FOR DINNER?
I'D LOVE TO. HOW'S SHE DOING?
GOOD.
SHE DOESN'T TALK ABOUT HER FATHER MUCH NOW.
SHE'S SUPER EXCITED TO SEE YOU.
AH!
WILL YOU PLAY WITH ME?

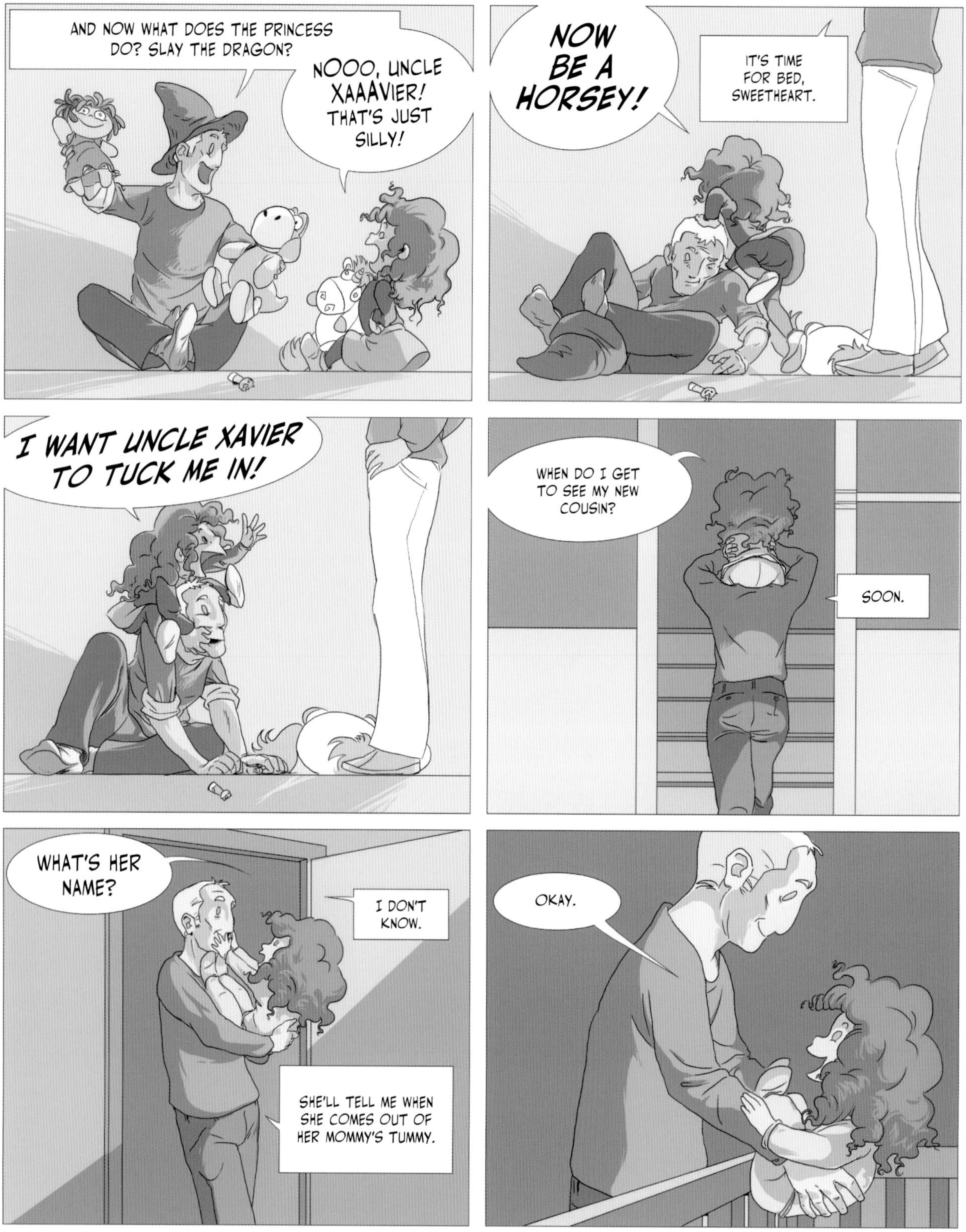
AND NOW WHAT DOES THE PRINCESS DO? SLAY THE DRAGON?
NOOO, UNCLE XAAAVIER! THAT'S JUST SILLY!
NOW BE A HORSEY!
IT'S TIME FOR BED, SWEETHEART.
I WANT UNCLE XAVIER TO TUCK ME IN!
WHEN DO I GET TO SEE MY NEW COUSIN?
SOON.
WHAT'S HER NAME?
I DON'T KNOW.
SHE'LL TELL ME WHEN SHE COMES OUT OF HER MOMMY'S TUMMY.
OKAY.

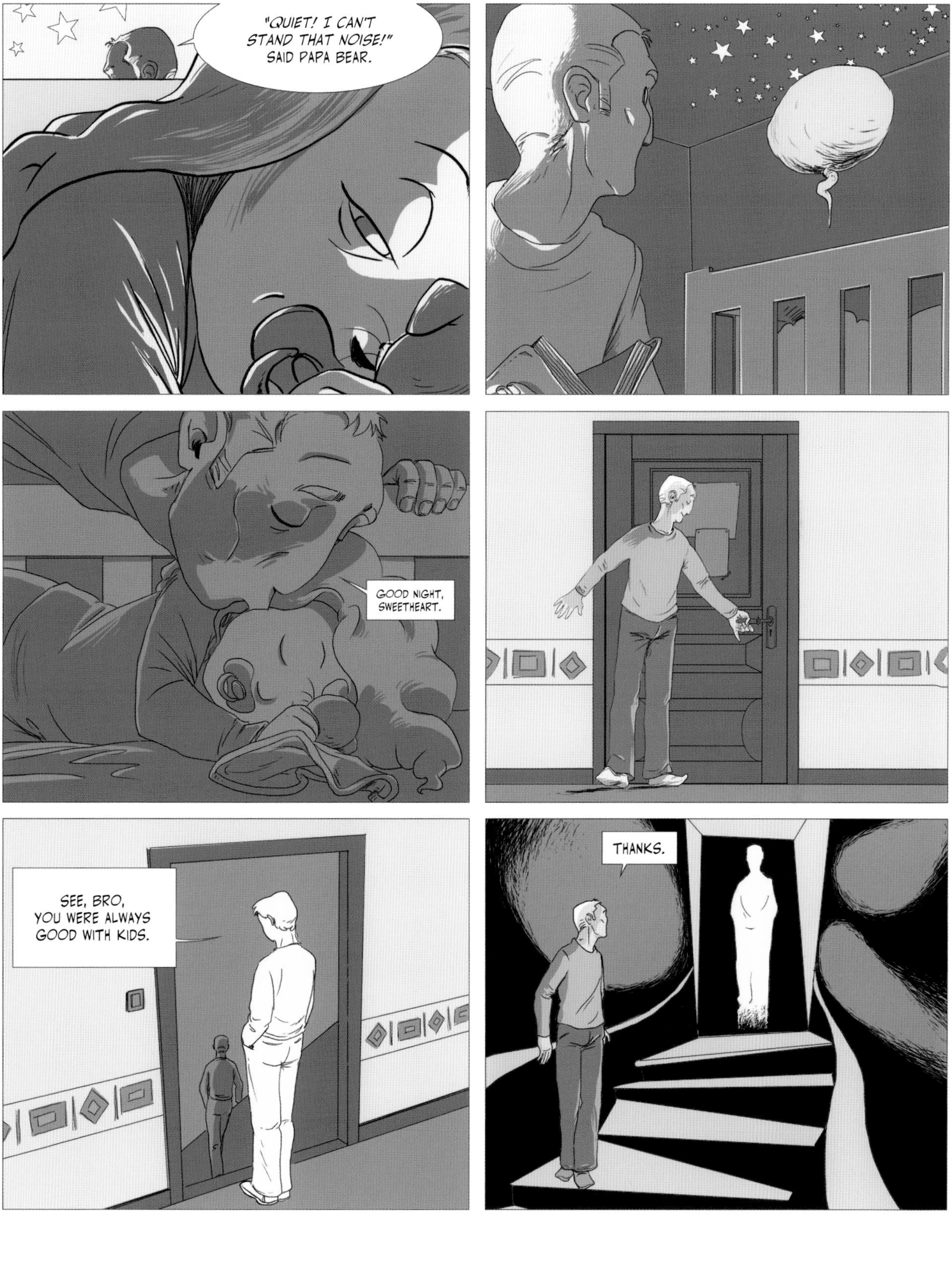
"QUIET! I CAN'T STAND THAT NOISE!" SAID PAPA BEAR.
GOOD NIGHT, SWEETHEART.
SEE, BRO, YOU WERE ALWAYS GOOD WITH KIDS.
THANKS.

Monday the 28th

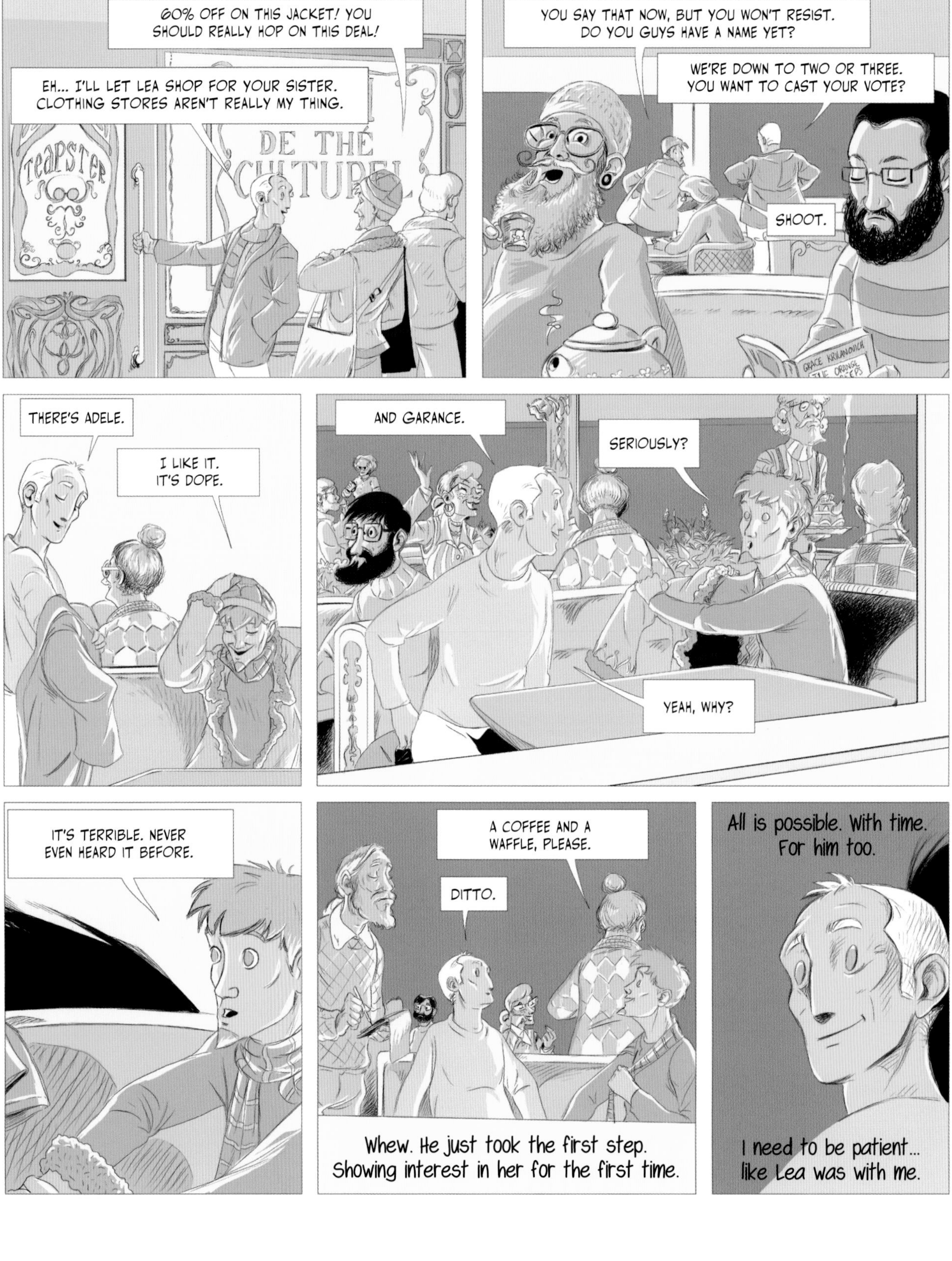

60% OFF ON THIS JACKET! YOU SHOULD REALLY HOP ON THIS DEAL!
EH... I'LL LET LEA SHOP FOR YOUR SISTER. CLOTHING STORES AREN'T REALLY MY THING.
TEAPSTER
DE THÉ
YOU SAY THAT NOW, BUT YOU WON'T RESIST. DO YOU GUYS HAVE A NAME YET?
WE'RE DOWN TO TWO OR THREE. YOU WANT TO CAST YOUR VOTE?
SHOOT.
THERE'S ADELE.
I LIKE IT. IT'S DOPE.
AND GARANCE.
SERIOUSLY?
YEAH, WHY?
IT'S TERRIBLE. NEVER EVEN HEARD IT BEFORE.
A COFFEE AND A WAFFLE, PLEASE.
DITTO.
Whew. He just took the first step. Showing interest in her for the first time.
All is possible. With time. For him too.
I need to be patient... like Lea was with me.

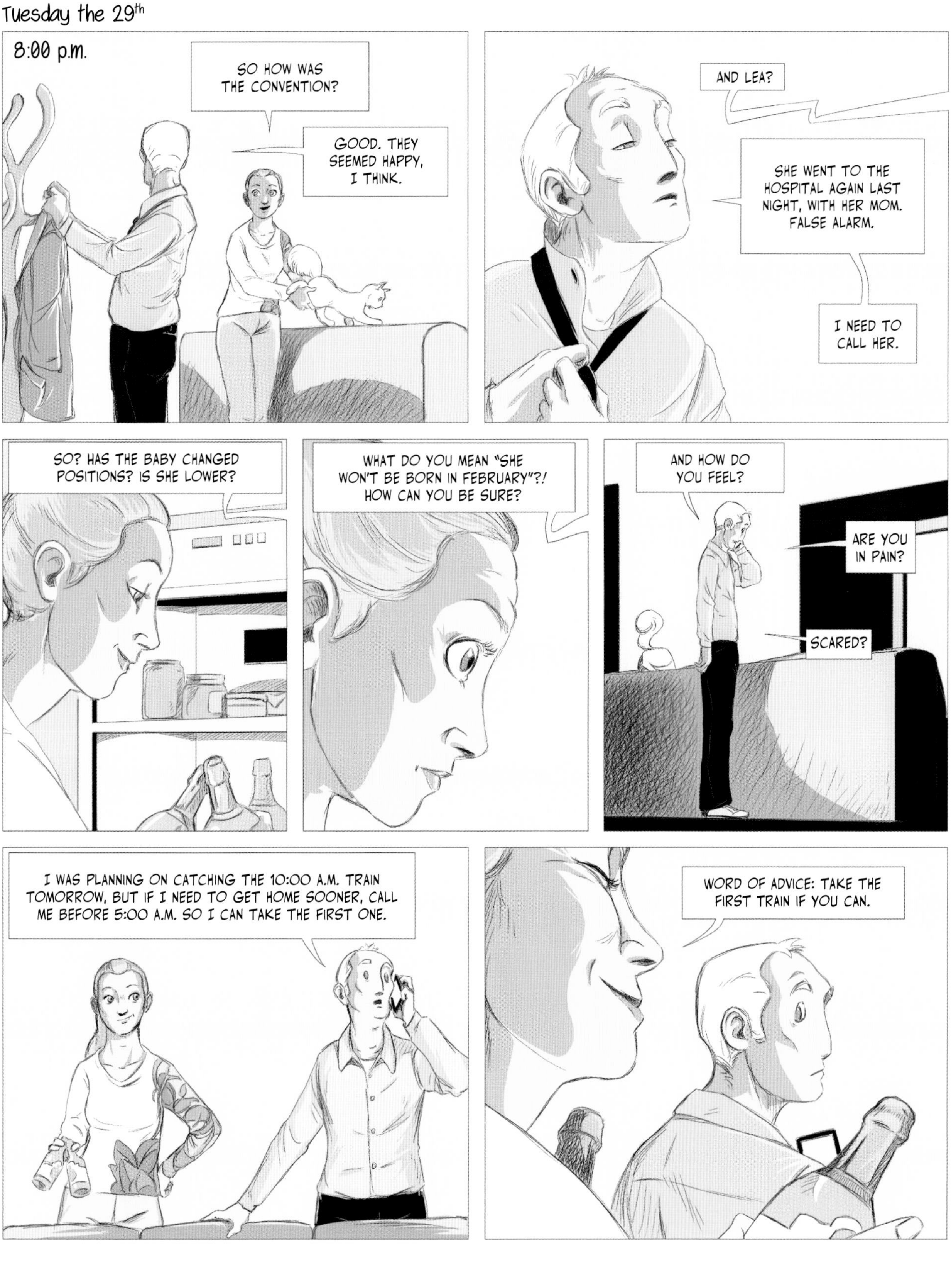
Tuesday the 29th
8:00 p.m.
SO HOW WAS THE CONVENTION?
GOOD. THEY SEEMED HAPPY, I THINK.
AND LEA?
SHE WENT TO THE HOSPITAL AGAIN LAST NIGHT, WITH HER MOM. FALSE ALARM.
I NEED TO CALL HER.
SO? HAS THE BABY CHANGED POSITIONS? IS SHE LOWER?
WHAT DO YOU MEAN "SHE WON'T BE BORN IN FEBRUARY"?! HOW CAN YOU BE SURE?
AND HOW DO YOU FEEL?
ARE YOU IN PAIN?
SCARED?
I WAS PLANNING ON CATCHING THE 10:00 A.M. TRAIN TOMORROW, BUT IF I NEED TO GET HOME SOONER, CALL ME BEFORE 5:00 A.M. SO I CAN TAKE THE FIRST ONE.
WORD OF ADVICE: TAKE THE FIRST TRAIN IF YOU CAN.

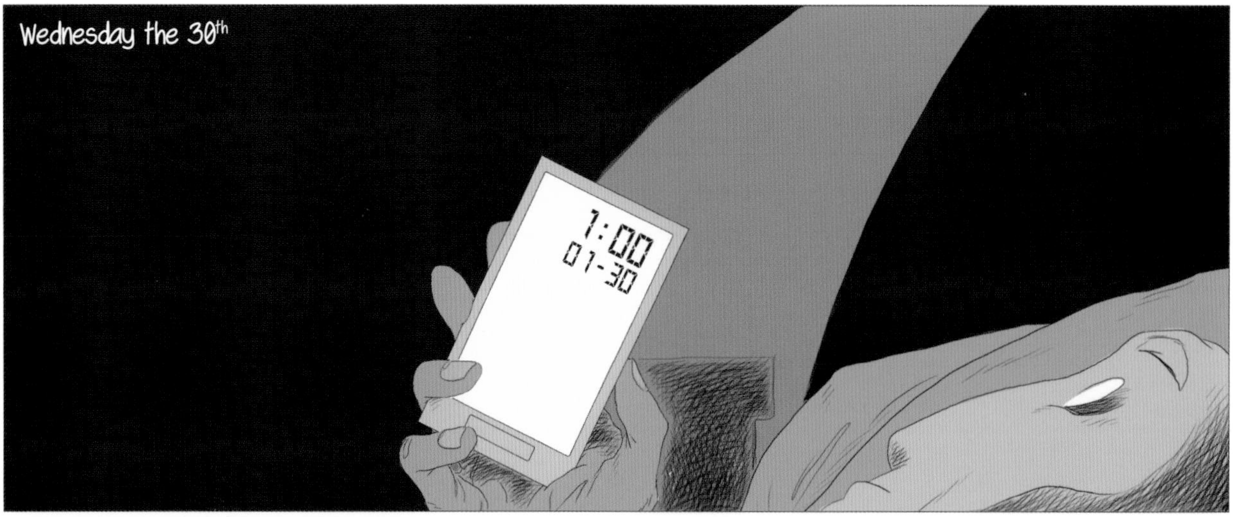
Wednesday the 30th
7:00
01-30

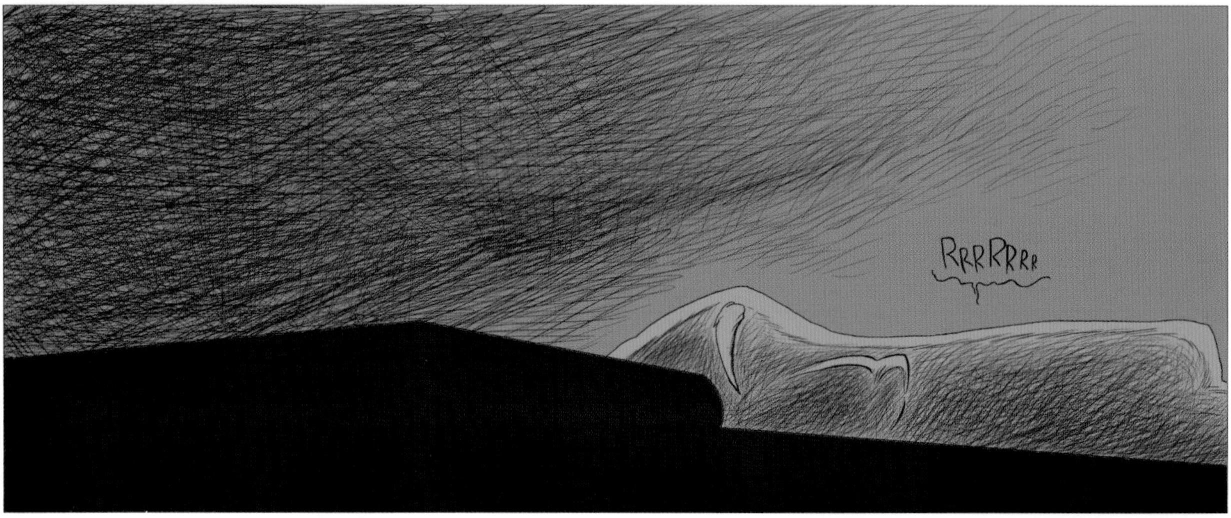
RRRRRRR

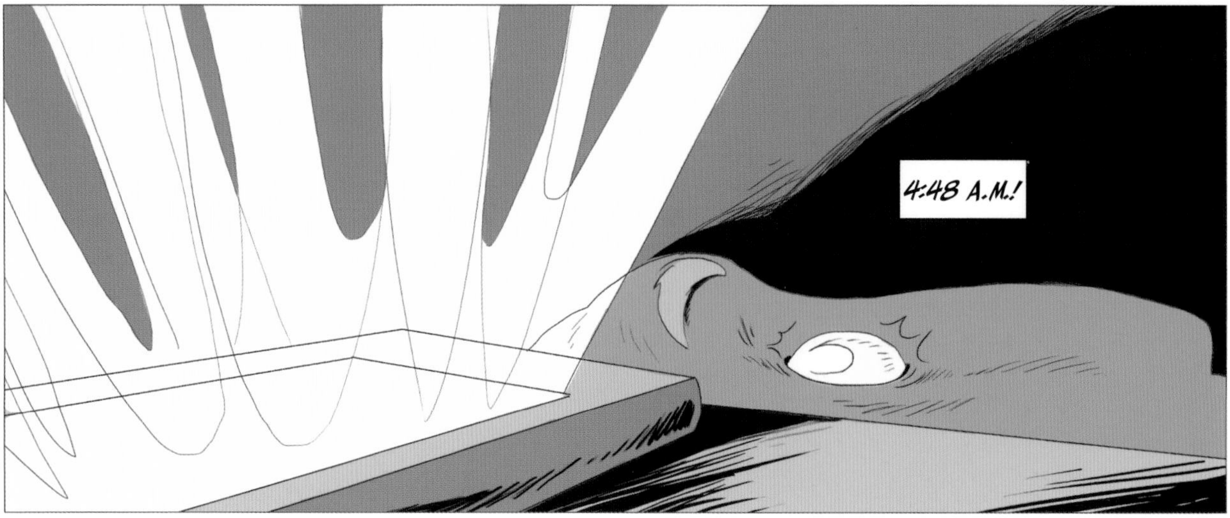
4:48 A.M.!

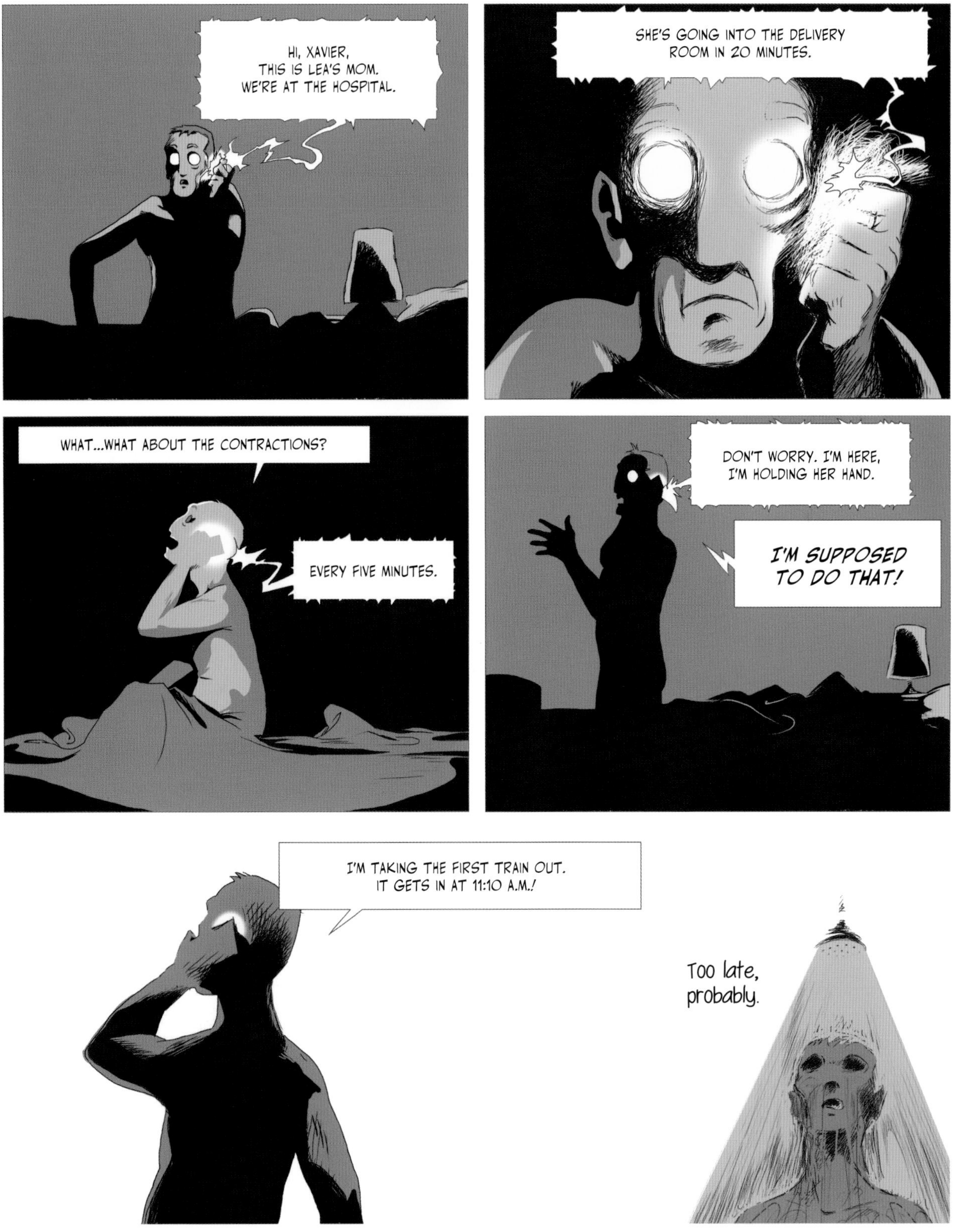
HI, XAVIER,
THIS IS LEA'S MOM.
WE'RE AT THE HOSPITAL.
SHE'S GOING INTO THE DELIVERY ROOM IN 20 MINUTES.
WHAT...WHAT ABOUT THE CONTRACTIONS?
EVERY FIVE MINUTES.
DON'T WORRY. I'M HERE, I'M HOLDING HER HAND.
I'M SUPPOSED TO DO THAT!
I'M TAKING THE FIRST TRAIN OUT. IT GETS IN AT 11:10 A.M.!
Too late, probably.

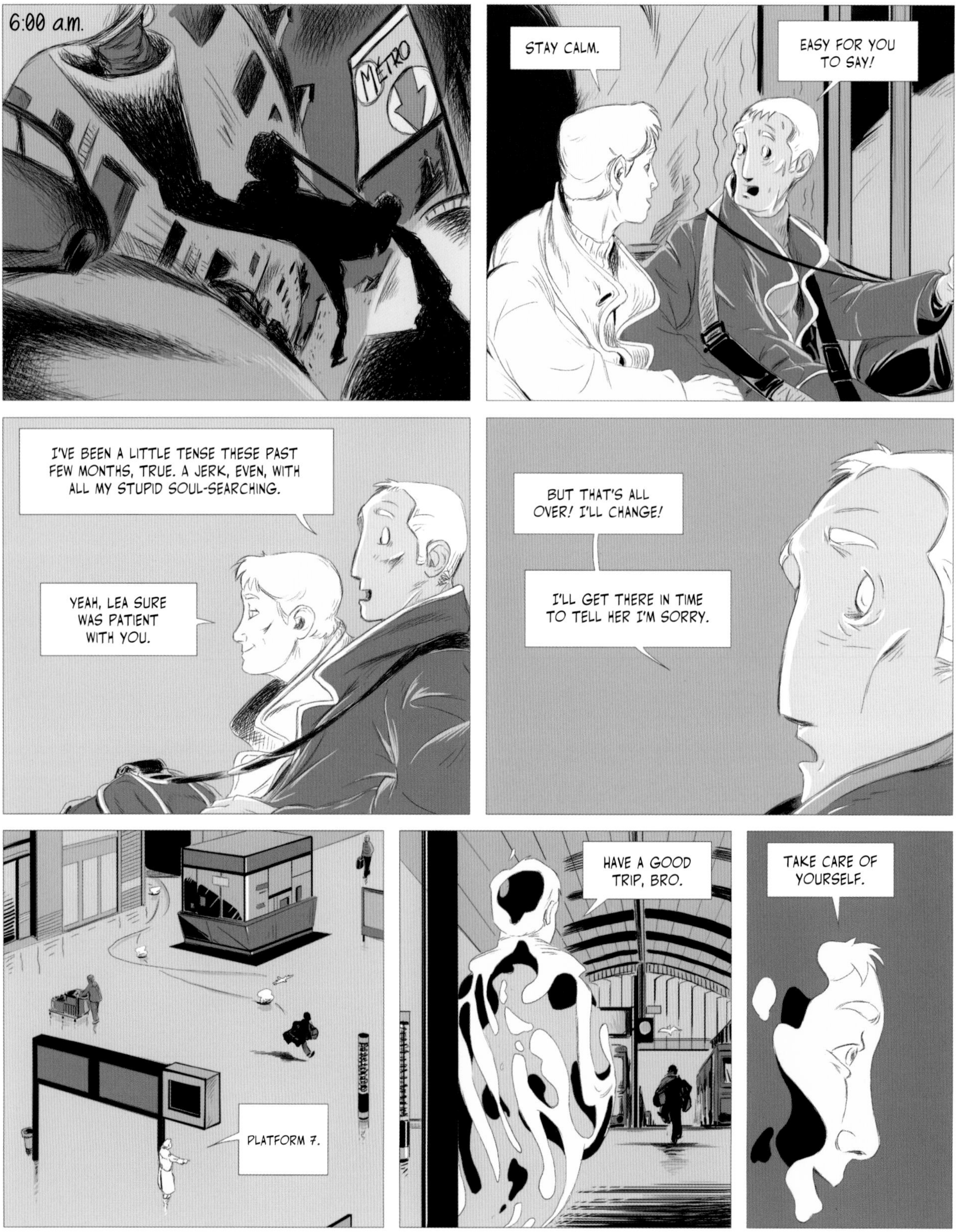
6:00 a.m.
MÉTRO
STAY CALM.
EASY FOR YOU TO SAY!
I'VE BEEN A LITTLE TENSE THESE PAST FEW MONTHS, TRUE. A JERK, EVEN, WITH ALL MY STUPID SOUL-SEARCHING.
YEAH, LEA SURE WAS PATIENT WITH YOU.
BUT THAT'S ALL OVER! I'LL CHANGE!
I'LL GET THERE IN TIME TO TELL HER I'M SORRY.
PLATFORM 7.
HAVE A GOOD TRIP, BRO.
TAKE CARE OF YOURSELF.

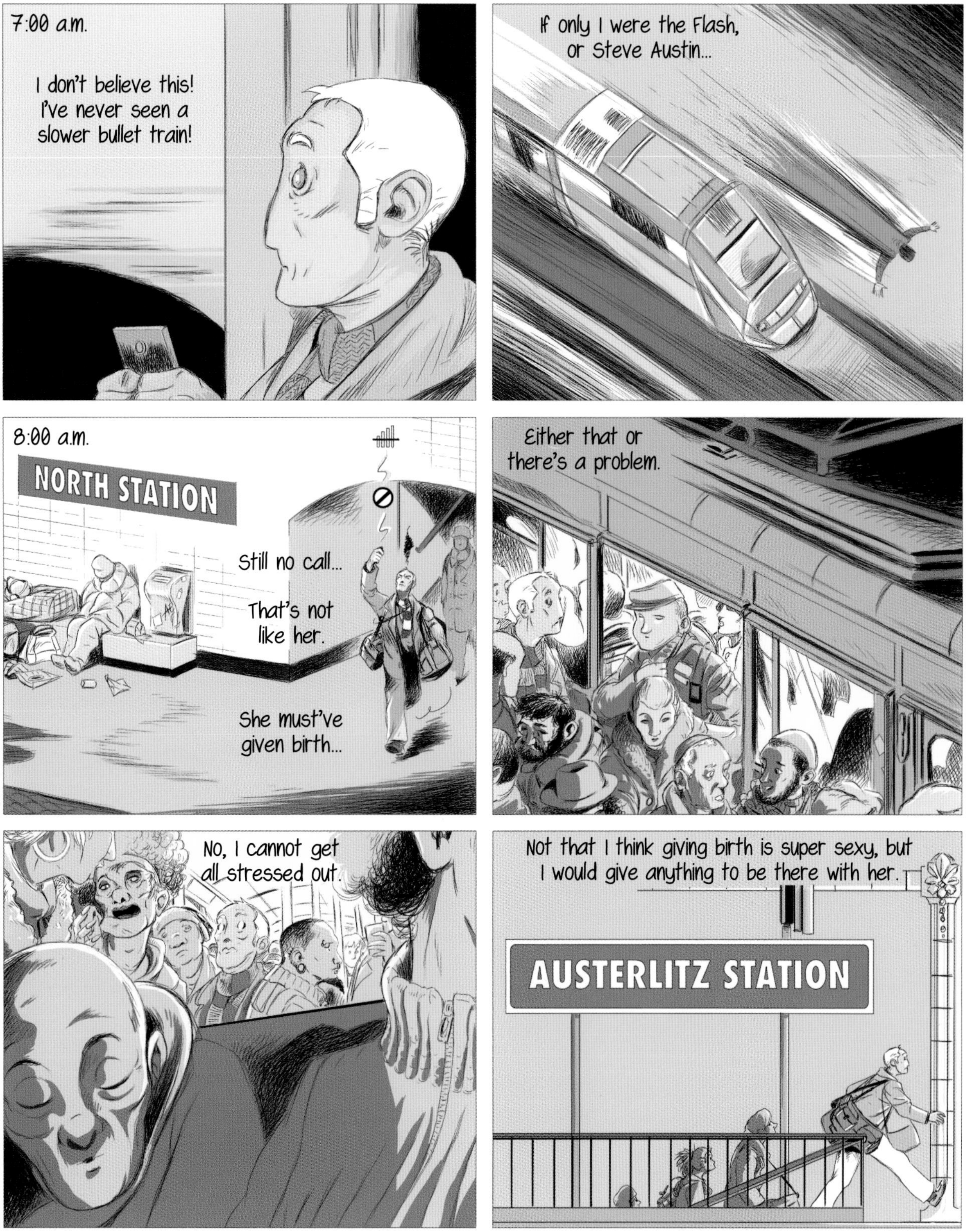
7:00 a.m.
I don't believe this! I've never seen a slower bullet train!
If only I were the Flash, or Steve Austin...
8:00 a.m.
NORTH STATION
Still no call...
That's not like her.
She must've given birth...
Either that or there's a problem.
No, I cannot get all stressed out.
Not that I think giving birth is super sexy, but I would give anything to be there with her.
AUSTERLITZ STATION

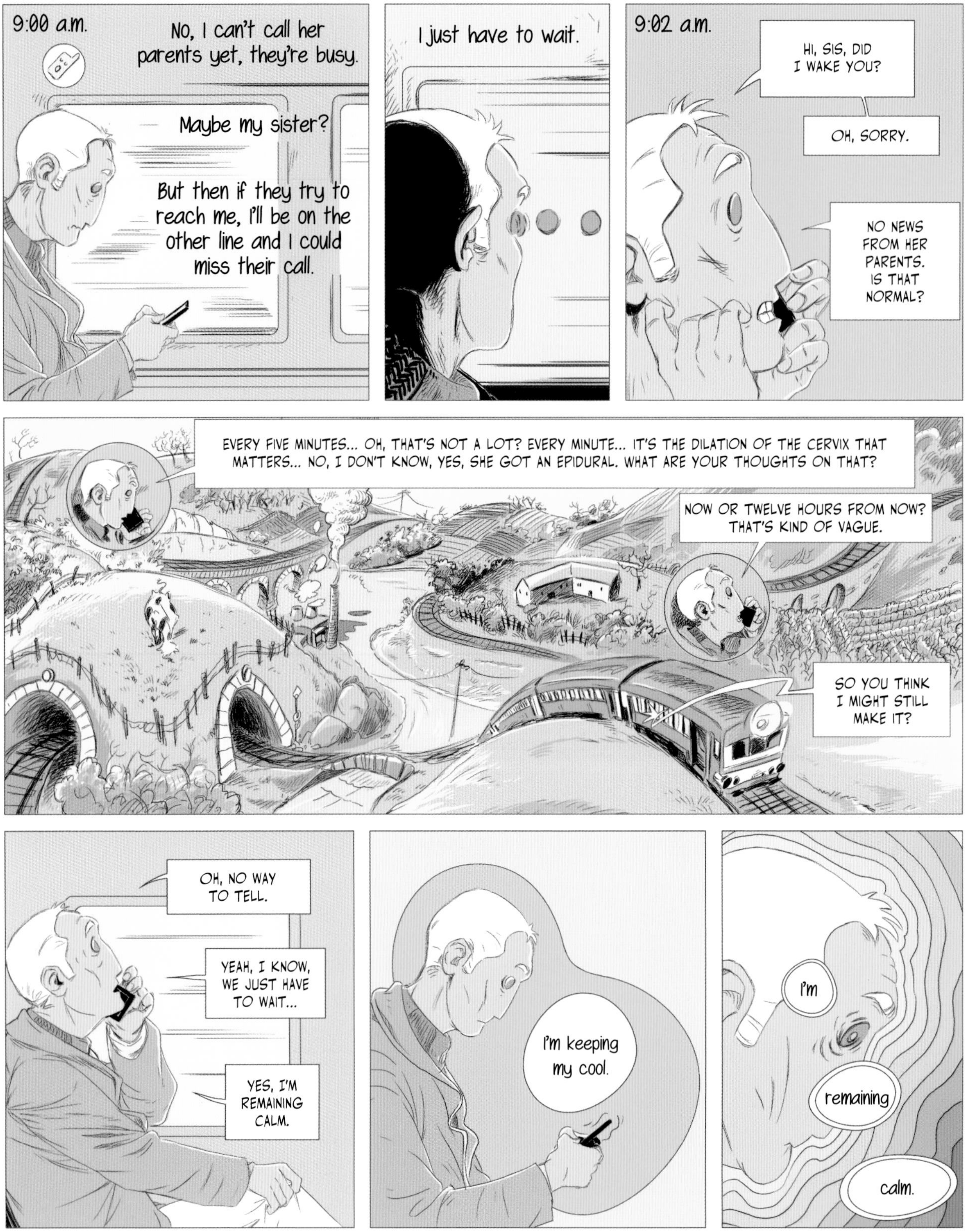
9:00 a.m.
No, I can't call her parents yet, they're busy.
Maybe my sister?
But then if they try to reach me, I'll be on the other line and I could miss their call.
I just have to wait.
9:02 a.m.
HI, SIS, DID I WAKE YOU?
OH, SORRY.
NO NEWS FROM HER PARENTS. IS THAT NORMAL?
EVERY FIVE MINUTES... OH, THAT'S NOT A LOT? EVERY MINUTE... IT'S THE DILATION OF THE CERVIX THAT MATTERS... NO, I DON'T KNOW, YES, SHE GOT AN EPIDURAL. WHAT ARE YOUR THOUGHTS ON THAT?
NOW OR TWELVE HOURS FROM NOW? THAT'S KIND OF VAGUE.
SO YOU THINK I MIGHT STILL MAKE IT?
OH, NO WAY TO TELL.
YEAH, I KNOW, WE JUST HAVE TO WAIT...
YES, I'M REMAINING CALM.
I'm keeping my cool.
I'm
remaining
calm.

LEA
PARENTS

SOOO?

SHE HASN'T GIVEN BIRTH YET?

REALLY?

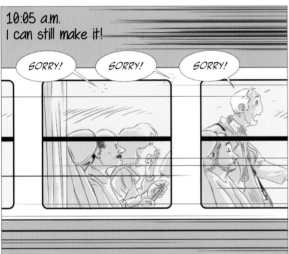

10:05 a.m.
I can still make it!

SORRY!

SORRY!

SORRY!

I fee like a teenager on his first date.

Anxious to be there, scared too.

Our train pulls into the Bourges station right on time. That's a good sign.

BLIP
BLIP

THIS IS IT, SHE'S ON HER WAY...
HOW LONG TILL YOU GET HERE?

NOOOOOOO

11:10 a.m.

TOO LATE!
TOO LATE!
TOO LATE!

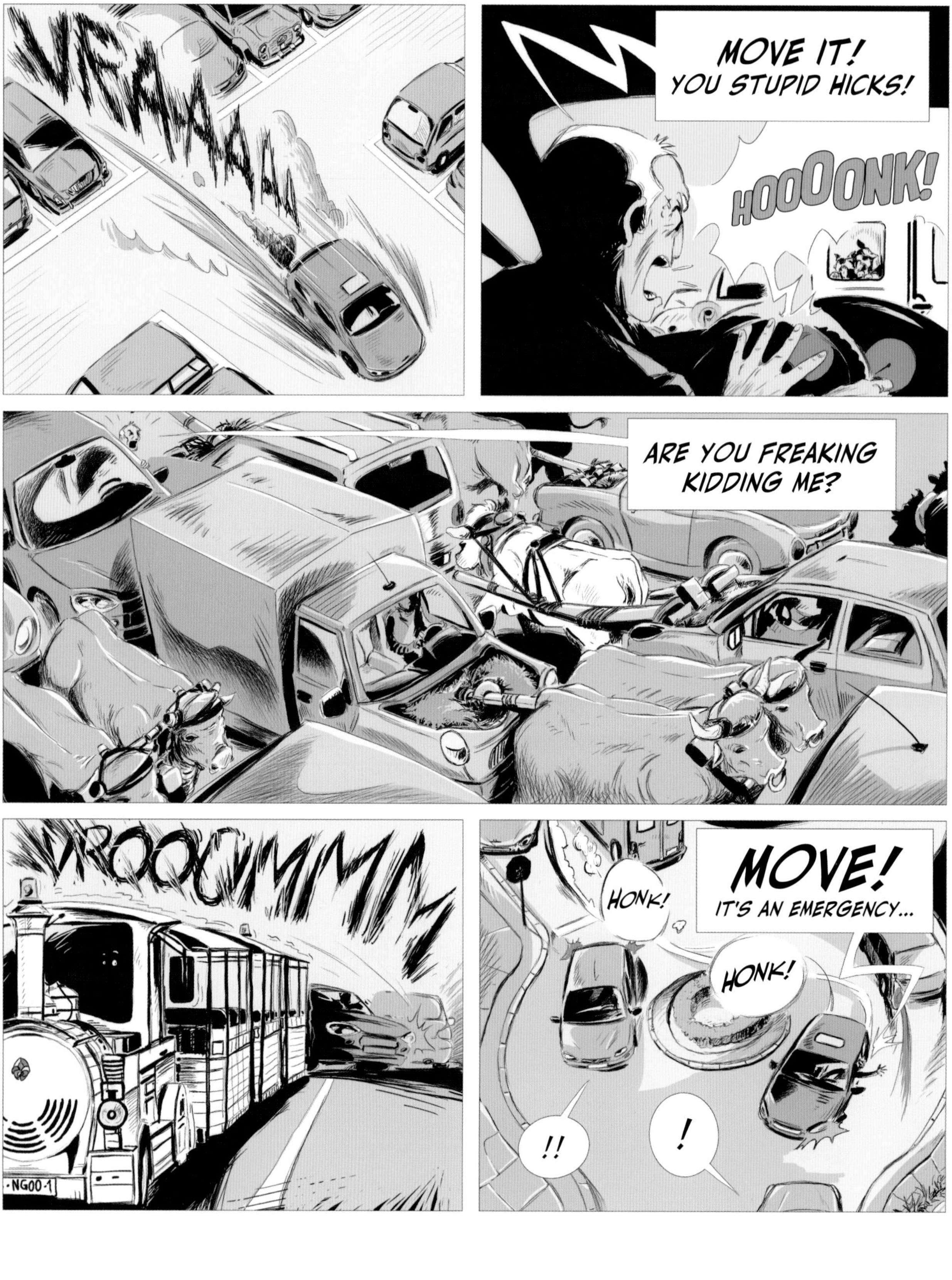
MOVE IT!
YOU STUPID HICKS!
HOOOONK!
ARE YOU FREAKING KIDDING ME?
MOVE!
IT'S AN EMERGENCY...
HONK!
HONK!
!!
!

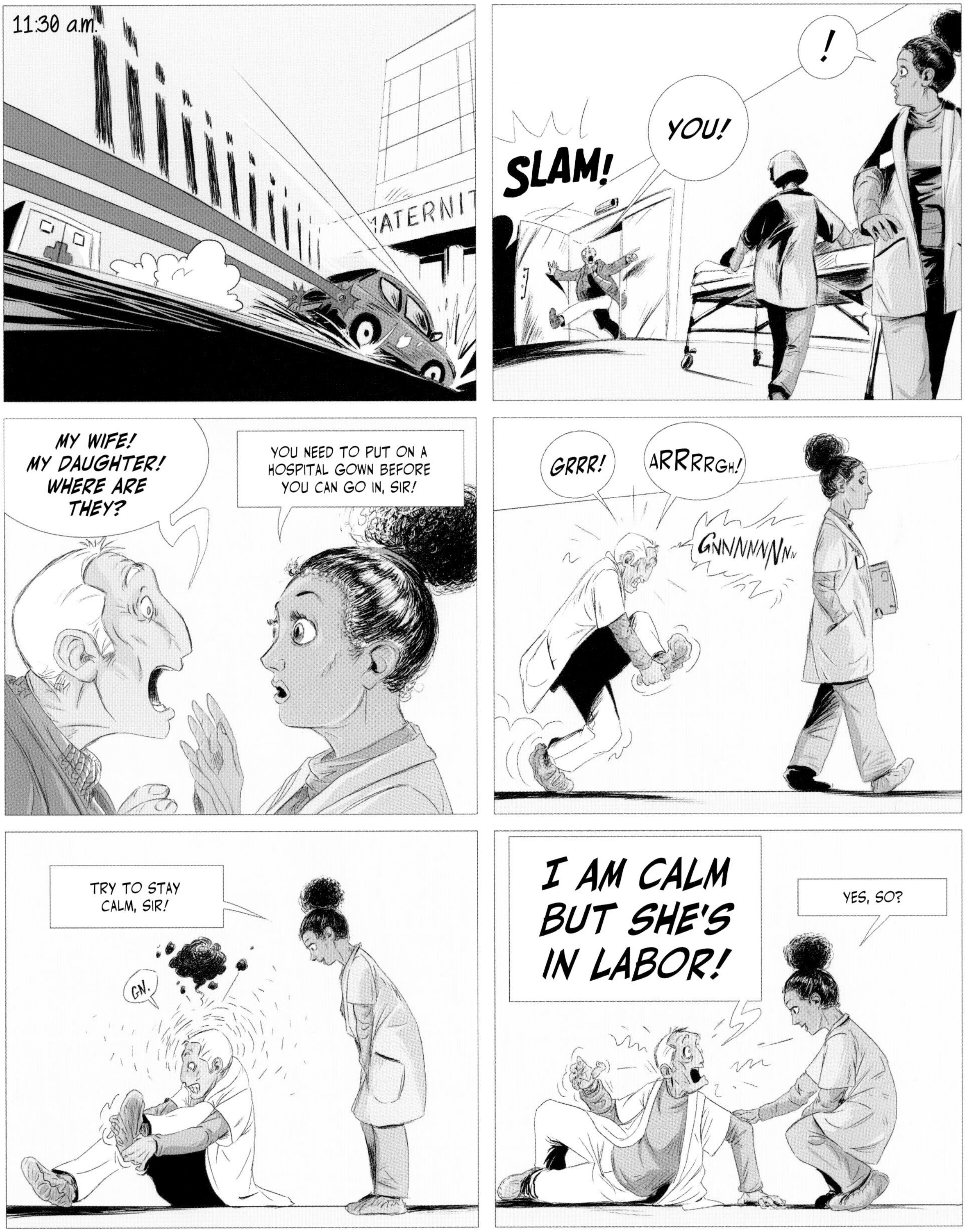

11:30 a.m.
MATERNIT
SLAM!
YOU!
!
MY WIFE! MY DAUGHTER! WHERE ARE THEY?
YOU NEED TO PUT ON A HOSPITAL GOWN BEFORE YOU CAN GO IN, SIR!
GRRR!
ARRRRGH!
GNNNNNNN
TRY TO STAY CALM, SIR!
GN.
I AM CALM BUT SHE'S IN LABOR!
YES, SO?

YOU'VE GOT TIME. THE BABY'S NOT HERE YET.

REALLY?

I'M HERE!

...like Ulysses after a very, very long journey.

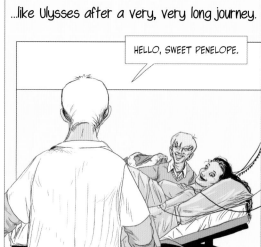

HELLO, SWEET PENELOPE.

HOW DO YOU FEEL? ARE YOU IN A LOT OF PAIN?

IT'S TAKING FOREVER BUT I'M SO GLAD YOU'RE HERE.

I HOPE IT HASN'T BEEN TOO HARD FOR YOU.

OH, YOU KNOW, ALL I DID WAS SIT QUIETLY ON THE TRAIN.

I'LL HAVE TO ASK YOU TO LEAVE, MA'AM.

OKAY, HERE WE GO. YOU NEED TO PUSH.

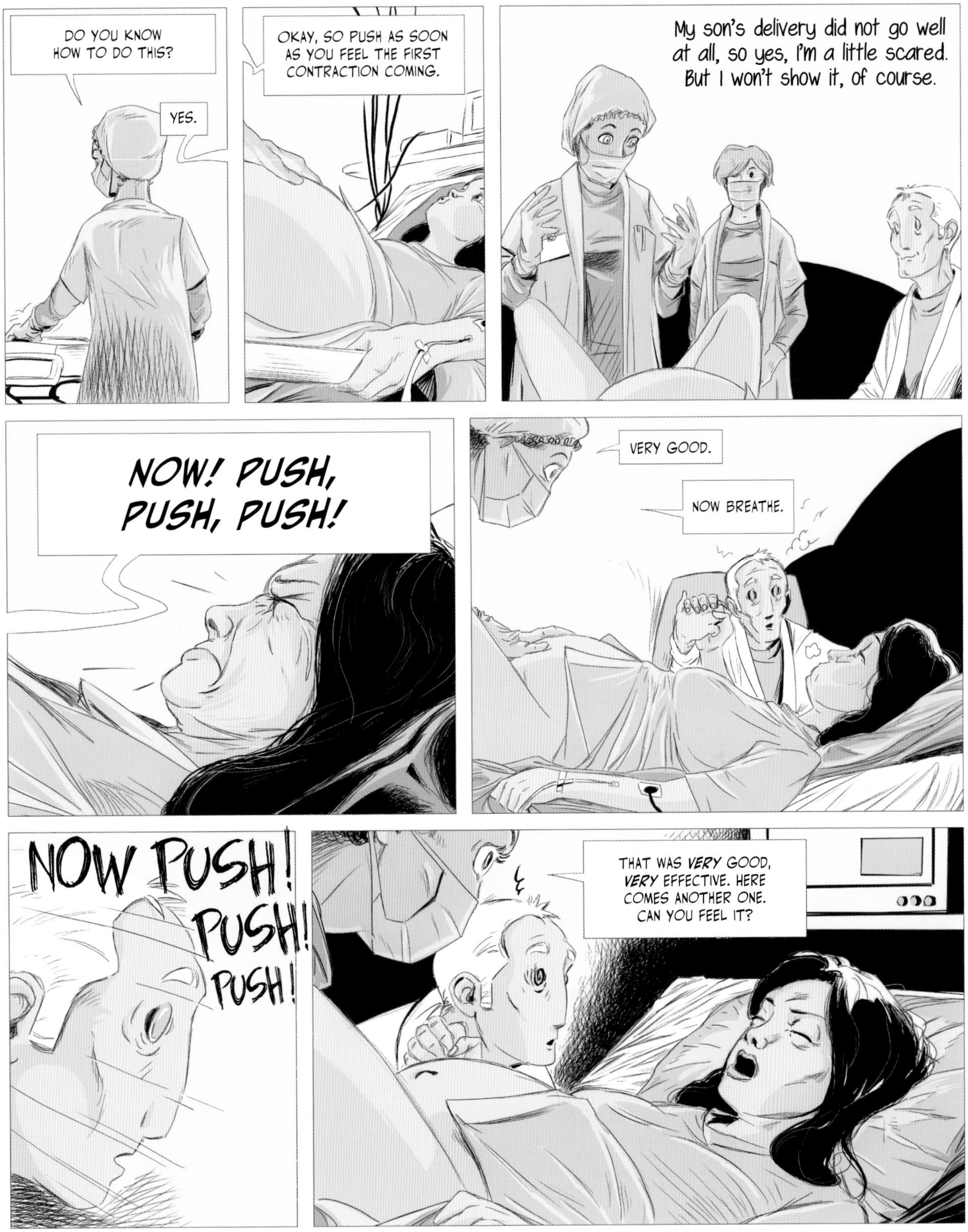
DO YOU KNOW HOW TO DO THIS?
YES.
OKAY, SO PUSH AS SOON AS YOU FEEL THE FIRST CONTRACTION COMING.
My son's delivery did not go well at all, so yes, I'm a little scared. But I won't show it, of course.
NOW! PUSH, PUSH, PUSH!
VERY GOOD.
NOW BREATHE.
NOW PUSH! PUSH! PUSH!
THAT WAS VERY GOOD, VERY EFFECTIVE. HERE COMES ANOTHER ONE. CAN YOU FEEL IT?

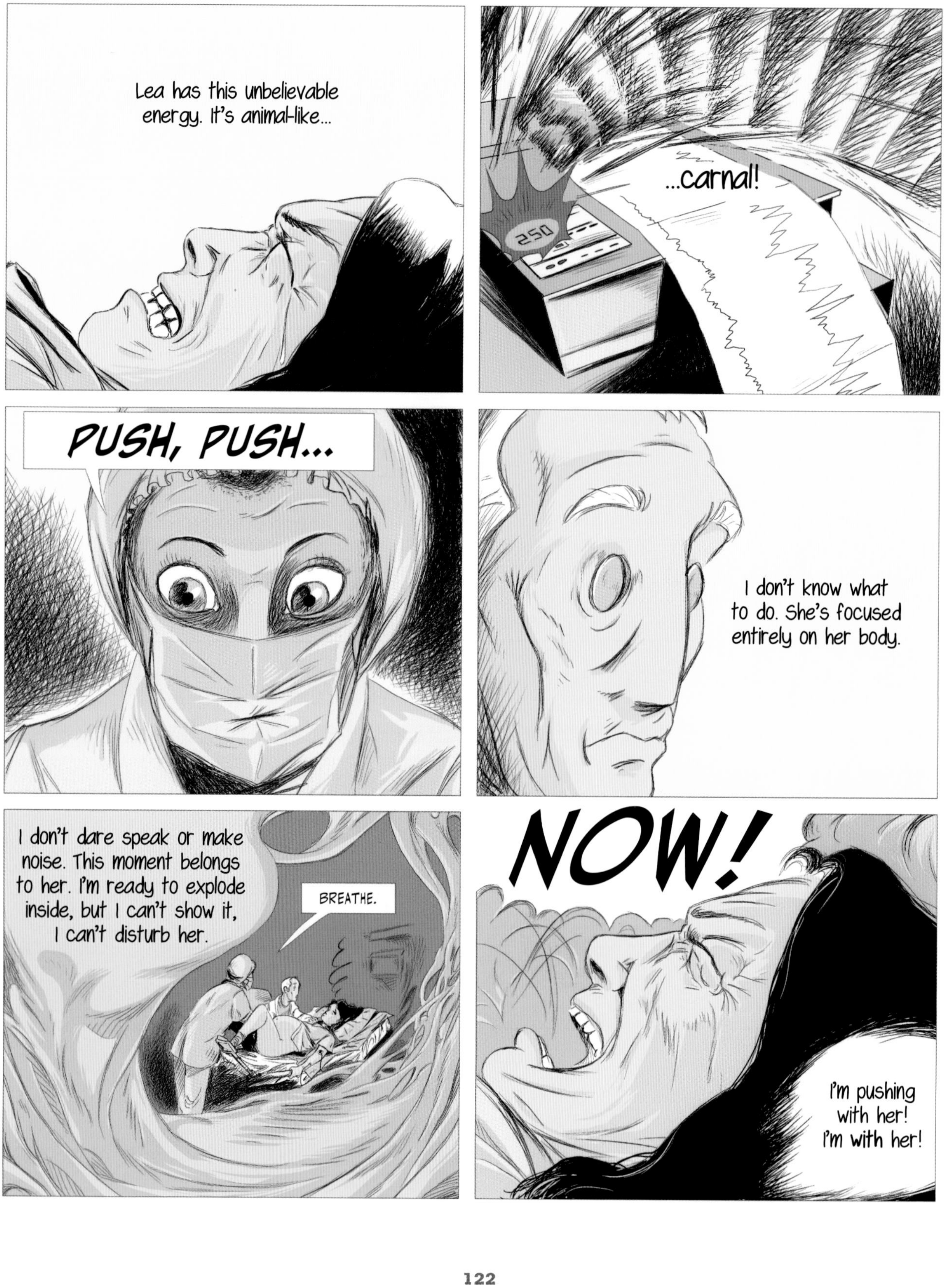
Lea has this unbelievable energy. It's animal-like...
...carnal!
250
PUSH, PUSH...
I don't know what to do. She's focused entirely on her body.
I don't dare speak or make noise. This moment belongs to her. I'm ready to explode inside, but I can't show it, I can't disturb her.
BREATHE.
NOW!
I'm pushing with her! I'm with her!

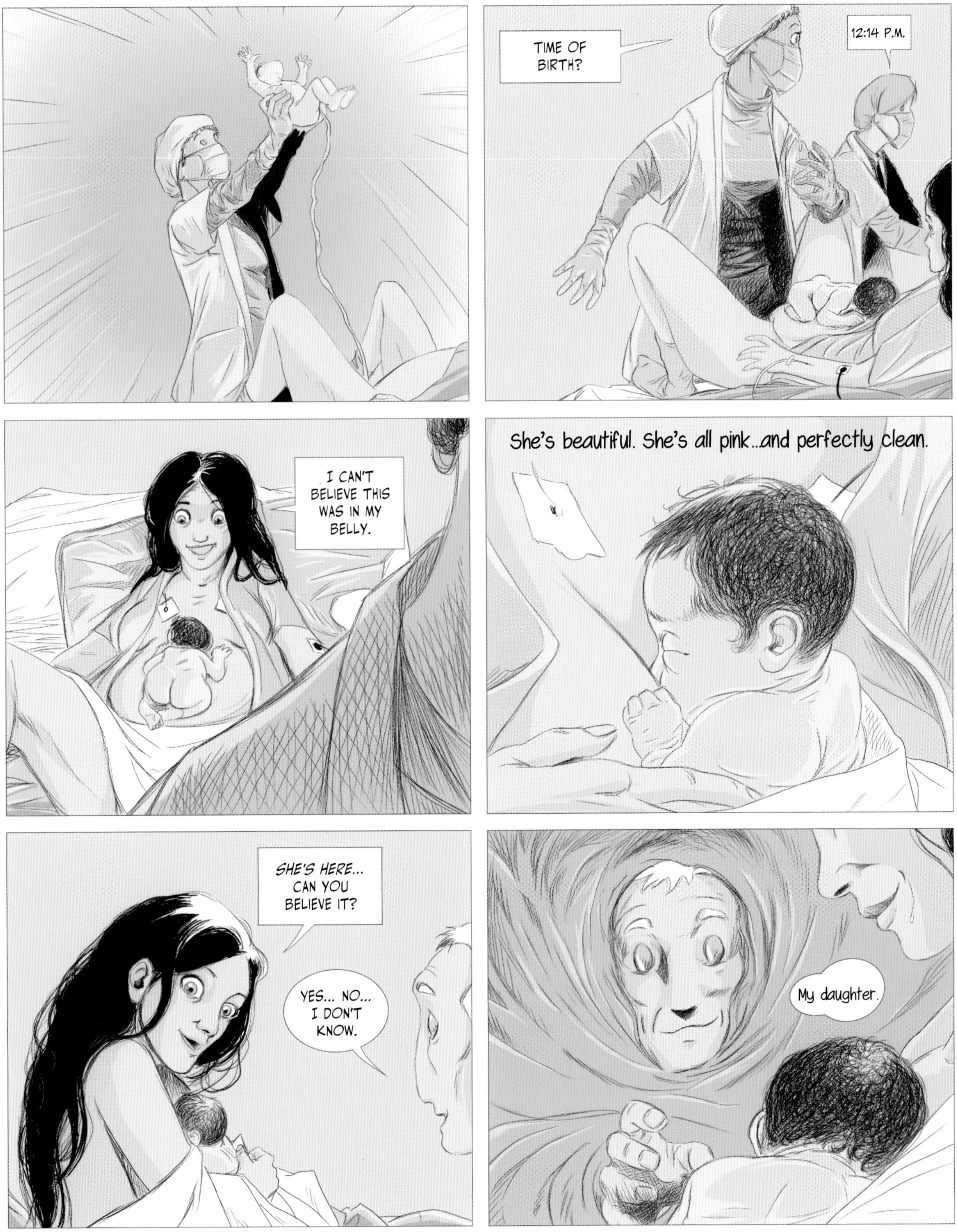
TIME OF BIRTH?
12:14 P.M.
I CAN'T BELIEVE THIS WAS IN MY BELLY.
She's beautiful. She's all pink...and perfectly clean.
SHE'S HERE... CAN YOU BELIEVE IT?
YES... NO... I DON'T KNOW.
My daughter.

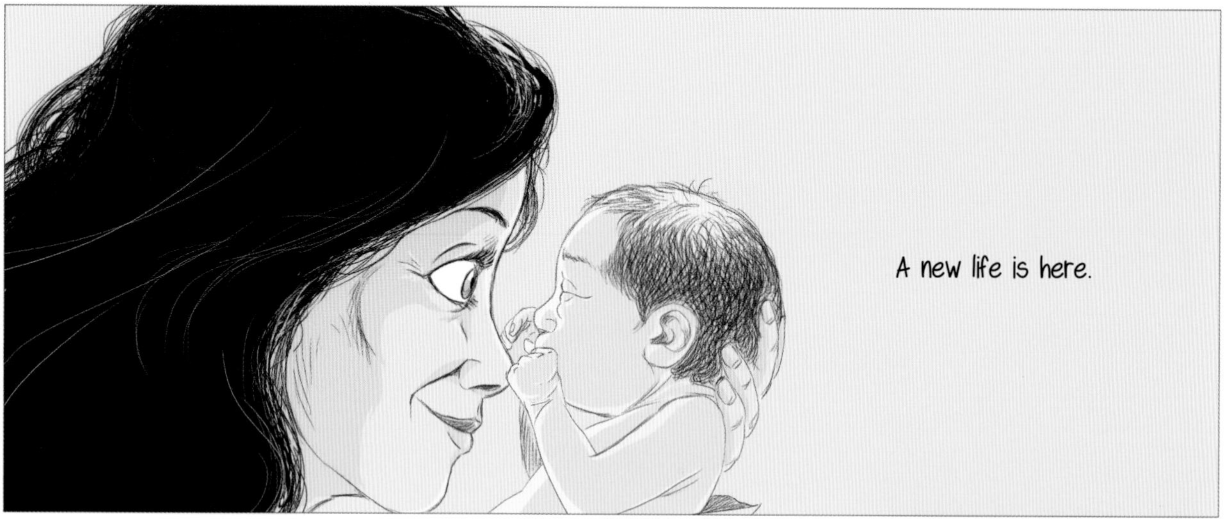
A new life is here.

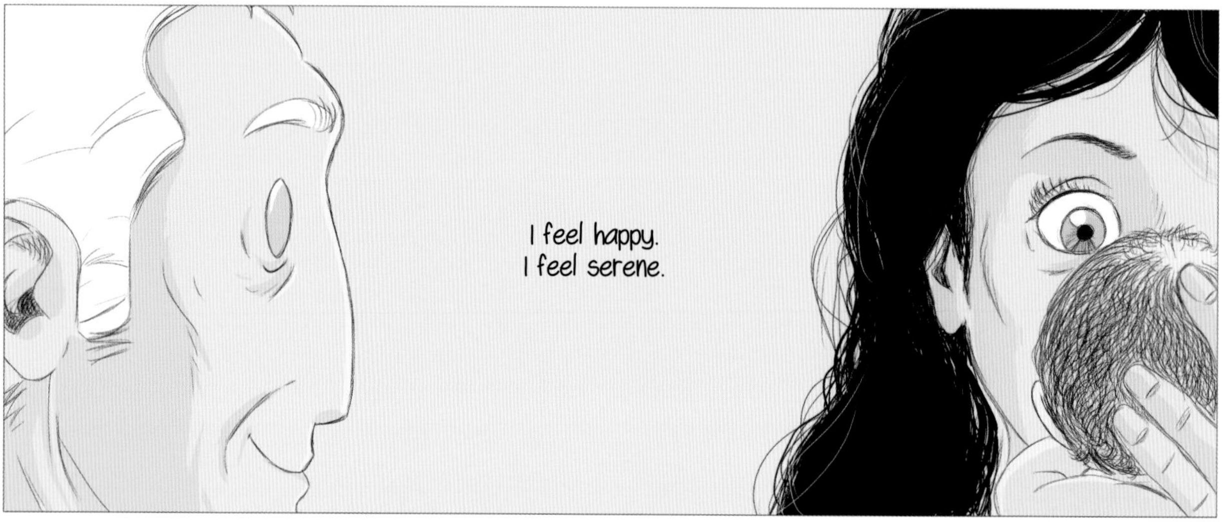
I feel happy.
I feel serene.

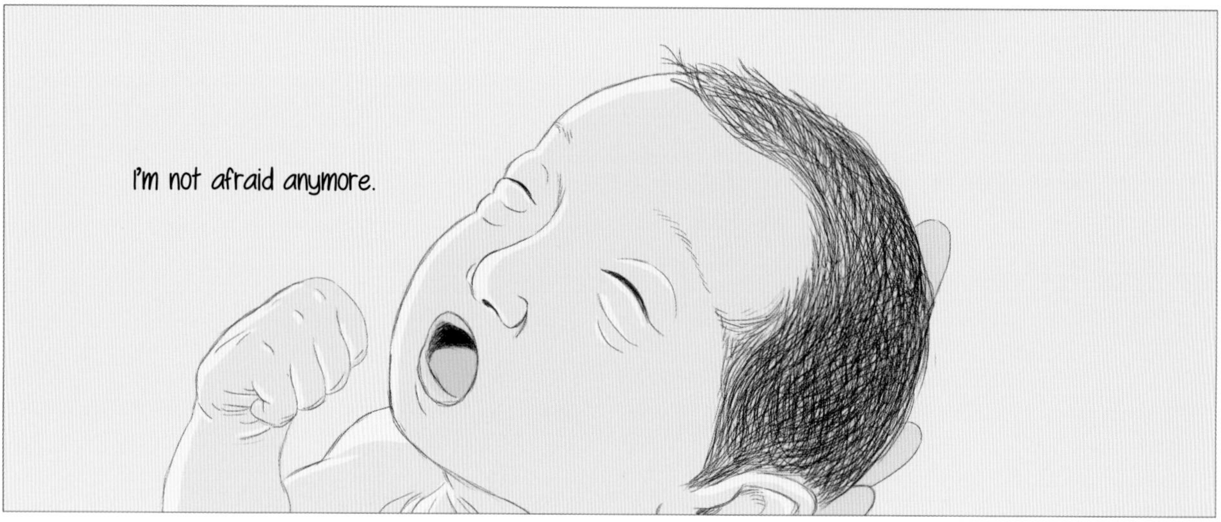
I'm not afraid anymore.

The Beginning.

BONUS MATERIAL BY ARTIST YANNICK MARCHAT

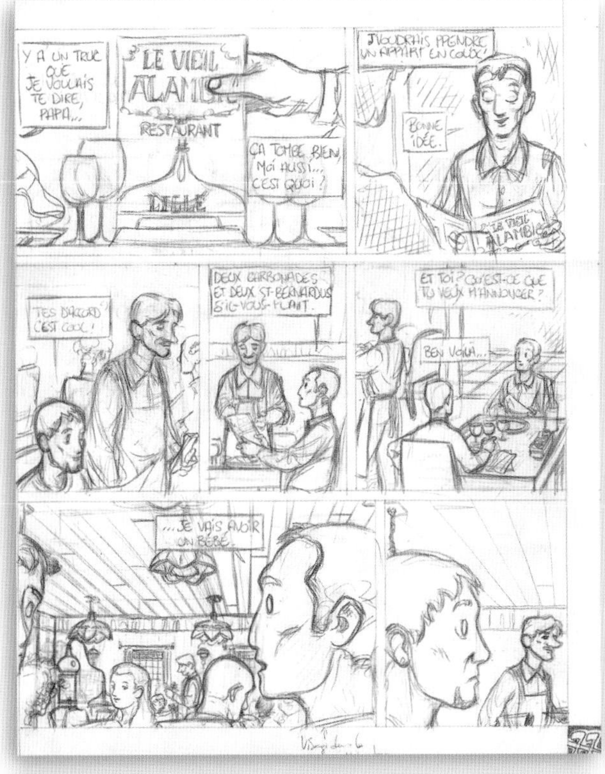

Y A UN TRUC QUE JE VOULAIS TE DIRE, PAPA...
LE VIEIL ALAMBIC
RESTAURANT
ÇA TOMBE BIEN, MOI AUSSI... C'EST QUOI ?
J'VOUDRAIS PRENDRE UN APPART EN COLOC'.
BONNE IDÉE.
T'ES D'ACCORD C'EST COOL !
DEUX CARBONADES ET DEUX ST-BERNARDUS S'IL-VOUS-PLAIT.
ET TOI ? QU'EST-CE QUE TU VEUX M'ANNONCER ?
BEN VOILA...
...JE VAIS AVOIR UN BÉBÉ.

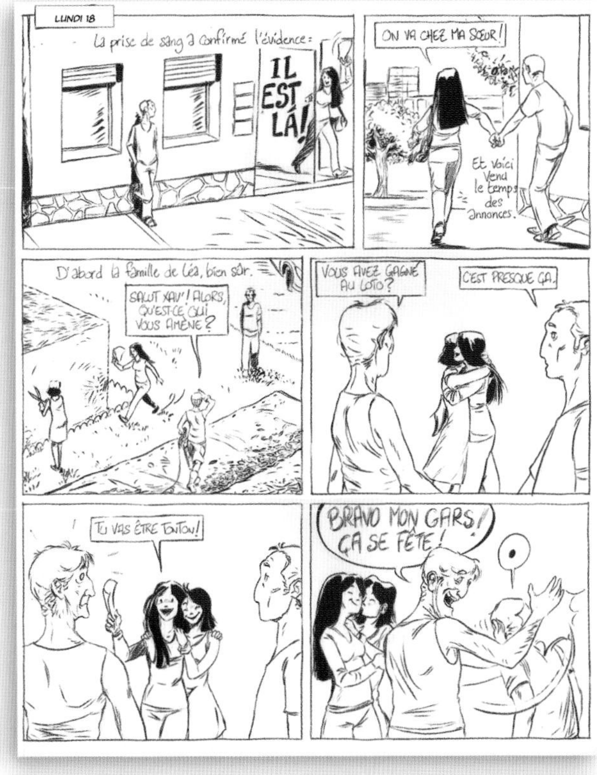

LUNDI 18
La prise de sang a confirmé l'évidence :
IL EST LÀ !
ON VA CHEZ MA SŒUR !
Et voici venu le temps des annonces.
D'abord la famille de Léa, bien sûr.
SALUT XAV' ! ALORS, QU'EST-CE QUI VOUS AMÈNE ?
VOUS AVEZ GAGNÉ AU LOTO ?
C'EST PRESQUE ÇA.
TU VAS ÊTRE TONTON !
BRAVO MON GARS ! ÇA SE FÊTE !

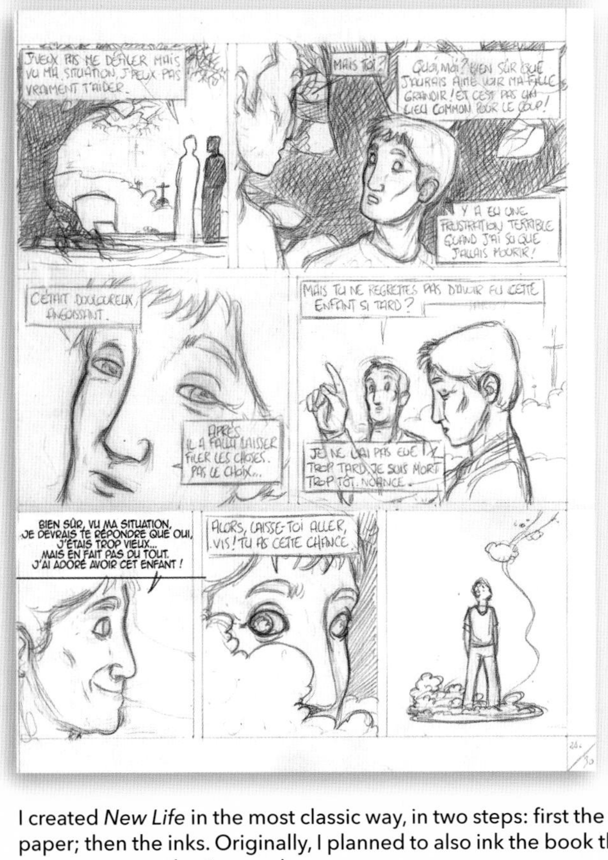

J'VEUX PAS ME DÉFILER MAIS VU MA SITUATION, J'PEUX PAS VRAIMENT T'AIDER.
MAIS TOI ?
QUOI, MOI ? BIEN SÛR QUE J'AURAIS AIMÉ VOIR MA FILLE GRANDIR ! ET C'EST PAS UN LIEU COMMUN POUR LE COUP !
Y A EU UNE FRUSTRATION TERRIBLE QUAND J'AI SU QUE J'ALLAIS MOURIR !
C'ÉTAIT DOULOUREUX, ANGOISSANT.
MAIS TU NE REGRETTES PAS D'AVOIR EU CET ENFANT SI TARD ?
APRÈS IL A FALLU LAISSER FILER LES CHOSES. PAS LE CHOIX...
JE NE L'AI PAS EUE TROP TARD, JE SUIS MORT TROP TÔT. NUANCE.
BIEN SÛR, VU MA SITUATION, JE DEVRAIS TE RÉPONDRE QUE OUI, J'ÉTAIS TROP VIEUX... MAIS EN FAIT PAS DU TOUT. J'AI ADORÉ AVOIR CET ENFANT !
ALORS, LAISSE-TOI ALLER, VIS ! TU AS CETTE CHANCE.

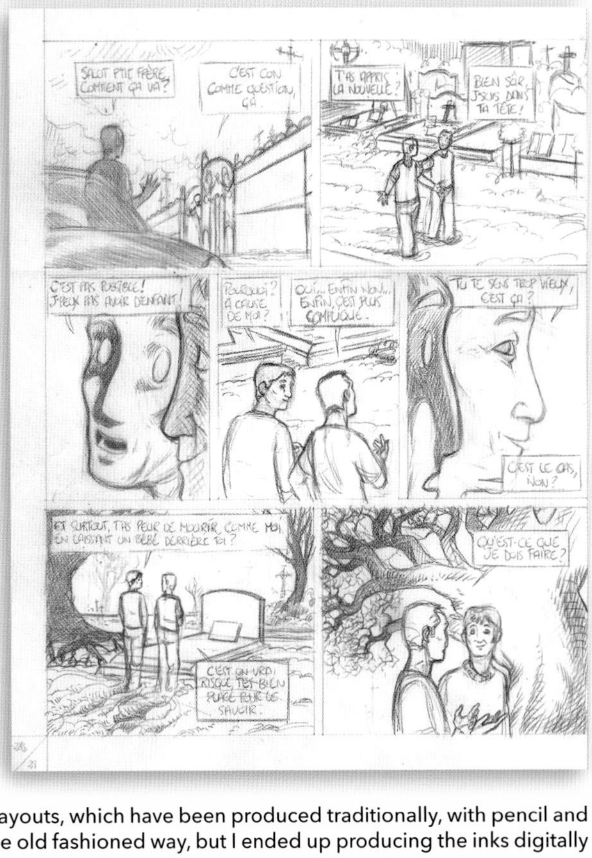

SALUT P'TIT FRÈRE, COMMENT ÇA VA ?
C'EST CON COMME QUESTION, ÇA.
T'AS APPRIS LA NOUVELLE ?
BIEN SÛR, J'SUIS DANS TA TÊTE !
C'EST PAS POSSIBLE ! J'PEUX PAS AVOIR D'ENFANT !
POURQUOI ? À CAUSE DE MOI ?
OUI... ENFIN NON... ENFIN, C'EST PLUS COMPLIQUÉ.
TU TE SENS TROP VIEUX, C'EST ÇA ?
C'EST LE CAS, NON ?
ET SURTOUT, T'AS PEUR DE MOURIR COMME MOI EN LAISSANT UN BÉBÉ DERRIÈRE TOI ?
QU'EST-CE QUE JE DOIS FAIRE ?
C'EST UN VRAI RISQUE. T'ES BIEN PLACÉ POUR LE SAVOIR.

I created *New Life* in the most classic way, in two steps: first the layouts, which have been produced traditionally, with pencil and paper; then the inks. Originally, I planned to also ink the book the old fashioned way, but I ended up producing the inks digitally to get a more cohesive result.

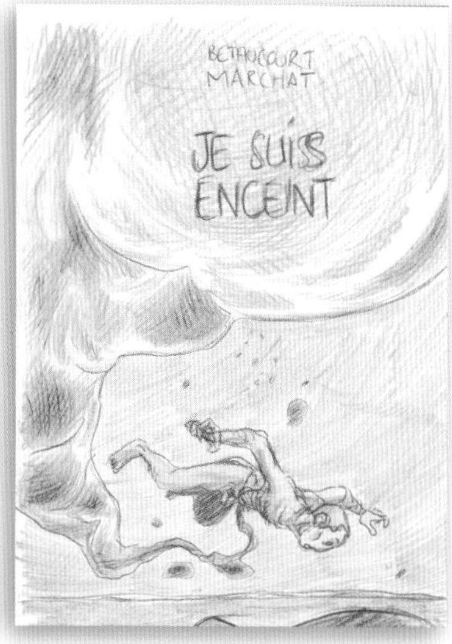
BÉTAUCOURT
MARCHAT
JE SUIS
ENCEINT

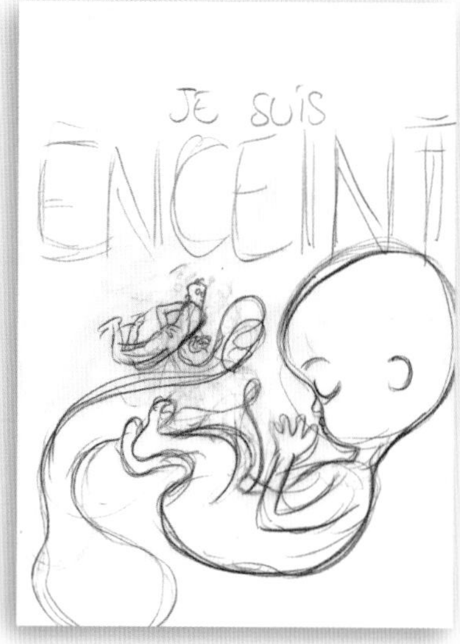
JE SUIS
ENCEINT

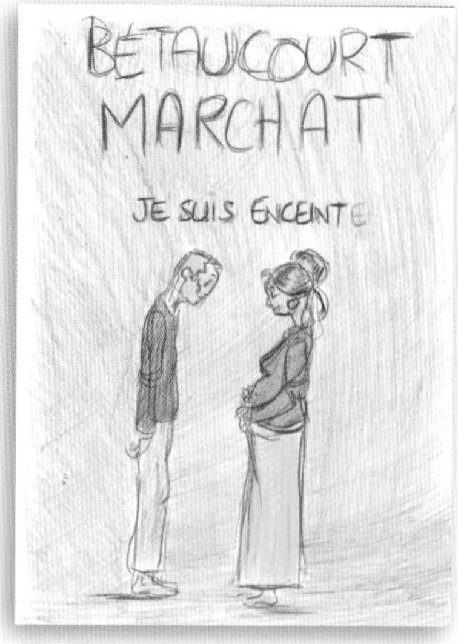
BÉTAUCOURT
MARCHAT
JE SUIS ENCEINTE

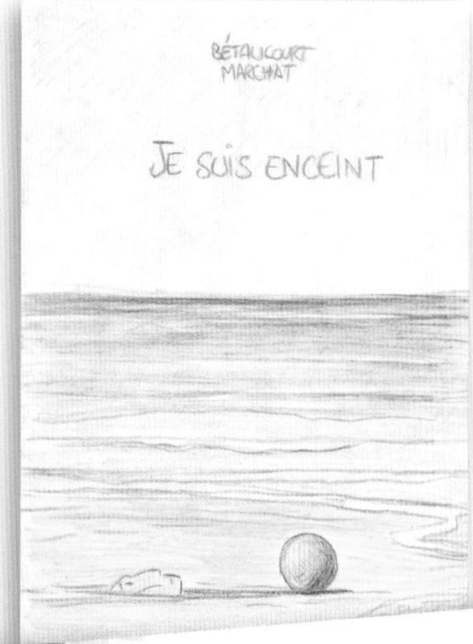
BÉTAUCOURT
MARCHAT
JE SUIS ENCEINT

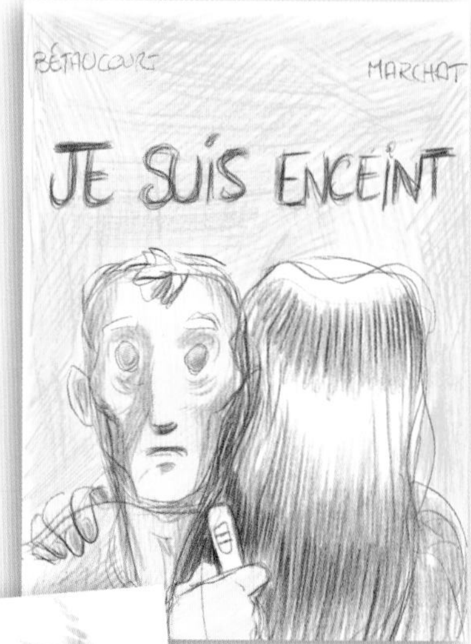
BÉTAUCOURT
MARCHAT
JE SUIS ENCEINT

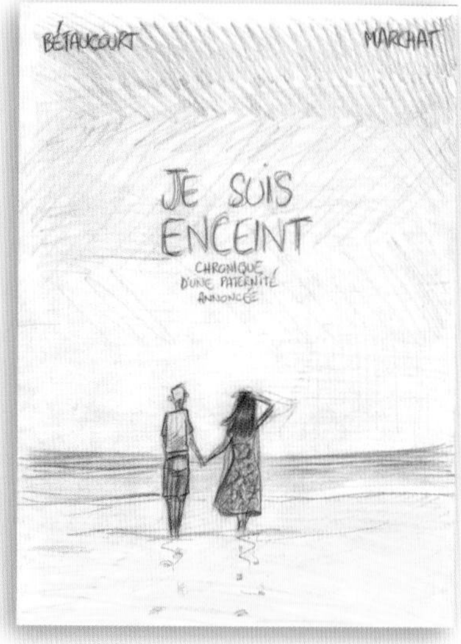
BÉTAUCOURT
MARCHAT
JE SUIS
ENCEINT
CHRONIQUE
D'UNE PATERNITÉ
ANNONCÉE

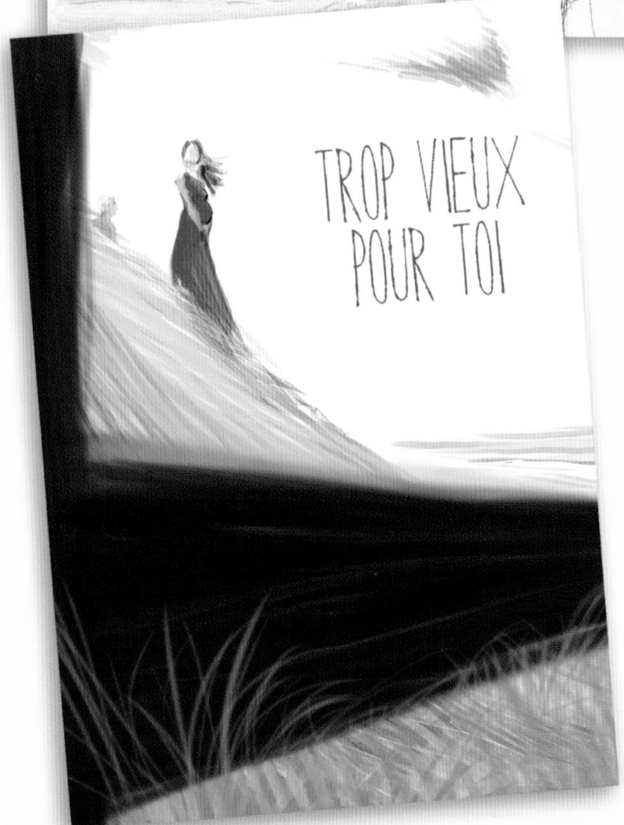
TROP VIEUX
POUR TOI

It's never easy to come up with a great cover for a graphic novel right off the bat. I toyed with different concepts, between symbolism and surrealism, and finally chose the sea as the main element. Water is as much a border as it is an invitation to travel beyond your natural ground. Water serves here as a metaphor for the radical change of life Xavier experiences.

Very quickly, the image of Lea and Xavier looking at the horizon on the beach made sense to me as a possible cover. I tried different ideas to represent the soon-to-be-born baby – first as a ball on the beach, then as sand castles, as in this version – but I eventually went back to a cover completely focused on the couple: Lea, smiling and at peace, and behind her, Xavier with his ongoing stress.

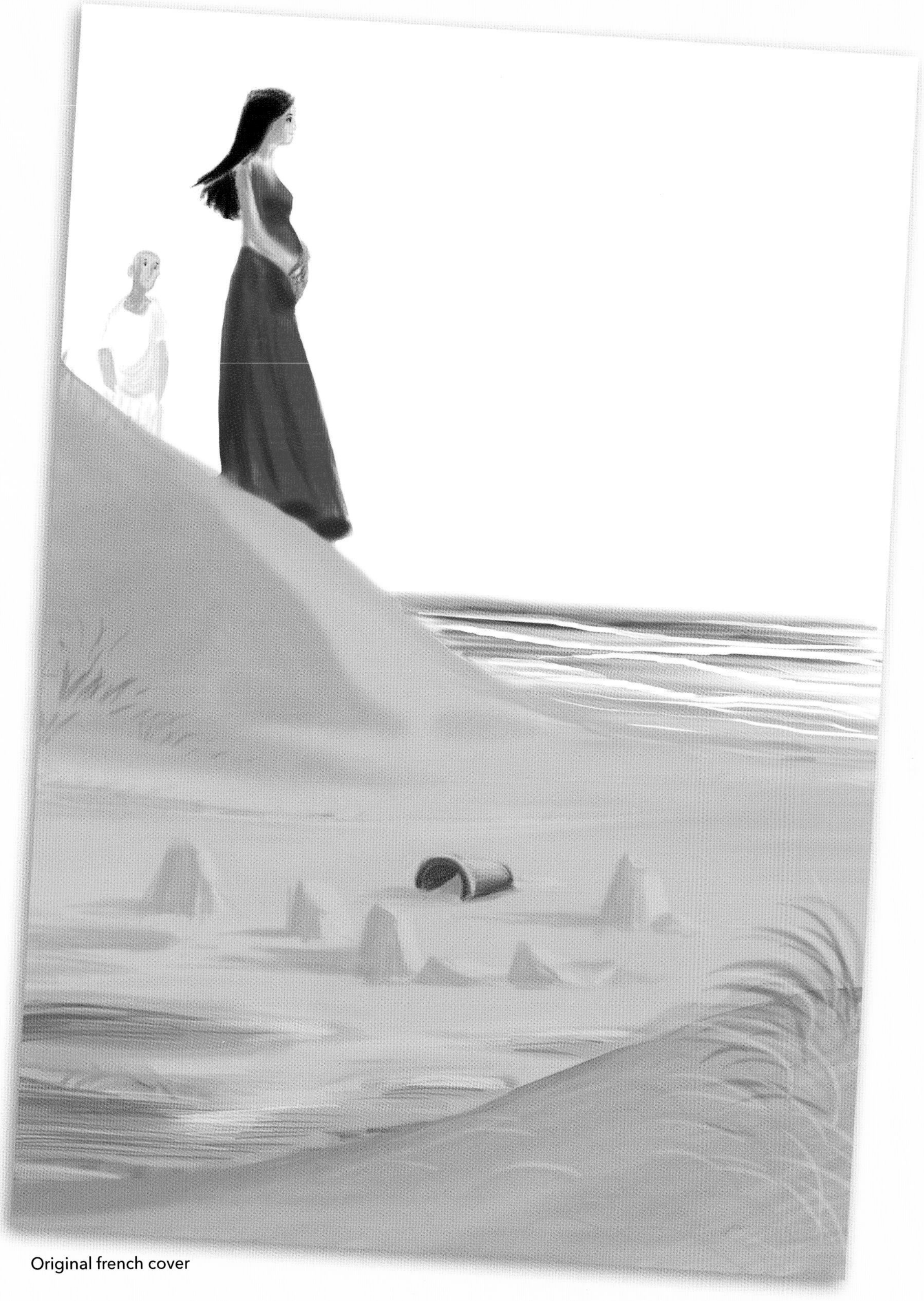

Original french cover

Léa a quarante ans
et pas d'enfant.
Elle ne peut pas en avoir.
Il paraît que l'utérus des femmes a des petits bras musclés qui retiennent les œufs pour la nidification.
Léa n'en a pas.
Pour devenir mère, il lui faudrait passer par la case Procréation Médicalement Assistée.
La vie a fait qu'elle n'y a jamais eu recours.
Cette situation me convient parfaitement.

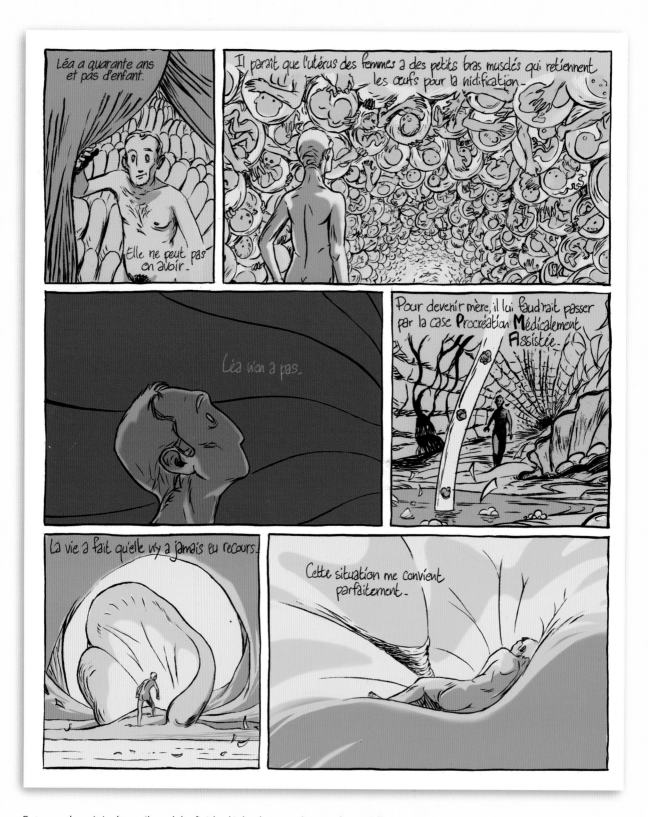

Between the original pencils and the finished inks, there can be significant differences. This color test with inks was one of the first we produced. It was rearranged and partially redone in the final version of the book to appear leaner and more legible.